LANGUAGE ALONE

Geoffrey Galt Harpham

LANGUAGE ALONE

The Critical Fetish

of Modernity

 Routledge
Taylor & Francis Group

NEW YORK AND LONDON

Published in 2002 by
Routledge
29 West 35th Street
New York, NY 10001
www.routledge-ny.com

Published in Great Britain by
Routledge
11 New Fetter Lane
London EC4P 4EE
www.routledge.co.uk

Routledge is an imprint of the Taylor & Francis Group.

Printed in the United States of America on acid free paper.

Library of Congress Cataloging-in-Publication Data
Harpham, Geoffrey Galt, 1946–
    Language alone : the critical fetish of modernity / Geoffrey Galt Harpham.
        p. cm.
    Includes bibliographical references and index.
    ISBN 0-415-94218-7 (hbk) — ISBN 0-415-94219-5 (pbk. : alk. paper)
    1. Language and languages—Philosophy.   I. Title.

P107.H37   2002

401—dc21   2002024904

To my mother, Mardel Harpham,

who always has an opinion

Contents

Preface

This book has two purposes, one modest and service-oriented and the other critical. The first is to provide a guide to the roles played in critical thinking of the past century by the concept of language, by which I mean not languages in particular but language in general, language as such, language itself, language alone. Many of the defining intellectual debates in the past century have relied on this concept, and I try to show how, why, and to what effect.

What I will call the thought of language centers theoretical or general linguistics, with its scientific aspirations and ethos, and has informed as well the working premises of other fields, including psychoanalysis, philosophy, structural anthropology, political theory, and literary theory. Over the past century, these other discourses have sought to ground or anchor themselves in the thought of language, especially as that thought was developed by Ferdinand de Saussure. They have made theoretical progress by referring, and deferring, to language as if it were a solved problem, a stable and determined entity, even while claiming on occasion to have undermined the concept of determinate knowledge itself. Two of these theoretical discourses, concerning ethics and ideology, are treated at length here.

The second, less modest purpose of the book is to critique the thought of language by exposing the limitations of language as an object of knowledge. Nothing meaningful, I argue, can be said about language as such, both because language "as such" is not available for direct observation and because the features, aspects, characteristics, and qualities that can be attributed to language approach the infinite. Language is inadequate as an object of knowledge both because there is too little information available, and because there is too much. Somewhere in the vast domain of the linguistic can be found tokens of virtually anything at all, including order, arbitrariness, social cohesion, individual creativity, rationality, freedom, the unconscious, excess, nature, culture—anything. This is why all characterizations of the essence or true nature of language are tendentious, but it is also why the thought of language has been able to serve so effectively as a proxy for other thoughts, a way of addressing recurrent questions about human life that have become difficult to address directly in a posthumanistic and rationalist climate.

If the thought of language stands in for concerns that cannot, for some reason, be addressed directly, then it should, in principle, be possible to determine what those concerns are, and so usher in a new era of honesty or directness. But we should not be too quick to embrace a principle of literality that, if realized, would put an end to speculative inquiry and to the vivifying sense of progress that has long provided the best excuse for our faltering and imperfect efforts to lead the examined life. Instead, we should perhaps try to appreciate the real productivity of indirection and surrogacy, the dynamism of false consciousness; we should try, that is, to find a way to live without the direct apprehension of truth even as we seek nothing less and nothing else.

One

LANGUAGE FOR BEGINNERS

There is nothing in the real world corresponding to
language. In fact it could very well turn out that there
is no intelligible notion of language . . . the notion
language might turn out just to be a useless notion.
— NOAM CHOMSKY, *The Generative Enterprise*

It may be that "What is a language?" is held to be a
question to which some academic discipline, e.g.
linguistics, is trying to give a definitive answer. But that
would not automatically make it a genuine question.
— ROY HARRIS, *The Language Makers*

It may even be in the cards that there is no such thing
as "Language" (with a capital L) at all!
— BENJAMIN LEE WHORF, *Language, Thought, and Reality*

There is no such thing as a language.
— DONALD DAVIDSON, "A Nice Derangement of Epitaphs"

1. Turning (in)to Language

If the cultural and intellectual life of a century could be expressed in a sentence, then a leading candidate for that honor, as far as the twentieth century in the West is concerned, is the following from Wittgenstein's *Philosophical Investigations:* "And to imagine a language means to imagine a form of life" (1997: I 19: 8). Widely quoted and variously construed, this sentence suggests many things, among them the possibility that cultural forms may be inferred from language because the properties of a given language contain the culture's essential structures of feeling, its collective sensibility, the intelligible form of its otherwise inchoate character, the tools with which it constructs its sense of things in general. So paraphrased, Wittgenstein seems to be making the pragmatic recommendation that we might study a language as a way into a particular culture, on the premise that an understanding of the one will lead to an understanding of the other.

But as readers of the entire *Philosophical Investigations,* rather than just this sentence, know, Wittgenstein has already said just the opposite. Language, he has been arguing in this passage, is a far more problematic concept than we would like to believe. The accounts of it that have been proposed have, he suggests, typically falsified the subject by reducing it to a few principles, even to a single essence, when there are, in fact, many different operations, varieties of usage, kinds of linguistic units. When we look closely at language, we see not simplicity but a warren of interlaced elements, codes, and levels, and mysterious horizons beyond which it cannot venture. Our confidence that we understand language is utterly misplaced; in fact, language is the site of a massive confusion. As he says later, "we do not *command a clear view* of the use of our words" (I 122: 49).

We can make a start, however, by imagining that language is composed of a number of self-contained, rule-governed operations that Wittgenstein calls "language-games." To get a handle on language as the totality of such games, we might, he suggests, think of "an ancient city: a maze of little streets and squares, of old and new houses, and of houses with additions from various periods; and this surrounded by a multitude of new boroughs with straight regular streets and uniform houses"—these representing the recent additions to the language of such elements as the symbols of chemistry and the notation of calculus (1997: I 18: 8). Here a "form of life" serves as the model for understanding language, not the other way around. Complex as it is, language can be understood by comparing it to another human production, one that, like language, seems both natural and cultural, improvised and given, old and new, material and ideal, an all-round environment when one is in it but a limited thing when one is not. "What has to be accepted," he says near the end of his book, "is—so one could say—*forms of life*" (II xi: 226).

Which is the model for which? The stakes involved in this simple question are unexpectedly high, for if an understanding of language comes first, and forms of life only later, then linguistics becomes the paradigmatic human science and the master-key to knowledge itself. But if, on the other hand, we are urged to model our understanding of a language on things like cities, then very different consequences follow. We could not even hope to imagine a language at all without first thinking our way through that great unfiltered mass of cultural, historical, economic, psychological, and other factors both material and immaterial—objects of competing and perhaps unscientific disciplines—that a scientific linguistics would have to strain out in order to focus on language itself. Imagining a language would, in fact, become strictly impossible, because the attempt to do so would summon forth not clean linguistic facts (of the sort Wittgenstein thought he had discovered and described in the *Tractatus*), but the vast debris of the world. Wittgenstein actually seems to anticipate this consequence when, immediately after proposing the concept of the language-game, he adds, "I shall also call the whole, consisting of language and the actions into which it is woven, the 'language-game'" (1997: I 7: 5). Its object hopelessly immured in an untheorizable mass of "actions," the project of a scientific linguistics would lie in ruins, unable even to begin.

The proliferating definitions of "language" even within the discipline of linguistics over the past century suggest that those whose specific task is the systematic understanding of language have been uncomfortably aware of the dilemma signaled by Wittgenstein's ambivalence. The same cannot, however, be said for those thinkers of the past century who turned to language as a way of solving conceptual or theoretical problems that stubbornly resisted clarification. Throughout this period, thinkers in a number of fields, including anthropology, literary theory, philosophy, political theory, and psychoanalysis, have sought to transform their discourses from speculative enterprises into scientific or at least somewhat more empirical disciplines by turning to the facts of language. It is a well-known fact that intellectual disciplines often advance by grounding themselves in ideas drawn from other disciplines, sometimes turning, in a spirit of amateur enthusiasm, to ideas that sophisticated thinkers in those presumably "grounded" disciplines are energetically trashing. For the past century, the dominant grounding idea for intellectual culture as a whole has been the thought of language. And the best general formula for that thought can be achieved simply by dropping a couple of words from the sentence of Wittgenstein's with which we began: "To imagine language means to imagine life." We can, this modestly revised sentence suggests, place the study of human existence on a sound and rational footing by proceeding as if language were a cache of evidence, a privileged site of human reality.

This kind of emphasis on language itself is characteristically modern. A "premodern" orientation, we might say, is signaled by a faith in the primacy of concepts on the one hand and the possibility of an unmediated observation of material fact on the other. A "modern" orientation dispenses with both kinds of faith and pursues instead a rational inquiry into representation as the site of a reality that can be tested and verified. The modernist moment is achieved when immediacy in either direction is renounced as an illusion, when the limits of language are seen as the limits of the world, and linguistic mediation itself becomes the object of observation. Both metaphysics and the "things themselves" are telescoped into "language itself," which becomes the one thing we can know, but the thing that will yield knowledge about all the rest. An exemplary modernist, Bertrand Russell was assured that "with sufficient caution, the properties of language may help us to understand the structure of the world" (23). The crucial and specifically modern note, the note that will be the subject of this book, is announced in Russell's promise of knowledge not about a mere form of life but about "the structure of the world," a knowledge of reality as such.

The modernist break erupts within a humanist tradition that enfolds it, a tradition that extends from antiquity to the present, in which language is held up as the defining achievement or attribute of the human species, an inborn capacity that enables human beings to exercise legitimate dominion over the rest of creation, and defines them as distinct from the brutes. What distinguishes the modern emphasis on language from this traditional humanism is not just a more concentrated attention paid to language, but something more radical, a presumption that language could be studied as a thing apart from human beings and human behavior, and that it could therefore serve as the object of a rational inquiry, even of an empirical science. From this point of view, language is a uniquely powerful and complex, but still limited and determined, entity that is available for observation.

Perhaps the ruling cliché concerning European cultural modernism—a cliché so pervasive and effective that its consequences have gone largely unremarked—concerns the new importance attributed to language. In the work of such iconic figures as Mallarmé, Cézanne, Wilde, Joyce, Stravinsky, Picasso, Braque, Schoenberg, Stein, Kandinsky, Le Corbusier, Mies van der Rohe, Apollinaire, and others, the medium of expression attains a new autonomy, being considered for its own sake, with form eclipsing content, surface dominating depth. Painting, music, dance, and literature become modern when artists divert their attention from the objects of representation, including the material world and their own subjective states, and devote themselves to a "technical" exploration of representation itself, for which "language" serves as a convenient synecdoche.

Modernity is actually more clearly marked in the history of painting than it is in literature. If Monet signaled the end of the premodern era of representation by plunging, in the spirit of a scientist, into the strictly optical phenomena of vision and visuality, attempting to render light rather than light-reflecting things, visual sensations rather than objects or the concepts that inform them, it was Cézanne who made the decisive modernist break by decoupling the work both from the object painted and from the effect of the object on the perceiver in order to force a concentration on the painting, and even on the paint, itself. Paradoxically, it is Cézanne's fierce dedication to the demands, constraints, and properties of his own medium, to what Christopher Butler calls "the language of the work," that aligns him with artists in other fields who were exploring the resources of their media (12). For, increasingly during this time and even beyond, artistic or cultural media were conceived as languages, with pigment, stone, tones, or human motion being credited with a "syntax," a "grammar," a "rhetoric," even a "phonology" (see Powers). In his authoritative general introduction to *Early Modernism: Literature, Music, and Painting in Europe, 1900–1916,* Butler speaks of the "withdrawal from consensual languages" as the key to the modernist innovation, followed by the construction of a new "language" of artistic expression that the audience would then be forced to learn, this time as nonnative speakers (4–14). The most programmatically modernist art did not affiliate itself with particular national traditions of expression, but cultivated an abstract "language of art" that could address a broadly European, even a universal audience.

For the art produced during this period, Butler says, the "application of the concept of language to the non-verbal arts seems to be justified, in so far as the painter and musician also become competent in a style for their arts, very much as one may become competent in a natural language" (10). Just as one may learn with great effort a language that is not given whole, as it is to infants, who learn in a linguistic "environment," but acquired piece by piece, one word at a time, so—according to the new theory—one may learn the "language" of modern art. The art produced under this dispensation could be expected to display its parts in such a way as to encourage an appreciation of the labor of analysis and construction that went into its making. Thus Cubism, for example, may be classed with the poetic practice of Imagism as instances of what the Russian formalist Victor Shklovsky called a "resurrection of the word," the emancipation of the part from the whole and of the minimal, essentially creative and subversive, unit of signification from the synthetic statement.

One should not misinterpret various modernist efforts to push language in the direction of music or painting as a sign that language was felt to be too abstract a thing to qualify as an art. For one effect of these efforts was to enlarge the domain of language so that it encompassed these other arts. Writing in 1916, a young Walter Benjamin reflected the spirit of the moment—and anticipated the spirit of a moment half a century hence—when he concentrated his attention, in the course of a stubbornly cryptic and elusive essay, on the imperial concept of *"language as such,"* and argued that all artistic forms must be grasped "as languages" with a definite connection to "natural languages" (65, 73). This urgent sense of language as an overriding and unifying imperative gives the various practices of modernist art their distinctive focus and thrust. During the period of the great avant-garde movements, from 1910 to 1930, numerous and often opposed accounts of language were, Raymond Williams notes, being advanced by parties with very different agendas (1989: 65–80). But while Williams argues persuasively for the conflicts that divided the language-based avant-garde, he also demonstrates the deeper point of agreement between all the contending parties on the revolutionary importance of the concept of language.

In fairly recent times, such thinkers as Richard Wollheim, Leonard Meyer, and Nelson Goodman have all testified to the success of modernism in this respect by affirming language's claim to preeminence as the privileged vocabulary for describing the work of art as such. Their works, published well after the era of modernism itself (c. 1895–1940), suggest that in this respect, the culture of the past hundred years constituted a single trajectory, and that a dotted rather than a solid line divides an elitist, technique-obsessed, and hermetic modernism from a theory-hungry, equivocally populist postmodernism. This limited but crucial continuity permits a kind of conversation between noncontemporaries, as when Pierre Boulez argues for the contemporary relevance of a modernist precursor, Schoenberg, whose music, Boulez says, deploys "a nonserial rhetoric" that stands as "the very model of a search for language. Arriving during a period of dissolution," Boulez says admiringly, "he pushed that breaking-up to its extreme result: 'suspension' of the tonal language" (12, 11).

In the twentieth century, the term *language* became, for many modern and postmodern artists and thinkers, a shorthand term for "atonality" in general, for everything that seemed nonnatural, artificial, broken up, discontinuous, theoretically complex, everything that rebuffed the human search for pleasure, immediate gratification, consolation, assurance. At the same time, of course, language never—especially in the embattled field of linguistics— fully relinquished its older meaning of "tonality" in general, a primordial and defining human endowment, the foundation of human cognition, human society, and human nature itself. And so, without abandoning its position at the center of humanism, language came to signify a supplementary and subversive antihumanism as well. *Language* says it all.

This distinctively modern subversion/extension of traditional humanism through a new kind of interest in language occurs with even greater force and clarity in the relatively contained field of philosophy. If Nietzsche is the

Monet of philosophical modernism, relentlessly stressing the psychological and worldly force of words and statements, insisting that language is not just a medium for the representation of objects and mental states but a thing—like light for Monet—that could be apprehended in itself, then Wittgenstein— "early" Wittgenstein, whose modernist indifference to the ordinary the mature Wittgenstein lived to regret—is its Cézanne. For Cézanne, painting constituted a critique of painterly representation itself; for Wittgenstein, "All philosophy is 'Critique of language'" (1961: 63). Wittgenstein's 1922 *Tractatus Logico-Philosophicus* does not demystify language or expose its deceptions, but inquires, in a morally nonjudgmental and scientific spirit, into its real nature, which he conceived as a form of "picturing." Largely under the influence of Wittgenstein, with Nietzsche, Gottlob Frege, Russell, and the American semiotician C. S. Peirce in the background, Anglo-American philosophy was able to perform what became the defining modernist gesture, a "linguistic turn."

The idea of the linguistic turn, as Richard Rorty described it in an important introduction to a 1967 book by that name, was to place philosophy on a more secure empirical base not by abandoning traditional questions, but by approaching these questions as though they were essentially linguistic problems that could be solved by therapy or observation—that is, by reforming language or by understanding more about the way language works (1967: 3). Rather than asking, "What can I know?" "What ought I to hope for?" "What is justice?" "Does God exist?" or "How should one live?" philosophers who were turning linguistic would ask, "How is it represented?" or "How does it signify?"

The result of this turn, it was presumed, would be a significant upgrading of philosophy in an intellectual climate dominated by science. By talking about language, philosophers could come to a consensus on what would count as evidence for or against a given proposition. While language might misrepresent, shade, misconstrue, confuse, or obscure the things represented in it, language itself was objectively real, accessible to the empirical method of observation and analysis. Such metaphysical entities as intentions, values, ultimate truths, or mental states could, after all, only be the object of a strictly amateur version of speculative common sense; but language could serve as a fit object for the scrutiny of a philosopher. Whatever philosophers used to think about, they could now think about more productively and professionally by focusing on language as a clearly defined shared structure that language-users know, albeit unconsciously, and apply to a variety of situations. If the problem of language has come to dominate the traditional problem of mind, this is in large measure because of the increasing currency of the convictions that the business of philosophy is not to produce meanings but to analyze them, and that language is, as Jürgen Habermas puts it, "the only thing whose nature we can know" (1971: 314).

Rorty actually described two turnings. In the first ("Cambridge") turning, philosophy sought to reform language by developing what Rudolf Carnap called the "logical syntax of language," or "ideal language theory." Legitimate philosophy, Carnap argued, was philosophy of language; and philosophy so defined constituted the syntax and even the semantics of the language of science. If only philosophers could process out all the metaphysical pseudoproblems that had obstructed clear vision, then, Carnap prophesied, "all the questions and theorems of philosophy [would] consequently find their place in the formal structure theory of language" (60). Behind such a pronouncement stood the luminous figure of Frege, whose teachings, strained through Carnap, Russell, and Wittgenstein, were to set the agenda for decades. The most influential aspects of Frege's work were concentrated in a series of arguments worked out in impressive abstraction: first, that the goal of philosophy was the analysis of the formal aspects of thought; second, that thought was to be distinguished from the dynamic and contingent—the merely psychological—business of thinking; and third, that the only way to get at thought was by analyzing language, especially a language purified of the defects and illogicalities that beset natural languages. In the second ("Oxford") turning described by Rorty, philosophy—wary of the possibility of cultivating bad faith and inauthenticity—renounced such grandiose aspirations and settled for trying to understand more about the pragmatics of "ordinary" or nonideal language. The task here was not one of purifying language, but of understanding it—and even, down the road, of discovering new, more interesting ways of talking (see Rorty 1967: 38).

Interestingly, Wittgenstein initiated the former in the *Tractatus* and contributed decisively to the latter in *Philosophical Investigations*. What unites these two movements, other than Wittgenstein, is, as Rorty points out, the empiricist effort to deal with direct perceptions, to be "presuppositionless." Philosophers who took the linguistic turn found themselves facing in the direction of words, which W. V. O. Quine described as "tangible objects of the size so popular in the marketplace." One could confront these objects directly by making a "semantic ascent," dragging philosophy out of the ambiguous wetlands of intentions, actions, sensations, and thoughts, not to mention Kantian transcendental synthesis, onto the dry ground of "a domain where both parties are better agreed on the objects (viz., words) and on the main terms concerning them . . . ascending to a common part of two fundamentally disparate conceptual schemes, the better to discuss disparate foundations" (169). Language became ubiquitous when the conviction began to grow among thinkers that none of the traditional grounds for philosophical thought—sensory perception, prelinguistic understanding, pure reason, moral intuitions, and so forth—worked any more. In the wake of this conviction, thinkers turned to language in hopes of finding a natural starting point, something that would be independent of cultural knowledge and even of questions of meaning (see Rorty 1991). The rhetoric of foundations and fundamentals underlay the linguistic turn(s), which sought above all to cast off illusions, myths, false ideas of all kinds, and begin afresh.

In the 1960s, an excited Rorty was prepared to count the linguistic turn "the most important philosophical discovery of our time," and added that its achievement in placing on the defensive the entire preceding philosophical tradition from the Greeks onward "is sufficient to place this period [roughly 1932–67] among the great ages of the history of philosophy" (1967: 3, 33). But according to the calculations of Jerrold Katz, Rorty may actually have understated the force of the linguistic turn by undercounting. Katz noted two separate turns, and expressed the hope that his collection of essays on *The Philosophy of Linguistics* (1985) might initiate a third. Rorty's two are counted as one, a single movement whose members include Frege, Wittgenstein, Russell, Moore, Carnap, Ryle, and others for whom the concept of language was the central concern. In a second movement, Katz says, philosophers turned not to language but to more advanced concepts being explored in linguistics. Prodded by Quine, such thinkers as Jerry Fodor and Katz himself began to approach the philosophically important aspects of language armed with professional expertise in linguistics, especially as Noam Chomsky had redefined and reoriented that discourse. For these thinkers, the premise that "meaning postulates are analogues of logical postulates" provided a warrant for casting philosophical problems in terms of linguistic problems, and linguistic problems in terms of logical relations (Katz 9).

Katz thus anticipates a third turning, toward the foundations of linguistics, in which linguistics itself would not merely contribute a certain rigor to the discourse of philosophy, but would itself become "an object of philosophical interest" (Katz 1985: 10). While the tools of this turn would be more refined than those of the first two, the goal would be the same, the drying-out of philosophy, the adequate description of a field of determined facts. For Katz, linguistics, or "the science of language," is such a field, and for this reason, "philosophy of linguistics can have the same theoretical value in attempting to answer epistemological and metaphysical questions as . . . philosophy of mathematics and philosophy of logic." Katz's ambitions are great, for he hopes with this third linguistic turn to arrive at an answer to "one of the most important questions in metaphysics, the question of what kinds of objects there are" (11).

Katz does not even mention yet another linguistic turning, whose roots are to be found in the work of Martin Heidegger, which announces a transition from a characteristically modern to a more specifically postmodern— and, intriguingly, a more fundamental—understanding of language. The prominence of language was a striking feature of Heidegger's first major work, *Being and Time,* but many French and German postmodern thinkers were even more responsive to the later Heidegger, especially to those texts in which language is described as the very essence not just of thinking but of thing-ing, the aspect of all things in which their essence was disclosed, or "unconcealed." The poetic text by Stefan George to which Heidegger turned in the 1950s suggests the necessity of renouncing a naïve sense of ontology, or what he described as "ontotheology," in favor of a more profound understanding of the nature, and especially the power, of language:

> *So I renounced and sadly see:*
> *Where word breaks off no thing may be.*

For late Heidegger, language is not the passive property or tool of language-users, but has its own self-generating and self-authorizing kind of being that brings man into conscious being. In Heidegger's texts, language is the object of a super-subtle discourse of agency whose large purpose is to gather and subsume human being into the quasi-divine being of language. If it "withholds its nature," if it "disregards precisely itself," if it "does not insist upon itself alone," if it refuses to advance itself or yield to our investigations, language is still everywhere, and everywhere a force (1971: 81, 131, 131).

Heidegger takes immense pains to reassure his readers that human nature is not canceled out by the majesty of language, whose only purpose and effect, he says, is to achieve or realize that nature. This humanistic dimension of Heidegger's thinking seems distinctly modern, but Heidegger's attempt to think of language alone leads him to a dimly lit mid-region in which nothing has a distinct identity at all. From the point of view of language, human beings do not possess their most distinctive trait, but rather are possessed by it, gathered into a language that "speaks" beyond their intentions and within their words, generating a kind of subsemiotic throbbing irreducible to expression, utterance, and representation. By urging a view of language as discontinuous with the aims or purposes of any speaker, Heidegger provides all the terms that would be needed by a postmodern antihumanism that could claim to base itself on his work. We do not truly possess the language we speak, Heidegger argued, and indeed, we cannot properly be said to "speak" in the sense of initiating discourse at all. Rather, language itself speaks and we speakers are spoken by language; when we speak, we speak as it were "*by way*" of language (1971: 124). We are, in short, possessed by a language that is "not anything human" (1975: 207). "Language is more powerful than we," he concludes, "and therefore weightier" (1971: 31).

Understandably, many readers of Heidegger closed his book convinced that man was never in control of the language that had formerly defined his place in the scheme of things; that man could no longer think of himself as a sovereign subject or even as an integrated psychic identity; and that, deep within man, posing as his living essence, was a functionally autonomous and disturbingly inhuman system. The potential effects go well beyond the demystification of traditional humanism. Heidegger (or rather, his English translator, who kindly invented this sentence as a friendly amendment) said that "the 'sign' in design . . . is related to *secare*, to cut"; and others, prominently including Jacques Lacan, took the hint, depicting language as a traumatizing "cleft" or "break" in the subject, a "signifying cut" that represents the force of castration, even of death, in human life (1971: 121).

In the 1960s, Heidegger's thought, understood in an aggressively antihumanistic way, served as the cutting edge of a multifaceted movement occurring on the margins of philosophy and beyond the pale of linguistics altogether. In this (fifth?) linguistic turn, the "renunciation" of which Stefan George speaks was extended to include the very bases of previous linguistic turns, direct perception, and the possibility of a presuppositionless scientific view of the world: for post-Heideggerians, language did not provide facts, but took their place. Man, too, was renounced, along with the "metaphysical questions" that plagued him. "We would," Heidegger wrote, in sentences that took on a second life during the "theory revolution" in the Anglo-American academy that began well after he wrote them, "reflect on language itself, and on language only," adding, with a marked absence of nuance, that "language itself is—language and nothing else besides"; and then, just to make sure: "Language itself is language" (1975: 190).

For many, the corner Heidegger glimpsed was decisively rounded at the moment in the mid-sixties when Jacques Derrida declared that the energies of "at least some twenty centuries" had at last produced an ethos that "*must finally determine as language the totality of its problematic horizon*" (1978a: 6). For others, it was when Michel Foucault, positioned at the same point, wrote that "man is in the process of perishing as the being of language continues to shine ever brighter upon our horizon" (1970: 386). Derrida and Foucault count as members of a para-philosophical avant-garde whose goal was to dismantle the notion of the self-mastering, self-aware subject and to reveal it as an illusion, an aftereffect, a mirage generated by language. In the post-Heideggerian moment, human being, human nature, and human consciousness are no longer issues. As a committed contemporary advocate of this moment insists, "*the paradigm of language has replaced the paradigm of consciousness*" (Benhabib 208).

In fact, even this sweeping pronouncement understates the case, for in the new paradigm, language holds the key to more than mere consciousness. For many postmodernists and fellow travelers, the defining discovery of the era was that language determines or structures society rather than the other way around. As Julia Kristeva says, "the conception of language as the 'key' to man and to social history and as the means of access to the laws of societal functioning constitutes perhaps one of the most striking characteristics of our era, and as such is definitely a new phenomenon" (1989a: 3). If, for previous linguistic turns, language was held to be "the only thing we can know," for the postmodern revolution, language is very nearly the only thing there is. "To a gaze forearmed by linguistics," Foucault writes, "things attain to existence only in so far as they are able to form the elements of a signifying system" (1970: 382).

While what I have been calling modernism continues, albeit in a compromised or even ironized fashion, the humanistic tradition based on the primacy of man as the only species capable of language, postmodernism attempts to turn this tradition inside out by representing language as the only thing capable of man. At some point—the very point, perhaps, where the modern grades into the postmodern—a concentrated attention to language itself as the key to human thought and human culture becomes not a scientific form of humanism but a coldly deliberate antihumanism of the sort expressed, in a fashionably offhanded way, by Jean-Jacques Lecercle, who paraphrases Gilles Deleuze and Félix Guattari and many others as well in describing language as "an unconscious machine. . . . It produces both concrete utterances and the subjects who utter them. Our discourse is produced by a machine. We are part of its arrangement ('*agencement*') and therefore do not control it. We do not use language as a tool, but are just a few of its innumerable cogs" (187). To consider humanity as "a few" inconsequential cogs in the language machine constitutes by any measure a serious insult to the notion that human beings have identities and destinies that bear some transcendental meaning and intrinsic value.

And so it is that both humanism, centered on the figure of the speaking lord of creation, and antihumanism, which posits man as the slave of impersonal forces, emerge under the ambiguous sign of language.

The most commanding articulation of the antihumanist ethos is surely the rhetorically magnificent conclusion of *The Order of Things*, where Foucault describes modernism from the point of view of incipient postmodernism, contributing his own emphases and enthusiasms in a way that posits a genealogical affiliation between himself and his precursors. As modern thought brings man himself into the field of knowledge, Foucault argues, it discovers a kind of "shadow," a factor of "the unthought" that remains unknown and unknowable, an "element of darkness, an apparently inert density" in which the known is embedded (1970: 326). The unthought is encountered and cultivated in psychoanalysis and ethnology, but it is in the discipline of linguistics that modernity is most decisively established and man most systematically both fetishized and "dissolved." Not only is linguistics "perfectly founded in the order of positivities exterior to man," but it provides, to a greater degree than the other disciplines, a "primary decipherment," a "general contestation" of the pieties of humanism (381).

Throughout his discussion of modern thought, Foucault, who found in language a power consistent with that which he discovered in prisons at a later point in his career, lends his warm endorsement to any sign of linguistic supremacy over the merely human, his appreciation of any incident in which man is humbled before the "untamed, imperious being of words" (1970: 300). Man has, he asserts, always been a precarious construct, a mere effect, a "fold" or "figure occurring between two modes of language" (386). While in the modern era (which, for him, begins with the French Revolution), language was seen as the essential testament to men's freedom, in the postmodern era just beginning when he wrote in 1966, language would, he promised, work diligently toward man's obliteration (291). Henceforth, the "right to conceive both of the being of language and of the being of man may be forever excluded"; an inerasable hiatus had intervened decisively between the reality of language and the "fantasy" of man. "The only thing we know at the moment, in all certainty," Foucault writes, "is that in Western culture the being of man and the being of language have never, at any time, been able to coexist and to articulate themselves one upon the other. Their incompatibility has been one of the fundamental features of our thought" (339). On those occasions where Foucault departs from historical description, he argues that language has always been master of man, but that this fact has only recently become fully evident. Before, men believed that speech was their servant, without realizing that they were merely submitting themselves to its structures, its demands; now, the truth is inescapable.

The most famous moment in *The Order of Things* is the very last, where the figure of man is "erased, like a face drawn in sand at the edge of the sea" (1970: 387). In this memorable image, Foucault attempts to capture human thought and even human being in a kind of twilight as they are about to be overwritten by a sovereign language. For Foucault, thought becomes modern by admitting language to a privileged place in the field of knowledge; it goes beyond modernity—he does not use the term *postmodern*—by abolishing itself in favor of language. In what we have come to call the postmodern condition, emergent but not yet dominant in Foucault's image, language is not merely what's left standing when man has been done away with; it is the mankiller itself.

From the vantage point of the present moment, it might well seem that all we have done for the last hundred years or so in the intellectual and cultural realms has been to turn to language, first to learn what is human, the specific terms of our mastery; and then, more recently, to learn what is not human, the specific terms of our servitude. In the past century, philosophy triumphed over its ancient problems by subjecting first the problems, and then the human beings that had the problems, to the solvent of language. And yet, despite a century of revolutions, the truth of language, and of man, still, I will argue, lies around the corner, always one turn away. To understand why this is so, we need to consider in greater detail not just the ends of linguistic turns, but their means, the style of the arguments that carry the burden of revolution.

2. Saussure and the Concrete Object of Language

In the beginning, there was Saussure, or so the story goes.
—MLADEN DOLAR, "The Object Voice"

The turning I have described as postmodern does not include such linguistic philosophers as Chomsky, whose interest in political and psychological issues appears, in a postmodern context, as a residual humanism out of touch with recent discoveries about the nature of man, namely, that it does not exist. Postmodern thought often refers to linguistics, but favors an account that is absent both from contemporary linguistics and from philosophical accounts of the linguistic turn. Unmentioned in Rorty's collection of essays on *The Linguistic Turn*, invisible in Martinich's anthology on *The Philosophy of Language*, absent from Katz's *The Philosophy of Linguistics*—and, amazingly, unrepresented in a book by Smith and Wilson called *Modern Linguistics*—the Swiss linguist Mongin-Ferdinand de Saussure is still referred and deferred to by many nonlinguists as the Founder of Modern Linguistics.

For most linguists, Hans Aarsleff reports, the decisive "epistemic break" separating modern linguistics from its prescientific precursor form came not with Saussure, but with the rise of comparative grammar early in the nineteenth century (1967: 127ff.). But for many of those outside the discipline of linguistics, modernism begins with Saussure, who has been revered and assailed as the essential modernist thinker, the originator of the whole constructivist, antihumanist paradigm, the inspiration for structuralism and post-structuralism as well as for French language theory in general, the leading figure in the development of semiology, the man who enabled the human sciences to become scientific, and much else.

Saussure's reputation is greatest among people who are largely indifferent to theories of syllabification, adduction and abduction, syntagmatic interdependencies, agglutination, and phonetic doublets—all of which are earnestly taken up in Saussure's *Course in General Linguistics*—but excited by other aspects of his thinking, which they have taken as the crystallized truth about language and the permanent North Star of the discipline of linguistics. At the very center of their discussion of "the role of critique in modern literary theory," Robert Con Davis and Ronald Schliefer include a heroic account of Saussure as the founder of structural linguistics and the progenitor of structuralism in general, Russian formalism, Prague semiotics, French structuralism, and even post-structuralism, right down to Derrida and Kristeva. The central principle of the entire intellectual genealogy is, in this account, derived directly from Saussure's founding recognition that a tree, called *arbre* in French, is called by other names in other languages, and that language therefore consists not of simple substances but relationships. "Within this analysis," they argue, "we can see that the science of linguistics, like the 'science' of psychoanalysis, or that of chemistry, is governed by a conceptual framework" based on relationships (Davis and Schliefer 125). Psychoanalysis may be an uncertain science, or "science," but linguistics is the master-discourse of science itself, including all the human sciences and even "hard" sciences such as chemistry, and Saussure is the central genius of language. And this is the way most literary thinkers see the matter. As the literary theorist Jonathan Culler says with impressive assurance, Saussure "provided a general orientation, a sense of the tasks of linguistics which has seldom been questioned, so much has it come to be taken for granted as the very nature of the subject itself" (94). In the critical theory community, "pre-Saussure" means "prescientific," and "post-Saussure" is inconceivable.

The main reason for this unwillingness on the part of nonlinguists to consider language in a non-Saussurean light is, of course, that Saussure is so rich in germinative conceptual energy that he has become indispensable. In a statement self-evidently meant to be uncontroversial and incontrovertible, Derrida commented in 1968 that "most of the semiological or linguistic research currently dominating the field of thought . . . traces its genealogy, rightly or wrongly, to Saussure as its common founder" (1973: 139). Many psychoanalysts, anthropologists, post-Marxist social theorists, and others might describe their own disciplines in the same way that Paul de Man characterized literary theory, which, he said, "comes into its own as the application of Saussurean linguistics to literary texts" (1986: 8). Saussure could be said to have contributed decisively to modernism through the principle of a social systematicity determining language, and to postmodernism through the principle of difference without positivity. He even makes a dark appeal, through means that will be the burden of this section to articulate, to both humanist and antihumanist arguments. Although neo-Saussurean thinkers in a number of fields who use language as a lever to dislodge transcendental pieties and replace them with scientific rigor often represent their project as a "critique of origins," Saussure looms very large among them as the authorizing father of the true account of language itself.

He is, incontrovertibly, the father-founder of the linguistics that most nonlinguists have preferred to call "modern," a linguistics, that is, that can be taken as a science by virtue of having reduced its object to the manageable field of the system of signs. But the theoretical eminence of Saussure's linguistics depends less on his success in achieving his expressed aim of making linguistics into a science than on the support his work lends to various intellectual or ideological projects. He made his initial reputation in 1878 with the publication of an historical study of Indo-European vowels, and taught general linguistics only three times, between 1906 and 1911. He had no thought of publishing the work on which his courses were based, and did not comport himself as a great pioneer or innovator. It would not, perhaps, have surprised him to learn that one day his work, like that of Freud, would be regarded by specialists as something like an ancient papyrus scroll dating from the prehistory of the discipline. His failure to publish or even properly to compose his thinking, a failure only partially remedied by the diligent efforts of his students and colleagues to gather and organize his lectures into what is now known as the *Course in General Linguistics,* suggests a surprising tentativeness that is confirmed by passages in his personal letters in which he confesses his frustration with the whole subject of general linguistics. "I have no dearer wish," he writes in 1894, "than not to be made to think about the nature of language in general" (translated and quoted in

Culler 24). And his long-standing, deep, and troubled interest in anagrams can, as we shall see, be interpreted as evidence of a lack of conviction concerning the very concepts for which he has become famous.

In fact, the comparison with Freud is, as Jean-Claude Milner has argued, inexact because Freud truly invented a new configuration, a new discourse, whereas Saussure was a conservative thinker who merely sought to describe a preexisting discipline of linguistics devoted to comparative grammar, a discipline that required elucidation because, as Milner puts it, it "was not cognisant of what rendered it possible" (1990b: 82). Among linguists today, Saussure is often seen as the last major figure in a now-discarded tradition—a decadent like, say, Wilde, to name another major thinker whose work was organized around the life of signs in society. Roy Harris and Talbot Taylor's authoritative *Landmarks of Linguistic Thought* is subtitled *The Western Tradition from Socrates to Saussure;* and Harris and Taylor, while fully understanding Saussure's originality, nevertheless treat him as the final blow struck against "the tradition of linguistic thought that began with Socrates," in which words were considered as integrally linked to the things they stood for (224). It is not at all uncommon to read appraisals of Saussure by the linguistically informed as timid, moderate, conservative, even backward (see Pavel 21). Surveying the history of linguistics, Foucault dismisses Saussure as a man who, so far from inventing the future, was "in fact rediscovering the Classical condition for conceiving of the binary nature of the sign" (1970: 67).

One of the ironies of Saussure's reception is that while many linguists and historians of linguistics regard him either as a critic or a representative of an exhausted line, he has become known among nonlinguists chiefly for the radical character of his beginning. Saussure earned his credentials as a hero and a sage, Roland Barthes said, by making a true beginning, by deciding "to choose one thread, one pertinence (that of meaning), and to unravel this thread: thus was constructed a *system* of language" (1972: 80; see also Lecercle 2). Firmly grounded by Saussure, linguistics could become a "new science" whose revolutionary effect, Barthes argued, could be compared to that of Galileo or Copernicus. Because Saussure understood where and how to make the first cut, modernism, that ethos of inauguration, was able to make it new; and postmodernism, that ethos of belatedness, was able to return to origins in order to critique them. The very name of Saussure seems to possess originative force: In the beginning was Saussure.

The greatest irony concerning the reception of Saussure concerns his founding gesture itself, his insistence that linguistics should make a beginning by an absolutely ruthless delimitation of its field. As Saussure saw it, linguistics had failed to become a science—an inquiry undertaken from a single, internally consistent perspective on a limited field of data—because it had permitted itself to become distracted by questions relevant to other fields, including ethnology, anthropology, history, and even prehistory. As a consequence, linguists had plunged into a mass of speculations on subjects other than language, permitting their true object, the *"objet à la fois intégral et concret"* of linguistics, to slip away unobserved (Saussure 1949: 23).

Walter Benjamin's essay "On Language as Such and on the Language of Man" was published at virtually the same moment that Saussure's lectures appeared, but took an altogether different approach. Benjamin criticized "the bourgeois view of language" as signs—a view, he said, that obscured the true nature of language. "Language," Benjamin insisted, "never gives *mere* signs" (69). Harkening back to a radically antimodern tradition that included Pietism and Jewish mysticism, Benjamin argued not for a tighter definition of language, but for a more expansive conception of a communicative "flow" that "runs through the whole of nature, from the lowest forms of existence to man and from man to God" (74). Almost as if in response to the argument Benjamin would make, Saussure contended in his lectures that linguistics must be a science, and that the infinite world of mind and matter in which language was diffused could never serve as a suitable object for an orderly inquiry. Linguistics, he said, could never hope to grasp language in all its manifestations and uses, an indefinite mass to which he gave the name *langage* but which might also be called "discourse." Noting that what was commonly called "language" straddled several fields—"physical, physiological, and psychological"—Saussure gave up on it immediately because "language as such has no discernible unity" (1997: 9, 10).

The main battle, however, was waged with those who, like Saussure, wanted to make linguistics into a science, but who were going about it the wrong way by treating language not as a social product deposited in individual brains, but as an autonomous growth, a kind of "fourth realm of nature." This premise, Saussure said, resulted only in confusion; indeed, "no other subject has fostered more absurd notions, more prejudices, more illusions, or more fantasies" than the study of language (1997: 4, 7). Linguistics could only become a science by eliminating all "external" factors in favor of an exclusive focus on what he called *langue*—"language alone" or "language as such," the socially constructed system of differences that positioned all linguistic units in relation to the others, thus permitting signs to function as vehicles of meaning. Saussure modernized linguistics and everything else for miles around, not by proposing a comprehensive unified theory of knowledge but rather by stripping away most of what had been regarded as integral parts of language, leaving the abstract notion of systematicity itself. He viewed the *langue* holistically, as a limited, determined entity, a discrete thing whose nature could be known. According to Milner, the "ethic of science" is based on a "renunciation" of total knowledge in favor of the partial knowledge available to a particular discipline (1990b: 79). By renouncing *langage* as its object in order to focus on *langue,* Saussure's linguistics was, or sought to become, an exemplary science.

Saussure regarded *langue* somewhat in the manner of a Durkheimian sociologist, as a "product of the collective mind of a linguistic community," a "social product stored in the brain" (1997: 5, 24). The linguist's task was to analyze this system as a "semiology," which meant "to define the units of a language, the relations between them, and their rules of combination" (Culler 94). Paradoxically, *langue* referred both to a given linguistic system such as French or Italian, and to the universal or essential condition of language as such. Even more paradoxically, while a true linguistics could only study *a language,* it had to treat as "external" all factors peculiar to that language in order to focus on the universal conditions of systematicity and difference themselves. Only in this way could linguistics realize its destiny of becoming "Queen of the Sciences," a discipline that could stand proudly alone where previous linguistics had relied implicitly on natural history, anthropology, psychology, physics, history, and various pseudo-versions of all of the above (see Pavel 19ff.). "*The only true object of study in linguistics,*" Saussure concluded with unusual emphasis, "*is the language*"—the system—"*considered in itself and for its own sake*" (1997: 230). And with this decisive formulation, Saussure felt that he had identified an object concrete enough to sustain a science.

It is fascinating to watch Saussure as, against his powerful will and deeply held convictions, he finds himself forced to dissimulate this laboriously achieved concreteness. This process begins immediately, with the account of the elementary linguistic unit, the sign. "Words" were burdened by disorderly histories and sometimes aberrant orthographic forms, both of which frustrated scientific inquiry; but signs, in which a sound component (signifier) was joined to a conceptual component (signified) as indissolubly as the recto and verso of a piece of paper, were not. Considered as a system of signs, language was a rational structure, a complex but orderly game, a vast grid of relational positions. From one point of view, this new focus benefits the would-be linguistic scientist immensely, since the posited object responds so readily to rational analysis. But there is a cost as well, for Saussure is able to rationalize the object of study only by installing, at the center of the concrete object of language, systematicity as such, the idea of an abstract structure composed, as he put it, of *differences without positive content.*

It was this strictly mental and yet, for the individual language-user, functionally unconscious structure itself that enabled the individual elements to possess definite meanings. The system did not consist of a mass of individually meaningful elements, but rather itself bestowed meaning on the elements by assigning them definite positions. Saussure clearly thought that the systematicity of language qualified it as an object of scientific study. And the key to this systematicity was, as he said in a fateful proposition that secured both his enduring eminence in other fields and his rapid superannuation in his own, arbitrariness. The link between signifier and signified was not natural, given, inevitable, or necessary, but "arbitrary," as was the fact that a given sound signified anything at all. While neither an individual nor a community could freely recast this relationship, there was no external constraining factor that attached a given sound to a given concept. It might seem paradoxical that an arbitrary system could be considered accessible to rational analysis, but as Roy Harris and Talbot Taylor point out, arbitrariness ensures that the relation between signifier and signified is "in no way dependent on factors external to the *langue*" and thus locks in at once the concreteness and the systematicity of the linguistic entity. "There is," Harris and Taylor write, "no contradiction between systematicity and arbitrariness unless we overlook the basic fact that all values are established contrastively; that is, in virtue of the differences between co-existing elements" (223; see also Harris 1987b: 64–69).

Just as important in the present context, arbitrariness is the principle that thinkers in other fields found most attractive for its suggestion of a self-contained and orderly system whose rules might be accessible to rational inquiry. Learning of Saussure through the work of Roman Jakobson, the anthropologist

Claude Lévi-Strauss, for example, came to believe that arbitrariness was "a prerequisite for the accession of linguistics to the scientific level" (1963: 209). Satisfied that linguistics was now a scientific discipline, Lévi-Strauss proceeded to model his own practice of anthropology on Saussurean principles, proposing the sign as the elementary unit deployed by the archaic "bricoleur" in the construction of myths, and the sign system as the key to what he called "the savage mind" itself (1966: 16–22). Impressed by the stunning success of Lévi-Strauss and others in transforming anthropology into a "structuralist" discipline, other thinkers began to turn to the concept of a system of signs as a way of modernizing their own disciplines along similar lines. Cut loose from linguistics and functioning as a free-floating principle of general theoretical utility, the notion of arbitrary systematicity came to represent not just the form of primitive thought, but also a revolutionary principle of freedom from material or transcendental necessity—the touchstone of advanced theoretical reflection in the politicized climate of the French 1960s.

While it might have been theoretically imperative on a number of levels, however, arbitrariness proved to be elusive. Where was it? Was it a feature of the relation between signifier and signified, as Saussure argued? Many readers felt, like Emile Benveniste, that Saussure had misplaced arbitrariness by locating it in what was in fact a functionally necessary relationship. Within the English language, the sound-image "rose" and the idea of a certain kind of flower are indissolubly wedded, for an English speaker can't help associating the sound with the concept. The true site of arbitrariness, Benveniste contended, was the relation between the sign as a whole and the real referent, some actual extra-linguistic flower. Saussure's reasoning on this point, Julia Kristeva agrees, "seems to have allowed an error" (1989a: 16). But Benveniste's relocation of arbitrariness may itself allow, or be, another error. For in a pragmatic, if not in a theoretical sense, the sign-referent relationship is no more arbitrary, no more negotiable, than the phoneme-concept relation. Things might have different names than they do, but one exercises this theoretical freedom at the cost of participation in the linguistic, and indeed the social community. Roses by any other name might smell as sweet, but if one held up a rose and praised the smell of "this lily," one would attract the wrong kind of attention. A compelling theoretical postulate, arbitrariness proves to be difficult to locate in practice.

Nor are linguists agreed that arbitrariness describes anything essential to language at all. Geoffrey Sampson finds the most vulnerable point of Saussure's entire exposition to be the relegation of syntax—which, from his point of view, is more necessary than it is arbitrary—to the domain of *parole*, the individual speech act, when it should, he feels, be grouped with the conventions of *langue*, and even given primacy among those conventions. Sampson detects in Saussure a "French" presumption that language is so "logical" that one need only learn the words, and not the conventions for ordering words, in order to make perfect sense. "The pattern of a scholar's thought," Sampson comments, "will often be influenced by presuppositions current in his intellectual milieu even though they involve beliefs which he would reject if he confronted them explicitly" (1980b: 55).

Indeed, for Sampson as well as for those linguists influenced by Chomsky, what is most arbitrary about Saussure is his unscientific—indeed, arbitrary—assimilation of language to semiotics. For Chomskyans, Saussure offers nothing more than a flabby sociology of language that misses altogether the real object, the hardwired mental capacity that enables us to learn language effortlessly. As one committed Chomskyan puts it, "Saussure made further linguistics impossible," and "had to be rejected if linguistics was to survive" (Graham 58). Thomas Pavel argues in a similar vein that the Saussurean themes of the "flight towards indetermination" and the "appeal to randomness," while abolishing classical metaphysics, also signal "the end of *methodology*" and thus represent a dead end for linguistics (71). For Milner, a Chomskyan linguist with connections to Lacan's Ecole Freudienne, the entire Saussurean account of language rests upon a set of exclusions with no more than a procedural justification; as a result, Saussure's "language" is "a mask arbitrarily constructed, one which touches upon no real" (1990b: 62). For Chomskyans and others, linguistics could only be scientific if it rejected arbitrariness and the horse (Saussure) it rode in on.

The total effect of arbitrariness on the scientific status of general linguistics is thus deeply equivocal. For those who regard language as an innate mental capacity, arbitrariness represents a fundamental mistake; and even for those who regard language as a social product, the principle of arbitrariness exacts a certain cost in terms of the sense of "concreteness" on which Saussure insists. But as we are beginning to see, arbitrariness is but one of the factors in Saussure's account that compromises concreteness. Even more subversive is the endemic binarism of Saussure's thinking—the *langue/parole* distinction, the internal division of the sign, the famous "speech circuit" of speaker and listener (which was, in fact, almost entirely the invention of the 1916 editors), the synchronic and diachronic aspects of language, and the "inner duality" of all linguistic facts. At every point, we find concreteness evaporated, as the sign imprints its ambivalent character on everything, even on the very terms of analysis themselves. The *Course* actually enacts a sustained crisis of concretion as it tracks the tendency of linguistic entities to doubling, mitotic self-division, and abstraction.

The deeper problem is that Saussure fails to establish a clean plane between language and not-language, to banish from view everything but an integral and concrete object of language alone. Throughout the *Course,* the nonlinguistic insistently returns in the foggy forms of "society," the "psychological entity" of the sign, the necessity of "subjective analysis," unconscious "knowledge" of the system, the "mental reality" of the sign, and "the role of abstract entities in grammar"—all of which bear witness to what is, or ought to be, excluded from language itself, and indeed from the domain of "objects." He addressed—rather than solved—the problem of abstraction by insisting that abstract linguistic entities rested ultimately on concrete entities, but this insistence only created a deeply problematic stratification of linguistic reality in which some levels are more real than others. And "that," Roy Harris comments, "marks the point that Saussure's reflections on language had reached when illness forced him to abandon the work" (2000: 280).

By leaving his work in such a provocatively unfinished and unresolved state, Saussure ensured a certain kind of reception. Not only has the discipline of linguistics found it necessary to repress its founder, but thinkers in other fields have invariably implicated him in scenarios of repression. For Derrida, the degraded or secondary status of writing in Saussure reaffirmed Western "metaphysics"; Saussure's claim that speech, rather than writing, enjoyed a natural intimacy with thought produced, Derrida charged, an account of language that could not be called scientific because it so manifestly reflected the force of repression (see 1978a; see also Roy Harris 1990: 158–79). Deconstruction is born as a "science of writing" in the lifting of Saussure's repression, the emancipation of the grapheme. Lacan's appropriation of Saussure is even more heavily invested in the notion of repression, for it begins with a mapping of the Saussurean sign onto the Freudian unconscious, with the "material" signifier representing a kind of ultimacy of unconsciousness. The bar that separates signifier from signified represents, Lacan suggests, repression itself, and its presence in the sign marks not just the inability of the signifier to grasp the signified but also the inability of the subject to integrate all its parts into a self-mastering totality (see 1977: 126). Saussure may have sought a cold, dry, and purely social linguistics that would make language fully available to disinterested scientific observation— a linguistics, and a language, of pure concreteness—but to many who came later, whether to bury or to praise him, the mind and repression are what he's all about.

3. Metaphor and the Law of Return: Saussure, Derrida, Rorty

> . . . the point where desire comes to corrupt a human science can be discovered, where, if one is willing to take the neces-sary trouble, an intelligible relation is tied to a possible theory of desire.
>
> —JEAN-CLAUDE MILNER, *For the Love of Language*

Given the prominent role of repression in the work and reception of Saus-sure, it cannot be surprising to discover what we might call a "law of return" operating in his text, as elements once banished rush back in un-guarded moments to reclaim their places. Among the banned elements are those "presuppositions current in the intellectual milieu" that seemed to Saussure impure because not drawn from a study of language alone. The *Course* is rich in milieu.

One such presupposition has already been mentioned, the Durkheimian notion of a "collective mind" responsible for creating "social facts" such as the system of signs (see Sampson 1980b: 43–48; Culler 85–94). Another is the work of Freud, who, Culler argues, should be linked to Saussure as co-inves-tigators of the social norms that make individual experience possible, and proponents of structural rather than causal explanations (85–94). A somewhat surprising third is Darwinism, which informs the "evolutionary" view of lan-guage development. Saussure had only scorn for those who saw language as "organic," and did everything in his power to exclude the temporal dimension from linguistics. But as Harris and Taylor point out, Saussure actually provided "what is in some ways a more convincing interpretation than any advanced by his neo-Darwinian predecessors of the notion that language is subject to the law of 'survival of the fittest'" by showing how linguistic elements could survive a process of change if they could find some role to play in the new system (216–18). A fourth presupposition can be traced back to the work of Hippolyte Taine, who developed the notion of relational identity in a way that clearly anticipates Saussure (see Aarsleff 1982: 356–71). Fifth, and perhaps deeper in the shadows, is Kant, whose antinomies might count as precursors of Saussure's binaries (see Milner 1990b: 83).

But really, there is no end of presuppositions that might be posited. Saussure was no Marxist, but that is no obstacle to a Marxist reading of him. Barbara Johnson has, for example, noticed something that only became fully legible after May 1968 in France—that Saussure's account of the signified bore an uncanny resemblance to "the fetishization of commodities resulting from bourgeois idealism's blindness to labor." The "liberation of the signifier" in Saussure's work is best read, she suggests, as a "rebellion against idealist repressions, and the unleashing of the forces of difference and desire against the law and order of identity" (41). There is in fact a good deal in the *Course* that suggests that Saussure was deeply and explicitly concerned with the crucial Marxian concept of value: Saussure frequently compares words to coins, and, at a deeper level, seems to draw his account of language from the marketplace. "Values," he says, "always involve:

(1) Something *dissimilar* which can be exchanged for the item whose value is under consideration, and
(2) *similar* things which can be compared with the item whose value is under consideration.
These two features are necessary for the existence of any value. To determine the value of a five-franc coin, for instance. . . . (1997: 113)

Perhaps Saussure's most productive insight, from a Marxian point of view, was that linguistic value, like the value of the commodity and cultural value generally, was produced not given, a function of historical and social rather than natural forces. With this insight, language became accessible to Marxian critique, and the unmanageable domain of history itself could be grasped by methods of linguistic analysis. Thus while Saussure was no Marxist in any of the most obvious senses, he did, in a generally conservative time, keep alive the Marxian faith in cultural materialism and the dialectic by hiding them in the ostensibly nonideological discipline of linguistics.

In light of such scholarly recoveries, Saussure seems now more than ever to be not just the central thinker of the past century, but the one thinker capable of crossing the great divide from the premodern to the modern and even beyond. His account of language begins with the central nineteenth-century notion of continuous change over time; but then, in a definitive modernist gesture, he brackets this change to isolate the linguistic system as it exists at a given moment. As William Everdell argues, "at the heart of Modernism is the postulate of ontological discontinuity," a concept that has been so effective that now, more than a century after modernism's first stirrings, "we cannot help seeing the objects of our knowledge as discrete and discontinuous—digital rather than analogue" (351). Everdell does not, in his vast book *The First Moderns,* mention Saussure, but it is Saussurean linguistics that provides the most fundamental and compelling instance of the "discovery" of the discontinuity postulate. By the same token, Saussure is ritually invoked by the thinkers of postmodernity as the genius who first articulated the two principles on which postmodernism is founded, the system without a center, and differences without positivity. Saussure's work, it now appears, was so powerfully transformative and influential because it had already absorbed so much.

It is in one respect comforting to think that Saussure, always cast as a lonely pioneer pursuing his narrow studies, lived in a rich intellectual environment. But if the real determinants of his thinking were found to be environmental, drawn from a general unfiltered atmosphere of current popularized versions of thinking on other subjects altogether, the scientific stature of his linguistics would surely suffer, as would Saussure's claim to have determined the nature of language alone. This claim was, as we have seen, complicated by Saussure's insistence that the true, innermost being of language was not strictly linguistic but semiotic, a property it shared with other symbolic systems. But it was further complicated, almost to the point of being subverted, by a number of thematic undertones that throb through the *Course.*

Perhaps the most intriguing evidence for the law of return in the *Course* is to be found in a rarely noted feature of the text, its reliance, for explanatory purposes, on figures of nature. Saussure is relentless in attacking those who regard language as natural or organic, but is for some reason unable to weed out all references to nature from his own discourse, as when he remarks, "Our definition of a language assumes that we disregard everything which does not belong to its organism, to its system" ["*à son organisme, à son système*"] (1949: 40).* Indeed, the entire fifth chapter of the Introduction is conducted in the key of biology, with references to "*l'organisme intérieur de l'idiome,*" "*la vie des langues,*" "*l'organisme grammatical*" (compared to "the inner organism of a plant"), "*le développement naturel, organique d'un idiome,*" "*l'organisme linguistique interne,*" and so forth. Onomatopoetic (i.e., nonarbitrary) signs are condemned on the grounds that they are "never organic elements of a linguistic system" (69). And throughout, the social product of language, the invention of the collective mind, is, for reasons never articulated, described in biological and merely organic terms.

These are, one might protest, merely metaphors, not integral elements of the theoretical system Saussure was constructing. And Saussure would, of course, agree that metaphors are not science. In fact, in a footnote at the end of the first chapter of his Introduction, he deplores the "illogical metaphors" in the terminology of previous linguists, and applauds the neogrammarians of the nineteenth century, who had fought against these metaphors so successfully that, after them, "it became unacceptable to say 'the language does this or does that', to speak of the 'life of the language', and so on, because a language is not an entity, and exists only in its users." But then, surprisingly, Saussure cautions against theoretical puritanism, warning that "such an attitude must not be carried too far." When describing language, one cannot restrict oneself to a strictly denotative literalism because we are, after all,

---

*My translation. With respect to the main terms of Saussure's discourse, the Roy Harris translation of the *Course* is to be preferred to the more widely available Baskin translation. But Harris feels alarmingly free to make both additions and subtractions in order to clarify Saussure's meaning. In several of the passages to which I will draw attention, he has deliberately mistranslated, as when he renders this phrase as "its structure as a system," eliminating Saussure's confusing reference to the "organism" of language (Saussure 1997: 21). Whenever I feel that Harris's clarity is more misleading with respect to Saussure's intentions than Saussure's confusion, I will provide my own translations, accompanied by direct quotations from the 1949 French edition, which, in all essentials, reproduces the 1916 text with which both Baskin and Harris worked.

still groping to discover the "facts of speech" and cannot yet describe them with perfect accuracy. And so we must employ, perhaps temporarily, certain "expressions which were formerly censured as inappropriate." If some metaphors seem arbitrary and irrational, Saussure concludes, "there are certain figurative ways of speaking which are indispensable" (1997: 5).

As it happens, it is precisely those metaphors in which the "life of language" is asserted that prove to be most indispensable of all, as when, in a characteristic moment, Saussure remarks that "language never stops interpreting and decomposing its units" ["*la langue ne cesse d'interpreter et de décomposer les unités qui lui sont données*"]—as if language had agency and intentionality, a formulation that could only be metaphorical (1949: 232). Sometimes metaphor leads on to metaphor in a manner that invites a separate act of interpretation and decomposition by Saussure's reader. Take, for example, the metaphor-rich discussion of the "immutability and mutability of the sign" in Part 1, chapter 2. Earlier, Saussure had described language as "a kind of contract" to which the individual is bound; but here he notes that it cannot be considered "simply as a form of contract," for the masses ["*la masse sociale*"] are not consulted: the language itself determines the signifiers, which are "*choisi par la langue*" (1997: 14; 1949: 104). Throughout this section, language is described, in metaphors whose motivation is uncertain, as a rule, a law, a brake on innovation, a depressant, a force that overrides individual agency and choice.

Oddly, subsequent Marxist thinkers have found this aspect of Saussure highly congenial. A Saussurean treatment of the sign system, they argue, could, if reread from a materialist perspective, help cure what Rosalind Coward and John Ellis call "a central failing in Marxist thought and practice," its inability to determine a ground for utopian aspiration. Since all social practices take place in language, they say, it becomes possible, in the climate of Saussure, "to consider language as the place in which the social individual is constructed," and also to undertake "a scientific analysis of the concept of the human" (2). Saussure, on this reading, offers a small, distant, theoretical, but firmly scientific support for the general proposition that people can transform or "construct" the conditions of their existence. His claim that meaning is the product of differences had, Coward and Ellis say, "a more radical potentiality" than he imagined, "since the signifier could be seen to have an active function in creating and determining the signified" (3). This reading is odd, if not precisely impossible, because it simply sets aside an entire pattern of insistence in Saussure's exposition of the ways in which language overrides individual and even collective agency. To read Coward and Ellis, and any number of other linguistically oriented post-Marxist thinkers, one would never imagine that Saussure felt that language offers "the most striking proof" of the fact that "the rules a community accepts are imposed upon it, and not freely agreed to" (71).

Saussure seems to approve of such rules, in the way that a conservative political thinker might approve of tradition and custom—which Saussure evokes with a banal eloquence in speaking of "the normal, regular existence of a language already established" or of the "collective inertia" to which language testifies (1997: 72, 73). It is in fact easy to provide "missing" political terms for entire passages in order to produce an account of an ideal conservative polis, in which the wisdom of tradition constantly restricts freedom of choice and, utopian hopes notwithstanding, defeats in advance any possibility of revolution. "Of all social institutions," Saussure concludes one such passage, "a language affords the least scope for such enterprise. It is part and parcel of the life of the whole community, and the community's natural inertia exercises a conservative influence upon it" (74).

What, then, has science informed us about the concrete object of language? That it is a kind of monetary system, saturated with value; that despite a general sense of individual freedom (in the production of speech), each element is subject to the rule of the system, or *langue*, from which it derives its identity; and that the names of politics and history must not be spoken. We learn, in short, that the sign is a metaphor for Switzerland in the European *langue*, with precisely the kind of appeal to warring nations that Switzerland, or the idea of Switzerland, has always had. Roy Harris notes other metaphorized "European" elements in Saussure, commenting that "the relevance of Saussurean doctrine to Europe's most critical social and political problems in the first half of the twentieth century is too striking to be ignored. Its quasi-mystical appeal to the absolute sovereignty of the community, its deliberate subordination of the linguistic role of the individual, and its presentation of *la langue* as a kind of psychological manifestation of collective uniformity can hardly have counted for nothing in its rapid and widespread acceptance" (Harris 1980: 157). Indeed, other disciplines were caught up in the same general context, so that Saussurean linguistics fit right in with "a variety of modern developments in academic disciplines as far removed from language studies as mathematics and physics, all manifesting comparable features. . . . If Saussure had not existed," Harris concludes, "it would have been necessary to invent him" (1980: 154–55; see also Harris 1981: 32–52; 1987a: 112–16; 1987b; 1990: 142–50).

Saussure was concerned to establish linguistics as a science in order to shield it from general social or moral influences. The *Course* registers a strong protest against the position that all knowledge is necessarily "embedded" in its particular cultural context, and insists that the object must be seen in its entirety and in itself. And so it is especially striking that elements of context can be so readily detected not only in Saussure's attempts to clarify abstract concepts but in the very features he posited of the linguistic object itself, which can easily be recoded as metaphors for a variety of extra-linguistic circumstances with political, cultural, and even personal determinants. Even more striking, however, is the fact that Saussure's account of language proved to be so responsive to contexts far removed from his own and so appealing to temperaments altogether opposed to his. A deeply conservative political thinker who was persuaded that his scientific undertakings were presuppositionless, Saussure might well have been horrified at the thought that his work would be deployed in the service of the theory revolution of the last half of the twentieth century, with its vaguely leftist jubilation, its utopian spirit of self-invention, its celebration of "difference."

How did this happen? The most general reason is that Saussure did indeed hit upon something crucial about language, but that he failed to realize exactly what it was. The *Course in General Linguistics* adapts so well to different contexts because what it actually describes is not the totality of language itself, but the word *language*. We can read the *Course* as a metaphorical meditation on the way in which *language* functions as both a master-signifier and a master-signified. As signifier, *language* exemplifies signification itself, pointing not just toward sounds, words, sentences, and signs, but also toward anything that may mean anything to anyone, such as rocks, rivers, trees (Nature's mighty hieroglyph), earthquakes, floods, plagues of boils (God's address to fallen humanity), lucky pennies, the Milky Way, the structure of DNA, cities, fashion, images, "texts" in the broadest sense, terrorist attacks—anything and everything capable of communication or expression of any kind. As signified, *language* is a meta-concept toward which all signifiers gesture, beyond their immediate referents. Like all signifieds, it carries with it a suggestion of "concreteness" and produces "substance-effects," but, when removed from the *langue* and considered by itself, alone, it dissolves into a smear of sounds, a trail of letters, with no object, either material or ideal, in sight. Installing difference-from-itself and context-dependency as the central principles of language, Saussure did not so much describe the concrete entity of language as he gave a powerful reason why such a description was impossible. Giving voice to the enduring singularity of the word *language*, a master-signifier and master-signified in all contexts, Saussure explains, finally, why he has become a theorist for all seasons.

So absorbed was Saussure in the scientific project of determining the irreducible facts of language that he did not seem to pause to suspect his own methods, his own conclusions, or his own rhetoric. Throughout the *Course*, he thinks *in* metaphors, but he does not necessarily think *through* his metaphors, nor does he think *of* the question of metaphor itself. He does, however, freely acknowledge, without seeming to realize the implications, that linguistics has a creative, even a poetic dimension that other disciplines do not. "Other sciences," he notes, "are provided with objects of study given in advance, which are then examined from different points of view." Linguistics, by contrast, has no such object. Take a simple word (his example is *nu*, "naked"): "careful consideration reveals a series of three or four different things, depending on the viewpoint adopted"—a sound, an expression of an idea, a derivative of a Latin word, and so on, with no guide as to which is logically prior to or more fundamental than the others. "The object is not given in advance of the viewpoint," he says; "far from it. Rather, one might say that it is the viewpoint adopted which creates the object" (1997: 8). Absent a fixed linguistic object, the linguist must decide on some (perhaps "arbitrary") basis what is going to count as language, and then describe it as if it were given.

Amazingly, Saussure then proceeds to do just that.

The crisis of concretion of which Saussure's metaphors are one aspect is perhaps more poignantly and comprehensively indicated by what has become known as "the other Saussure," a thinker of an altogether different stripe. This Hyde-like obsessive emerged into visibility with the 1971 publication of previously embargoed notebooks in which Saussure had collected and analyzed vast numbers of variously constructed anagrams—the letters of the name of a god scattered through the poem written in the god's honor, numerous kinds of homophony or echoes, and so forth—that he thought he could locate in archaic Latin poetry (see Starobinski; see also *Semiotexte* on "the other Saussure," and de Man 1986: 36–54). Manifestly linguistic and therefore something that ought to be included in the linguist's field of vision, the anagram does not behave like a "sign," being nonarbitrary, nondifferential, noncontingent, and unrelated to a "concept." In a brilliant, difficult, and consequently little-known book, Milner described anagrams as a "return of the foreclosed," tokens of a repressed "real" in language that was discernible only to the speculative inference of psychoanalysis, not to a scientific linguistics. In discovering that anagrams were always perceptible—indeed, they seemed virtually ubiquitous—but never fully demonstrable, Saussure came face to face with what Milner calls an "unconscious" dimension of language that intruded upon the waking dream of science.

Milner's Saussure is not the magisterial Founder of Modern Linguistics and the paradigmatic thinker of modernism, but a "shattered figure" driven mad by anagrams—who, however, still managed to presage the authentic genius, as Milner would have it, of Lacan (1990b: 109–17). Also on the basis of the evidence provided by Saussure's interest in anagrams, Jean-Jacques Lecercle constructs, in *Philosophy through the Looking-Glass* (1985), a Saussure who pointed the way to Gilles Deleuze and Félix Guattari. These thinkers, Lecercle says, contested all the essential postulates of a scientific linguistics in favor of a heterodox, "excessive," "pragmatic," untheorizable, power-strafed language; and they found what theoretical and historical support they required not, of course, in the Saussure of the *Course,* but in the "demented seeker of anagrams" who discovered a form of linguistic "delirium" that overturned all his scientific aspirations, but which led by a winding path to the truth of language (Lecercle 2).

Our conclusion about Saussure—that his integral and concrete entity of language is necessarily and extravagantly haunted by what it excludes—will anchor the rest of this chapter, and the rest of the book. From here on, the argument will be, first, that when it comes to language, metaphors are truly indispensable, for language cannot be described as an integrated whole without an arbitrary act of exclusion that establishes an essence or core by delimiting the field of the linguistic. In other words, any description that attributes to language a particular character, nature, or function will necessarily have the status of a metaphor. The second claim, following from the first, will be that metaphors in the description of language will typically reinstate precisely what has been excluded in the initial determination of what counts as language. I will argue, in short, that attempts to characterize language will fail and fail in the same way, by an action of return that restores what has been banished in the initial effort to purify and limit the data.

This action of return in the discourse on language is so inescapable that it determines even the most sophisticated attempts at description. Consider, for example, Jacques Derrida's early efforts to base a post-philosophical discourse about human existence on an account of language. Perhaps the most condensed version of his efforts in this respect is to be found in a 1967 essay published at the end of the English edition of *Speech and Phenomena* called "Form and Meaning: A Note on the Phenomenology of Language," in which he tracks Husserl's efforts to grasp the nature of language. With painstaking attention to detail, Derrida rebraids all of Husserl's distinctions, demonstrating how Husserl himself cannot maintain a clean plane between, for example, "expression" and its "bodily aspect," or between "meaning" and "sense." In fact, Derrida concludes, an "irreducible complicity"—the law of return by another name—works throughout Husserl to "[fuse] the two strata," and so defeat the idealizing gesture on which they are founded (1973: 126).

The triumph of Derrida's argument is the demonstration that the distinctions between the essential and the contingent aspects of language—distinctions that were motivated by the desire to replace what Husserl called "metaphysical interpretations" by proper analysis—were themselves metaphysical in their essence (1973: 107). Critiquing Husserl's failure of rigor, Derrida cautions that metaphysics can, like the devil, mime the form of its opposite. In the end, he suggests, we should not look to a self-deluding practice of theoretical rigor to defeat metaphysics, but rather to the antitheoretical, antimetaphysical properties of language itself. "Form and Meaning" constitutes a warning to any who would attempt to impose a false clarity on language by attempting to define and delimit it. It is not, however, a warning Derrida could afford to heed, and it is this point on which I wish to focus. Since his entire early project rested on "the phenomenology of language," he required some explication of that feature of language that qualified it to stand as the decisive refutation of metaphysical illusions. In pursuit of this feature, he abandoned his usual practice of close reading of theoretical or philosophical texts and delivered, at the Sorbonne in January 1968, a programmatic lecture, also bundled into *Speech and Phenomena,* called "Differance."

Derrida uses this cryptic neologism to indicate not just the kind of differences to be found *in* language, but also the difference introduced *by* language into traditional notions of consciousness, agency, rationality, intention, identity, and life itself. All of these differences, Derrida contends, must be seen as functions of the sign, arbitrary and differential. In one of its inaugural moves—the upgrading of the status of writing being the other—deconstruction expands the concept of the sign to cover the field of language, and then expands the concept of language to cover almost everything else.

Clearly, Derrida derives his emphasis on differences in language from Saussure. The exposition, in *Grammatology,* of Saussure's account of the sign was one of the early triumphs of the deconstructive method. But whereas the sign constituted, for Saussure, the kernel of the integrated and concrete object of language, for Derrida the bifurcated sign testifies to language's disintegration, its failure to harden into concreteness. "Differance" itself is not itself, for it actually denotes two different kinds of difference, a principle of distinction or discernability and a temporal principle of deferral or delay: the sign can never coincide with itself both because its meaning is determined by other signs, and because the signified concept is apprehended *later* than the perception of the signifier. Differance, according to Derrida, is a fact; but it is also a value, for it blocks the path to a certain kind of narcissism. Citing Saussure repeatedly, Derrida argues that since we think only in signs, we must conform to "the general law of difference," which means we cannot be self-mastering subjects but must remain divided, conflicted, at odds with ourselves (1973: 146).

Of course, Derrida is constantly on guard lest he repeat the very errors he criticizes, and so refuses any concrete or positive identity even to his own term. Differance, he says, is "neither a *word* nor a *concept,*" but a version of nothing, a mere "spelling mistake" (1973: 130). Specific differences could be said to be the "effect" of differance, but in fact the entire logic of causality is out of place here. Differences are effects without causes, for their putative "cause," differance itself, does not produce or create anything. Differance "commands nothing, rules over nothing, and nowhere does it exercise any authority"; it consists only of "an operation which is not an operation, which cannot be thought of either as a passion or as an action of a subject upon an object"; "there is no essence of differance; not only can it not allow itself to be taken up into the *as such* of its name or its appearing, but it threatens the authority of the *as such* in general" (153, 137, 158). The only way one can indicate it, and that imperfectly, is through the mannerisms that evolved into the critical-theoretical style of the 1970s and much of the 1980s, including crossed-out words, strings of questions with no answers, and a decided preference for negative formulations. All these tics and hedges are necessary, Derrida implies, to overcome the bad habits of a self-mystifying philosophical discourse that is virtually founded on the denial of differance. By laying bare the mechanisms of this denial, deconstructive critique tries to take a first step in permitting the repressed to return, inaugurating a new day in the history of thought in which the reality of language emerges to displace a host of pseudo-problems that had been occupying, or rather distracting, the attention of philosophers.

Within a differential system, differance is certainly different. The antidote to ancient confusions, the solution to ancient dilemmas, it would be a master-term, serving the same purposes for him that nature, reason, history, or power have served for other philosophers, if its meaning were not that there are no such terms. And this is the problem. Derrida's essay has passed comfortably into intellectual history with much the same foundational status for deconstruction and critical theory generally as Saussure had for modernism, and is seen by many as the final nail in the coffin of assured interpretations, incontestable meanings, and self-identical human subjects. In this respect, however, the term's very success may have compromised or undercut its ability to distinguish itself from the discourse of philosophy that it criticizes. Has Derrida's essay, then, somehow collaborated with the philosophical discourse it criticizes? Has it failed to establish a deconstructive difference, or to determine a specifically linguistic quality that authorizes deconstruction? The status of deconstruction, and of a certain highly influential view of language, rests on the answers to these questions.

The first thing to be noted is that, Derrida's extraordinary delicacy of phrasing notwithstanding, differance is not a difference without positivity. It takes various positive forms, as Derrida points out by locating traces of a meditation *avant la lettre* on differance in Nietzsche's meditations on power, Freud's account of the unconscious, and Levinas's theory of ethics. In all these discourses, the factor of differance exercises various kinds of agency even while remaining in the hollows. The silent *a* of differance, while "secret, and discreet, like a tomb," still "(provided one knows how to decipher its legend) is not far from signaling the death of the king" (1973: 132). So differance sends out powerful signals, and these signals are more powerful than the king himself. Nor does differance hesitate to undertake certain projects, opening up, for example, "the very space in which onto-theology—philosophy—produces its system and its history" (134–35). Other projects it forcibly discourages: "But while bringing us closer to the infinitive and active core of differing, 'differance' with an *a* neutralizes what the infinitive denotes as simply active," and even "forbids the essential dissociation between speech and writing that Saussure . . . wanted to draw" (137, 146). In short, differance is a player, even a man of action, *opening up*, *bringing*, *signaling*, *neutralizing*, *forbidding*, *preventing*, and *threatening*. And it is differance that empowers language to act in the peculiarly autonomous and self-governing way that Derrida especially respects, as when he posits as the site of the "originality" of language "the structure peculiar to language alone, which allows it to function entirely *by itself*" (92).

These inward-turning and negative, but still potent forms of agency—based, we might suggest, on "the authority of the *as such* in general"—eventually produce the return of metaphysics that dominates the end of the essay on differance, when Derrida concedes that differance, which is "'Older' than Being itself," "remains a metaphysical name" (1973: 159, 158). "There is nothing kerygmatic about this 'word,'" Derrida says (159). But a pure nothingness is kerygma itself.

Perhaps the most candid and least guarded of Derrida's accounts of differance came in a 1981 interview with Richard Kearney. Frustrated with Derrida's hesitations, qualifications, and evasions, Kearney finally asks, "If deconstruction prevents us from asserting or stating or identifying anything, then surely one ends up, not with 'differance,' but with indifference, where nothing is anything, and everything is everything else?" In response, a perhaps flustered Derrida undertakes a general defense of "philosophy" as the discourse by which disciplines interrogate themselves and come to a self-understanding:

Philosophy, as logocentrism, is present in every scientific discipline and the only justification for transforming philosophy into a specialized discipline is the necessity to render explicit and thematic the philosophical subtext in every discourse. The principal function which the teaching of philosophy serves is to enable people to become "conscious," to become aware of what exactly they are saying, what kind of discourse they are engaged in when they do mathematics, physics, political economy, and so on. (1984: 114)

The law of return could not be more clearly marked than in this recourse to precisely the categories and concepts that differance was supposed to dislodge. Responding to Kearney's worries about a wholly unproductive meaninglessness issuing from differance, Derrida describes philosophy as both an integrated discipline with special critical powers and an authoritative presence operating within and underwriting all "science." Announced with great clarity and confidence, philosophy's "principal function" is to make people conscious, to make them masters of their speech so that their words will express their intentions—and differance will be repressed once again.

Such moments are uncharacteristic in Derrida, but the question is whether they are altogether avoidable; or whether, as I have been arguing, any effort to determine the essence of language in general, no matter how scrupulous, rigorous, canny, or self-aware, will suffer such a relapse—a relapse, in Derrida's case, into "self-awareness" itself, and thus to the conscious subject defined and honored by traditional philosophy. Such an unwilled return in the work of this subtlest and most self-aware of thinkers suggests that others less canny than he will have an even harder time determining and describing language itself.

If deconstruction cannot avoid the law of return, perhaps we would have better luck with an approach that renounced the concepts and problems of traditional philosophy in favor of a "pragmatic" approach to language. This proposition is especially tempting, since pragmatism—by recognizing lines of force and power in language, by honoring the customary connection between words and things, and by attending to the contingencies of language use— seems as if it should be more sensitive to the concreteness of actual usage than the abstractions of rationalist philosophy and the reductions of linguistic "science" ever could be. As a relatively familiar and accessible instance of such pragmatism, we might consider the essay on "The Contingency of Language" that opens Richard Rorty's 1989 *Contingency, Irony, and Solidarity,* in which Rorty mounts a strenuous, or rather an aggressively relaxed, attack on idealisms, essentialisms, and metaphysical illusions of all kinds. Here, if anywhere, it seems, we have a chance at a conception of language without repression, and therefore without any unwanted "return."

Candidly identifying himself with the romantic revolutionary optimists of two hundred years ago who discovered that everything could change, through human agency, almost overnight, Rorty argues that people should simply rid themselves of unproductive beliefs in such things as perfect truth, ultimate meaning, final justice, higher purpose, and an authentic nature. Rather, we should try to imagine our lives in the manner of utopian thinkers or, better yet, of poets—free inventors of "vocabularies" that bring new realities into being. The task should not be one of providing a flawless mirror of the outer or inner worlds, but rather one of creating an attractive, useful picture of the world, and then of forging an attractive and useful way for people to live in it. The burden of this disarmingly informal argument *en pastel* is borne by a series of propositions placed at the beginning of the essay: "most of reality is indifferent to our descriptions of it," "the human self is created by the use of a vocabulary," "truth is made rather than found," and, most important, "*languages* are made rather than found" (1989: 7). Languages, or as Rorty prefers, "vocabularies"—a highly strategic reduction that permits him to focus on issues of word choice—are essentially tools, made things used to make other things.

The argument about how we should understand our position in the world hinges, then, on an argument about the nature of language. And here we come upon Rorty's version of the notorious "performative contradiction" that we have already witnessed in Derrida, and which beset so many theoretical pronouncements of the 1970s and 1980s in which contingency was asserted in absolute terms. "The difficulty faced by a philosopher like myself," Rorty says, "is to avoid hinting that this suggestion gets something right, that my sort of philosophy corresponds to the way things really are," because such a suggestion "brings back just the idea my sort of philosopher wants to get rid of, the idea that the world or the self has an intrinsic nature" (1989: 7–8). It is difficult indeed to keep the banished ideas at bay when one knows with such undisturbed assurance exactly what sort of philosopher one is, and what sort of thing language is. When Rorty praises one of his sort for facing up to the contingency of language, renouncing all truth claims, or eschewing foundations, wrong ideas come flooding back in the very assertion that they *have* gotten it right.

Ironically, this simple performative contradiction, which makes the entire argument difficult to respect or even to understand, provides the surest clue to the real pragmatism of language. Language works, creates, constructs, builds only insofar as it is presumed to express and represent, only insofar as it is credited with a certain passivity. When it is felt that language has assumed a power greater than that of reflection, transfer, or relay, it is distrusted and therefore becomes powerless to do anything at all. When the revolutionary pragmatist takes to the streets to denounce the king as a degenerate scoundrel, the worldly force of his description is pegged to the notion that the true character of the sovereign is adequately described by the phrase, not constituted by it; and, moreover, that the human force of individual conviction motivates the utterance in the first place; and, too, that nobody ought to be ruled by a degenerate scoundrel. If everybody was a philosopher of Rorty's sort, none of these assumptions would be in force, and nothing would follow from revolutionary redescriptions. Accounts that have no discernible purchase on the world and make no claim to reflect the convictions of some speaker or writer have no power to charm, motivate, or persuade, much less to create. When Hemingway's Jake Barnes remarks at the end of *The Sun Also Rises,* "Isn't it pretty to think so?" he registers a pragmatist's resistance to the notion of free self-invention. Flaccid, monosyllabic inebriate that he is, Jake can assure the desperately confused, inconstant, dissipated Lady Brett Ashley that, her creative suggestion notwithstanding, he and she would probably *not* have had a damn good time together.

The pragmatics of language use depend upon the force of such notions as "fit," accuracy, and adequacy, and when Rorty attempts to exclude these, he speaks not as a pragmatist but as a theoretical puritan, unwilling to admit the facts of use because they are irregular and untheorizable—because they are *too contingent.* The disorderly process of word-to-world, word-to-intuition, and word-to-word matching constitutes, however, the very processes by which linguistic force, linguistic intelligibility, and therefore linguistic utility are established. Ultimately, Rorty's pragmatism founders on a paradox: only if we believe that truths are found rather than made can we make truths at all.

This paradox actually finds expression in Rorty through an oscillation, bewildering at first glance, in his account of making. Truths, he says, are made because languages are made. To accept this proposition, he argues, is to enter into a secular, natural, and human world, one in which people struggle to achieve their ends, chiefly through the use of their primary tool, language. The most durable of the metaphors for language proposed by Rorty (which include the "coral reef," with dying metaphors constantly being replaced by new ones), the tool is, unfortunately, unsuited to the task. German idealists and French revolutionaries may have changed their vocabularies, and they may have become new kinds of people, but the language they used did not change them, at least not if language is still to be considered a tool. Tools do not change the nature of their users. While they may participate in a gradual process by which human beings modify their self-conceptions, tools do not function as agents in this process, for the nature of a tool is only to facilitate the execution of tasks formulated by the mind that governs the hand that holds them. In short, if language is a tool, it lacks the transformative power Rorty wants to accord to it; and if it has that power, it is not a tool.

Rorty himself discovers a second limitation in his metaphor when he notices that the development of the new vocabulary typically precedes the project for which it is especially useful. We "hit upon" a way of talking, and then gradually discover a purpose for talking this way. Once again, tools don't typically work this way; we don't hit upon a wrench and then discover to our delight that we can use it to twist things—"but," Rorty says, "I shall, for the moment, ignore this disanalogy" (1989: 13). He is wise to ignore it, but perhaps pragmatically imprudent to admit to noticing it at all, for by doing so, he forces the recognition that languages and tools, and so much else, resist a casual redescription, no matter how appealing or inspired.

The very possibility of a failed analogy provides a counter-revolutionary check on Rorty's romantic rebellion, and bears witness to the law of return that, I have been arguing, afflicts any characterization of language, any attempt to mark its limits and construe its essential nature. Of all words, *language* is the most resistant to Rorty's unpragmatic pragmatism, not because its true character repels false descriptions, but because it accepts, in its immeasurable vastness, an infinite number of descriptions. Any theoretically coherent account of language must exclude some observable or inferable features, dimensions, or aspects of language; and these denied elements will necessarily exert a certain pressure on the object that is produced by their exclusion. In Saussure, the vehicle of return was the indispensable metaphor through which the whole cultural and political world of the extra-linguistic milieu made its way into the inner fastness of language alone. In Derrida, difference became what it appeared to deny, an autonomous and effective source of agency. And in Rorty, the metaphors themselves were subject to partial cancellation through which disobedient aspects of the figure were noted, but "ignored."

Saussure was not interested in metaphor as such, but Rorty is. Indeed, for Rorty, "metaphor" represents the tip of the spear in terms of language's ability to refashion the world. Initially, he says, metaphors seem "strange, mystic, wonderful" (1989: 19). But they provoke fresh acts of perception, stimulating people to "get busy developing a new theory" in response to them (17). When they do, reality is refashioned, and the metaphor, once so alien and exotic, will "gradually require a habitual use, a familiar place" (18). Rorty undoubtedly meant to say that the metaphor would *ac*quire a habitual use, but may have missed the typo because *require* is required by his argument even if that requirement is not acknowledged. Rorty wants to argue that metaphor is cognitively empty, independent of both world and mind. But in order for phrases to function as metaphors, they must be seen to possess some occluded or fragmentary cognitive content, based on the conventions of habitual use. To describe my Tommy Hilfiger T-shirt as "a serrated beaker of green liver condescension" is to produce a strange and mystic phrase, but not—unless you know something about T-shirts, beakers, liver, and condescension that I don't—a metaphor. Of course, an ingenious and determined person might see some distant principle of intelligibility in the phrase—perhaps keying off the "condescension" of Tommy Hilfiger or male fashion generally—and that person might be said to perceive a dimly metaphorical function in the phrase, and may get busy theorizing in response. But without a bit of meaning, which is to say a bit of reference, up front and a promise of more to come, there is nothing to work with and no incentive to work.

Rorty is radical in two directions. He deploys a rhetoric of purposive freedom based on the singular power of language as a creative agency, and a rhetoric of haphazardness in which people "hit upon" vocabularies, a rhetoric that draws upon a view of language as a made thing, like a tool. The full ambivalence of his clearheaded and lucidly expressed argument converges on his terminal pronouncement—which recalls Derrida's "nothing kerygmatic about this 'word' "—that we ought to "get to the point where we no longer worship *anything*, where we treat *nothing* as a quasi-divinity" (1989: 22). This is a very hard point to get to, or even to locate. Does the sentence prohibit worship in general, or just worship of things? Should we not worship anything, or worship something called *nothing*—in the form, perhaps, of metaphor? Informing this uncertain recommendation are the two distinct phases of Rorty's argument, each of which insistently returns to disturb the other.

The point of these demonstrations of the inevitability of the law of return is not that Saussure, Derrida, and Rorty are sloppy thinkers. In fact, the returns of unwanted elements in their discourse actually provide a measure of the real integrity of their thought, their principled inability altogether to exclude or repress disorderly but finally undeniable elements of language in the interests of mere coherence. In any discourse on language as such, clarity and order constitute temptations, reductions achievable only by metaphysicians or logicians; only in more rigorous or honest discourses will the excluded elements be permitted to return in order to expose and undermine the logic of exclusion that structures them.

4. Language and Human Nature

> Why does language behave as if it were a person? Because
> it does.
>
> —J. HILLIS MILLER, " 'Reading,' Part of a
> Paragraph in *Allegories of Reading*"

What most insistently and subversively returns to language is man, and the various forms of human life in which language figures. This return is acknowledged only rarely by those heavily invested in the thought of language, although it is occasionally approached. The American linguist Edward Sapir argued that "every fragmentary science of man, such as economics or political science or aesthetics or linguistics, needs at least a minimum set of assumptions about the nature of man in order to house the particular propositions and records of events which belong to its selected domain" (1949: 579–80). Without a set of silent assumptions about human being, human nature, the human condition—without what Saussure calls a point of view—observations of language would be empty, data would fail to cohere into a meaningful pattern, and researchers in the human sciences would not know what their instances were instances of.

Sapir's point might be more or less freely conceded by many economists, political scientists, and aestheticians. But most scientists of language—linguists, and those who regard language as an object of empirical scientific knowledge—would reject it. If something so speculative as the nature of man were to be admitted into the data, the field would be opened up to precisely those intellectual, political, and cultural factors that any true science would begin by excluding, and the study of language would be not a science at all, but a mere humanism, yet another way of asserting that man is the measure of all things. As we have already seen, language seems to be external to human beings in a way that the objects of other human sciences do not. I believe, however, that Sapir is right, and would only add that it is precisely in those discourses—linguistics and other discourses as well—most committed to establishing the objective truth of language that the denial of presuppositions about human existence will be strongest, and the return of man the most emphatic.

One reason that linguists may have been resistant to Sapir's argument was that many of them were busily exploring a different approach altogether, a more scientifically exciting project indicated by Sapir himself when he said that human beings were "very much at the mercy of the particular language which has become the medium of expression for their society" (1956: 69). Here, human nature is said to be subject to language, an alien force configured to human contours only in the sense that an iron maiden is a perfect fit for its tenant. One did not need, on this view, presuppositions about the nature of man in order to study language, for the empirical study of language yielded objective evidence about that nature. Given more resonant voice by Sapir's student Benjamin Lee Whorf, this way of thinking about language was easily assimilated to the antihumanism emerging in other fields, which it seemed to confirm.

What Whorf called cryptotypes—"covert" or "submerged" meanings with no surface reflection at all—revealed to him the power of language to structure the objects it denoted. Speaking a language with cryptotypes (such as English), people were not deploying a neutral and obedient tool, but were unconsciously subject to the "sway of pattern over reference," helpless to resist the "far-reaching compulsion from large-scale patterning of grammatical categories, such as plurality, gender and similar classifications" (261, 137). In English, we might think of "a glass of water," while in other languages, the abstract concept of water, water in general, might be unavailable; and the stuff found in glasses, streams, rain, and oceans might have different names. Differences between languages demonstrated to Whorf, as they had to Saussure, the "arbitrariness" of linguistic units; but Whorf placed a much heavier stress than his predecessor on the way in which language exercises a "power of the nature of magic" not just over concepts or objects, but over language-users themselves, who are programmed to regard language's categories as coordinate with those of reality itself (267). We are, Whorf insisted, limited in the thoughts we can conceive, even the perceptions we can have, by the language we think in, whose patterns "we all, unknowingly, project . . . upon the universe" (262).

Because language very nearly has a "mind" of its own, Whorf argued, our minds are not truly *our* own. But through a study of the languages of others, we may yet be able to cast off illusions and parochialisms, and enter onto "a great phase of human brotherhood," realizing universal kinship on "the cosmopolitan levels of the spirit" (263, 264). For although human beings are limited by their languages, all languages have equal claims to complexity, integrity, even beauty. Whorf invoked "the web of Māyā" and "the plane of Kāma" in an effort to guide his readers toward this larger view (263, 266). Whorf, we should note, fully understood the antiscientific tendency, even the sweeping irrationalism, of his arguments. In his most memorable and prescient essay, "Language, Mind, and Reality" (1942), he wrote that "science's long and heroic effort to be strictly factual has at last brought it into entanglement with the unsuspected facts of the linguistic order" (246). Chief among these is the fact that the necessity of thinking in a given language inhibits our ability to think of, or even to perceive, language itself, whose data must be filtered through an arbitrary lexical grid. Moreover, the limitations of any given language ensure that we will have only a very partial and imperfect view of anything higher, anything universal. Whorf believed, however, that a study of the particularities of each language might yet provide us with a preliminary access to the "noumenal world—a world of hyperspace, of higher dimensions" that was about as close as we could get to divinity (247).

If we could make an honest effort to transcend our constraints by undertaking comparative linguistics, then, Whorf suggested in a moment of inspiration, we might be able to glimpse a "PREMONITION IN LANGUAGE of the unknown, vaster world" (248).

Such an argument is as easy to accept (it is *ease itself*) as it is difficult to prove. Like Saussure, Whorf believes that empirical study could disclose the truth of language and could thereby even bring us to the brink of a truth beyond language. And, like Saussure, he has great respect for the power of language to structure both world and mind. This second premise was felt by many nonlinguists to be so interesting that its conflict with the first premise was ignored; indeed, the first was felt to confer legitimacy on the second. For many thinkers who came after Whorf, knowledge of language was both reliable and inclusive; it was, indeed, the key to everything worth knowing.

But we may well ask whether Whorf has truly discovered the truth about language, or just unknowingly projected it onto language out of obedience to some unconscious compulsion, some imperative determined not by the data but by his language. It is difficult to know how Whorf would answer that question, because the choice of either alternative would undercut part of his case. Even if we reckon that his account is determined by something other than the facts, it is not easy to say what that something is. Has Whorf's language provided him with the categories, structures, conventions, and values that he attributes to it? Or do these presuppositions and assumptions derive from other circumstances—say, from Whorf's race, class, gender, and culture? It is, after all, stereotypically masculine to worry about abstract theoretical questions; and very Western to understand the world in terms of power and dominance; and entirely typical of overeducated Connecticut liberals to promote a guiltily exaggerated respect for those ways of life (the Hopi, the Chichewa, the Algonkians, the Zulu) obliterated by the West in its crushing drive to mastery, and then to urge, as a palliative, a deference to the ancient wisdom of the East—suitably assimilated, of course, to noumena and hyperspace. From this point of view, Whorf serves as an especially clear and powerful instance of the way in which a host of contextual presuppositions about life in general can be displaced onto the receptive pseudo-object of language.

The most indispensable metaphor for Sapir, Whorf, and many who follow in their footsteps, is that of power, which is said to extend from the more or less benign guidance provided by linguistic categories all the way to the violent coercion by language of a helpless human cognitive apparatus. Why are so many thinkers of the past century unable to think of language without thinking of power? No single answer will suffice, but we might make a highly speculative and tentative beginning by noting that language has been called upon to assume tremendous responsibility for human affairs at the historical moment when human agency has produced, in the form of wars, genocide, avoidable famine, and ecological devastation, the most appalling effects. Separated from human being, considered as a thing apart, language can be imagined as a kind of buffer between humanity and its self-imposed afflictions—the social or psychic pathologies that burden us, the limitations that inhibit us, the prejudices that blind us. An autonomous and dominating language might even seem to relieve humanity of an intolerable responsibility to atone for its crimes and to realize its ethical, ecological, political, and historical obligations. The notion that people are slaves of language cushions the recognition that human beings are more capable than had been supposed of realizing bad ends, and less capable than had been hoped of realizing good ones.

The argument for the agency of language can, in other words, be seen as one expression of a widespread if unfocused sentiment that the record of human agency cannot be defended. Language can absorb a good part of the responsibility for our shortcomings, and as Whorf suggests, can also provide some hope that we might yet realize our dreams of a new universal community, on the cosmopolitan levels of the spirit, under the direction of a former servant that has cast off its chains in a way humanity has found impossible to do. In the intellectual culture of the past century, in which the power of language is a given, human solidarity comes at the cost of a new servitude against which resistance seems almost inconceivable.

The appetite for servitude seems especially healthy among intellectuals of the last half-century who refer to the facts of language as though these had been determined by scientifically impeccable means. In the work of these thinkers, what might be called "the return of the native" through figures of agency and even character is often startlingly abrupt because nonlinguists are, in general, even more assured than linguists concerning the nature of language, and so take fewer precautions against anthropomorphic contamination. Foucault, for example, was so preoccupied with the erasure of the figure of man by the wave of language that he failed to notice that the wave itself, like a drawing of a storm with a furrowed brow and bulging cheeks, had taken virtually human form. To demonstrate in richer detail the covert rehumanization of an ostensibly inhuman language, however, we should turn not to *The Order of Things*, but to the even more austerely antihumanist text written as an explanation of the implicit methodology of that work, *The Archeology of Knowledge* (1969). For it is in this subsequent work that the concept of "discourse," an unstressed concept in *The Order of Things*, stands revealed as the cornerstone of the entire project, as well as a safe house for the fugitive human.

Foucauldian discourse is language minus the subject, a counterintuitive notion that Foucault represented as a distillation of cold fact from the warm slush of humanistic illusions, language at its most authentically linguistic. Thus, discourse is not the expression of human mind, a notion Foucault mocks as a "gentle, silent, intimate consciousness," but is rather a series of documentary surfaces structured by an "obscure set of anonymous rules" (1972: 210). Not foundations, but transformations occupy the archaeologist of language; not the natural, immediate, and universal, but the regular, objective, and specific facts of discourse; not the living will of the speaker or writer, but an "immense density of systematicities, a tight group of multiple relations"; not voices or subjectivities but an anonymous, undecipherable murmuring (76). To dwell nostalgically on the theme of "the founding subject" is, Foucault insisted, to "elide the reality of discourse" (227).

The hard kernel of language, discourse itself has an even harder kernel, "the statement." And yet it is just here that the predicted return occurs. Not just any collection of signs makes a statement, Foucault notes; nor are sentences equal in all respects to statements. For a collection of signs to be a statement, there must be "something else," a "particular relation with a subject" (1972: 89, 92). Of course, this "subject" is not to be confused with a person, because the idea of a person, a consciousness capable of intending or causing something, is confusion itself. How much clearer and cleaner it is to think of a purely linguistic "function" that merely resembles a person, or, more accurately, provides a theoretical space, a "particular vacant place that may in fact be filled by different individuals" (95). But this last phrase is somewhat misleading, for in Foucault's own analysis, this vacant place *must* be filled with some "individual" or other. Without some posited "founding subject," some substantial human being filling that empty space, marks remain marks, and cannot even become statements. The vacancy of which Foucault speaks is merely theoretical, and is always filled in practice. It has much the same force as the notion of a day "without" weather. By naming "the weather" as if it were an independent thing, we suggest—but only in theory—the nonsensical possibility of having no weather at all. A subjectless statement is like a weatherless day, and to dwell on them is as productive as dwelling on the weather.

In fact, the subject had not awaited Foucault's permission ("may in fact be filled") to return. For even in Foucault's account, language comports itself exactly like (a very powerful and autocratic) man, with something of the same all-licensed aggressivity as that attributed to Spiro Agnew, "Nixon's Nixon." Language in Foucault's account is man's man, even a man among boys. "Standing above all these words," Foucault writes of a Borges story, "is the rigorous and sovereign language which recovers them, tells their story, and is actually responsible for their birth" (1977: 66). In the admirably austere work of Blanchot, Foucault wrote in 1966, "language alone is allowed to speak"; any subject that may appear within its "formless rumbling" is "no more than a grammatical fold" (1990: 26, 55, 54). In fact, language has the full range of subjective attributes, being at one end lordly and overbearing, and at the other end ephemeral and self-effacing, "that softest of voices, that nearly imperceptible retreat, that weakness deep inside and surrounding every thing and every face" (1990: 57). Retrieving the gentle, silent, intimate consciousness he had ridiculed and banished as a humanist illusion in *The Order of Things,* Foucault relocates it in the dark but fully humanized heart of language. More than a poetic lapse, such a passage testifies once again to the necessity of return, the impossibility of an adequate conception of language that does not include assumptions about human nature and human life, assumptions that crowd in on the concept in the form of explanatory metaphors. In Foucault, these assumptions provide not just the background to an understanding of language, as Sapir indicated, but the features of language itself.

In Paul de Man the appetite for servitude in the presence of an "inhuman" language takes a distinctively paranoid form. Again and again—and yet, with considerable variety and unpredictability—de Man replays a virtually Kafka-esque scenario in which a reader stands with impotent longing before the law of language, the portal to which is guarded with dour humor by de Man himself. The reader, in this scenario, brings hypotheses, perceptions, interpretations, hopeful guesses—to which language returns no answer. To readerly desires for a coincidence of form and meaning, and, in a more general sense, for a meaningful integration of human beings into a social and material world, language responds with an unmoved insistence on discontinuity and on its own indifference to human purposes, including communication.

On a few memorable occasions, the features of language that de Man describes actually make their way into his own language, so the reader can feel their force in the course of understanding them notionally. Introducing a collection of essays, de Man confesses that he cannot quite bring them together into the unified form of a book: "I feel myself compelled to repeated frustration in a persistent attempt to write as if a dialectical summation were possible beyond the breaks and interruptions that the readings disclose" (1984: ix). Such a sentence, an unbuttoned attempt at direct communication, provides readers of de Man with the opportunity to relish the same knots and tangles he so doggedly pursued in the texts of Rousseau, Rilke, and Nietzsche. What does the sentence actually say? That de Man is frustrated in his efforts to sum things up? That he is compelled by some force to try to sum things up? That he is compelled to be frustrated? (How does that work?) That summation is possible? That it is impossible? That "breaks and interruptions," no matter how repetitively disclosed, cannot be grounds for summation? What we have here, de Man's more sympathetic readers might say, is not just an adventitious failure to communicate, but a brilliantly condensed instance of the very principles that de Man is talking about.

The principle of principles is conflict. De Man's discourse stages a series of little battles in which rhetorical figures clash with a mechanical grammar, metaphor crosses swords with metonymy, and readers try to wrench meanings from texts that withhold them because they are too busy interacting with themselves to respond to a reader. As de Man says, "the paradigmatic linguistic model is that of an entity that confronts itself" (1978: 153). Under these circumstances, the better a reading is, the deeper the understanding of its own redundancy it will register. Language becomes a self-contained theater of violence, disclosing its furious conflicts to readers who, like the spectators at a Civil War battlefield reenactment, can only gape. All the interest, all the agency, belongs to language, including even the power to deconstruct:

"The deconstruction of the figural dimension is a process that takes place independently of any desire; as such it is not unconscious but mechanical, systematic in its performance but arbitrary in its principle, like a grammar" (1978: 299).

While de Man sometimes described the operations of language in terms of "defacement," "decomposition," "radical annihilation," and even "sheer blind violence," the dominant emphasis, especially in his later years, falls on the mechanical, arbitrary, and "inhuman" randomness of language. In these years, in fact, the concept of the inhuman itself becomes an object of his attention. As he says in one late text, "the inhuman is: linguistic structures, the play of linguistic tensions, linguistic events that occur, possibilities which are inherent in language—independently of any intent or any drive or any wish or any desire we might have." The record of human endeavor, history itself "is not human, because it pertains strictly to the order of language." In fact, de Man concludes, warming to his subject, "there is, in a very radical sense, no such thing as the human" (1986: 96).

The message now coming from language, via de Man, is not just that all human hopes and fears are vanity, but that the very concept of the human is vanity as well—although the question of whose vanity it is remains unsettled. In the most radical turn of this radical argument, de Man declared that "Actual language . . . has invented the conceptual term 'man'" (1978: 153). Human beings "exist" as a kind of quivering mirage only so that language can exist, in much the same way that God created man so that he could be, truly, God. The entire nonverbal world may well be "a speculative hypothesis that exists only, to put it in all too intentional terms, *for the sake of* language" (210). Despite the flickering suggestions throughout his *oeuvre* of powerful feelings of disgust and even revulsion at the very notion of humanity, de Man's admirers revere him not just as a literary critic but virtually as a sage or a philosopher. As Stanley Corngold says, de Man is "a great philosopher of the inhuman condition" (83).

De Man may or may not be a great philosopher, but the humanity that he siphons off from man in his later work is immediately redirected to language. For in de Man's account, language is more inhumane than inhuman, for it displays a full measure of coldly intentional agency, and such agency is not an attribute of machines. The terms of de Man's "speculative hypothesis" are "all too intentional" because they suggest that language is essentially and even thoroughly human, behaving just like other subject-agents, with creative projects, enemies, sibling rivalries, conflicts, even self-consciousness. When de Man writes of "language, regardless of whether it conceives of itself as a consciousness or not . . . ," he explicitly allows the possibility that language can be conscious and even self-aware, and so presupposes what can only be called the humanity of language (1978: 219 n).

So powerful was de Man's conviction of the intentionality of language that he even attributed his own agency to the texts he read. In his one disagreement with Derrida, de Man argued that Rousseau's texts did not await the interpretive touch of the master, as Derrida seemed to suggest, but literally deconstructed themselves (see 1983: 102–41). In a late interview, he described the difference between himself and Derrida as a distinction between passive reading and active creation: "The difference is that Derrida's text is so brilliant, so incisive, so strong that whatever happens in Derrida, it happens between him and his own text. He doesn't need Rousseau, he doesn't need anybody else; I do need them very badly because I never had an idea of my own, it was always through a text . . ." (1986: 118). One understands de Man pretty well if one comprehends that this is both a confession and a boast.

Whatever it is, it was not taken seriously by de Man's admirers, who took very seriously his views of language. Discussing a knotty de Manian passage on the incongruously "human" behavior of language, J. Hillis Miller refers repeatedly to de Man's ideas: "I suppose de Man means . . ."; "No, de Man is anxious to have us understand . . ."; "I take it he means that . . ." Miller's profound respect for the mind that never had an idea marks a fault line in the very argument he's trying to explicate. For Miller praises in de Man precisely the kind of interpretive accomplishments that de Man denies. Moreover, when we look at de Man's arguments themselves, we see that while he describes language as inhuman, he also attributes to language intentionality and agency. The passage Miller cites requires lengthy explication—Miller's article is called " 'Reading' Part of a Paragraph in *Allegories of Reading*"— because de Man continually struggles to keep these heterodox energies in line, and the text is contorted as a consequence.

The frailty of the argument for the inhumanity of language becomes even more apparent in Miller's retail version of it. In Miller, we find de Manian claims to the effect that language "takes precedence over human consciousness," that it "exceeds" human intentions, that the act of rigorous reading reduces the human subject to a "relay station . . . in a purely linguistic transaction," and so on (1989c: 22). But the humanity of language, denied by de Man in dictum but embraced in metaphor, rears its head in Miller's discourse in the kind of evocative moment that he, no more than de Man, could not avoid: "Something human might remain if every separate human being were effaced," Miller writes; "Language might remain . . . " (1983: 183). Language might be able to survive the disappearance of man—for all we know, it engineered that disappearance—but it remains "something human."

Perhaps the most triumphant return of the native, however, is to be found in the field of general or theoretical linguistics, which had modernized itself by asserting its independence from all general assumptions about humanity. Forty years after the publication of Saussure's *Course*, Chomsky effected a revolution in linguistics by reversing Saussure at every point, identifying a language that was necessary not arbitrary, given not constructed, centered not on the sign but on grammar, and psychological not social. For Chomsky, a study of language yields crucial evidence about a cognitive structure common to and distinctive of human beings. In short, Chomsky sets out to do what thinkers such as Foucault and de Man would regard as impossible on the face of it, to think the being of language and the being of man together. In Chomsky's version of Foucault's image, the crashing wave of language leaves not a smooth expanse of sand, but solid rock, on which is etched an even sharper and more detailed image of man.

So dramatically has Chomsky expanded the field and raised the stakes of linguistics that it often goes unnoticed by nonlinguists how severely restricted his account of language really is, and how much depends upon the restrictions. Chomsky has a strict construction of the linguistic that focuses on syntax as the kernel of the "purely linguistic" to the exclusion of what he calls "other cognitive systems—in particular, our system of beliefs concerning things in the world and their behavior" (1979: 142). Where other thinkers made a semantic ascent up to a plane on which everyone could agree on the object—words—Chomsky makes a syntactic descent into the domain of the invisible, the intuitive grasp of the "logical form" of grammar.

Chomsky is almost completely uninterested in the concept of a language, which he describes as "an obscure sociopolitical concept having to do with the colors on maps" (see 1979: 527 n, 509; and 1990: 145–46). Nor is he concerned with the content of language, which seems a distraction from the main point. Indeed, he says, if "beliefs, attitudes, etc." were incorporated into the concept of language, "I would conclude that language is a chaos that is not worth studying—but personally I do not believe that any evidence or substantive arguments have been brought forward in favor of such a hypothesis" (1979: 152–53). His entire project is based on the possibility of identifying the properties of the human language faculty, the "distinct cognitive structure" of "universal grammar" that underlies the grammar of natural languages. Hence his resistance to the claims of semantics, functionalism, or communicative pragmatics, which have been advanced from time to time by dissident linguists. On one side of the linguistic fence is syntax—universal, autonomous, and rational; on the other is the unfiltered debris of other cognitive systems. And good fences, Chomsky argues, make good neighbors.

Chomsky repeats, then, Saussure's insistence on discriminating between the essential kernel of language that is available to rational inquiry, and the margins of language that are not. Like Saussure, he believes that a science of language is possible, but is reluctant to call the object of such a science *language:* what *langue* is for Saussure, syntax is for Chomsky, the legitimate object of inquiry. Typically, he will appear to call into question some hazy commonsense definition of language, but will not foreclose on that term altogether. "There is," he declares, "nothing in the real world corresponding to language"; but he immediately adds a softer qualifier to the effect that "it could very well turn out that there is no intelligible notion of language," that the notion of language "might turn out" to be useless (1982: 107). Or he will put the term in quotation marks, but then appear to reconsider his own skepticism: "'language,' if such a notion can become an object of serious study . . ." (1979: 190). He points out that "in work devoted to language, the term 'language' barely appears"; his own *Aspects of the Theory of Syntax,* for example, contains no index entry for "language" at all (1986: 29). And yet, other works bear titles such as *Language and Mind, Knowledge of Language, Reflections on Language,* and "Language and Freedom."

If it is not *precisely* language that Chomsky studies, what is it? What is the actual object of his work? It is not the grammar of a given natural language, for that is only the field of evidence for an evolved property of the human brain, a faculty or capacity that inheres in the chemical compounds and electrical impulses within the brain. Chomsky is attempting to describe "a system of digital computation of a highly restricted character, with simple principles that interact to yield very intricate and complex results" (1990: 517). This systematicity, he argues, is the kernel of the language faculty: "rules" are "fundamental," while "representations"—the realm of *language*—are "epiphenomenal" (see 1980). While he insists that these rules are real, they are also purely formal, and must be inferred rather than described on the basis of direct perception. They consist of "patterns in the mind," as Ray Jackendoff calls them, that enable people to generate an infinite number of grammatically correct sentences using a finite number of combinatorial elements (see Jackendoff 1994). The Chomskyan version of linguistic science results, in other words, in a flight from concreteness, a purging of language of all traces of the local, the social, the material, all contingent content, so that what remains is a systematicity so purified, so idealized and abstracted, that even while, from the point of view of many scientists including linguists, it approaches the condition of "imaginative literature," its rhetorical modality is symbolic rather than "linguistic" in the quotidian sense (Chomsky 1982: 68).

And yet it is this abstraction, so pure that words can only describe it at a kind of metaphorical distance, that Chomsky, in a gesture that defines both his singularity as an intellectual and the inevitability of what I have been calling the law of return, identifies with human nature itself.

At this point, we can venture an hypothesis about the typical course of general, theoretical inquiries into language as such. The first step must be the reduction of the totality of language—an imponderably vast, contradictory, and amorphous mass that defeats rational inquiry by its unsorted immensity—into a more manageable form. For Saussure, this was the socially constructed sign system, whereas for Chomsky, it was syntax; for others, it has been communicative pragmatics, differance, discourse, or specific "vocabularies." This reduction then serves as the actual object of inquiry, even while the general term *language* is retained. The reason the larger, rejected, and misleading term is retained is clearly in order to give the inquiry the kind of weight, scope, and significance that would naturally follow from a knowledge of language as a totality.

The results of the inquiry are necessarily influenced to a very great extent by the initial determination of the object of study, for language is so various that anything, any quality or characteristic at all, can be discovered somewhere within it; and as Saussure well understood, there is no single way of determining which aspect of language is logically prior to or more fundamental than the others. The initial determination of the linguistic core must therefore be arbitrary, and since it is, it will typically reflect extra-linguistic presuppositions about human nature, human agency, and human society. Secreted in the linguistic core, these presuppositions return, often in the form of explanatory metaphors. Chomsky's shocking revolution, in which a specific account for human nature is derived directly from grammar, simply lays bare the mechanism of all attempts to isolate the essence of language.

5. The Critical Fetish of Modernity

> There is a long history to the inability . . . of the vision
> of thinking to see directly the unifying unity of the being
> of language.
>> —HEIDEGGER, *On the Way to Language*

> The essence of language is hidden from us.
>> —WITTGENSTEIN, *Philosophical Investigations*

For thinkers in a wide range of disciplines, language has the status of a point of origin on which everyone can agree, a kind of base camp at which one can rest in preparation for some final assault on the summit, a "pilot science" capable of guiding all the rest. Impressed by the success of linguists in establishing the truth of language, thinkers in other fields have turned to language in order to achieve the same result in their disciplines. For such thinkers, and they are legion, language constitutes a body of settled fact, established with great scientific integrity by credentialed linguists, preeminently—for reasons we must explore—Saussure.

In the discipline that happens to be named linguistics, however, the situation is, and has always been, otherwise. The history of linguistics is a history of beginning, with each generation of linguists believing that they were standing at the rosy dawn of a true understanding of language. Max Müller, the first to proclaim a "Science of Language" devoted to the study of "language itself" as "the sole object of inquiry," acknowledged in 1861 that it was "a science of very modern date," and one "scarcely received as yet on a footing of equality by the elder branches of learning" (I: 23; II: 3). Nearly half a century later, the Father of Modern Linguistics, Saussure, described his role as that of a pioneer or a scout, clearing away the misconceptions of many years in order to prepare the ground for a true science of language that might arise later. A generation later, Whorf said that linguistics was "still in its infancy" (232). And Chomsky, untraditional in so many ways, is mainstream in this, describing linguistics as an "underdeveloped field," an immature and even "semi-existent" discourse whose current "infantilism" will gradually disappear as the discipline matures (quoted in Randy Allen Harris 255). Rejecting theoretical linguistics in general, Roy Harris still repeats this essential point, saying that "our understanding of [the intricacies of communication] is still in its infancy" (1990: 149). Thinkers in other disciplines may feel that linguists have solved the problem of language, but linguists themselves seem—and have always seemed—to feel that they're just getting started.

Where does a science of language begin? What is the epistemological status of language? In his 1990 *Introduction à une science du langage*, Milner posits as the first "primitive fact" confronted by linguistics the fact "that there are speaking beings." To speak of language, he says, "is simply to speak of the fact that speaking beings exist." In order to make interesting statements about this fact, it would be necessary to call it into question, but this is precisely what linguistics cannot do. "For linguistics," Milner argues, "this existence can be neither deduced nor explained in general. It is thus possible to understand the sense in which linguistics does not have language as its object: language is its axiom" (1990a: 41). Linguistics, unlike philosophy, must study the properties, chiefly grammatical, of natural languages—it is only there, Milner asserts, that "science" has a role. All other questions—of the origin of language, the existence of language, the nature of language—must be referred to philosophy. Language remains, as Milner says in this *Introduction* and elsewhere, stubbornly resistant to scientific inquiry; the very phrase "universal grammar," proposed as a subject for scientific description, comes very close to being meaningless from a scientific point of view, since "language can only ever be observed in a particular language" (232).

Milner is not alone in the belief that language exceeds the boundaries of anything that science could determine as an object of knowledge. Even linguists—beginning, as we have seen, with Saussure himself—have made the same charge. Indeed, the discipline of linguistics has been for many years distinguished by the extraordinary stridency of its internal critique. Not only have particular methodologies, orientations, or schools of linguistic thought been assaulted, often in the most direct and even personal terms, by other linguists, but the legitimacy of the entire field is called into question by linguists themselves on a regular basis. In such a context, Geoffrey Sampson is not as iconoclastic as he seems to want to be when he claims that there is simply "no room for a 'general theory of language', of the kind that so many contemporary linguists see themselves as contributing to" (1980a: 19). Theoretical linguistics, he charges, has never properly determined its object; rather, it has simply announced that it has determined an object when it has in fact created a theoretical fantasy. Sampson describes the entire enterprise of Chomskyan theoretical linguistics in particular as a mighty group delusion, a self-created, self-governing, academic hoax, "a mirage" (210; see also Sampson 1979).

The most withering "internal" attack on the scientific pretensions of general or theoretical linguistics is surely that of Roy Harris, Professor of General Linguistics at Oxford University and the most distinguished historian and critic of linguistic thought working in the English language. In a long series of books beginning with *The Language-Makers* (1980), Harris argues with authority and conviction that general linguistics has no object for its researches at all. Harris does not commit himself to a particular view of language and then claim that every other linguist gets it wrong. Rather, he argues that particular views are the problem, for they all falsify the heterodox immensity that is gathered into the term *language*.

Typically, Harris notes, linguists relegate to the domain of the nonlinguistic all cultural practices, beliefs, and traditions, and to the domain of the imperfectly linguistic everything that is spontaneous, disorderly, or irreducible to rule. In the layman's lexicon, *language* is a hazy term with numerous and conflicting meanings, and a huge variety of functions, including exercising control over one's environment, exchanging information, persuading or seducing or coercing or deceiving others, adopting certain public roles, expressing one's own individuality, forming compacts and contracts, passing the time, creating an impression of thought, exercising the imagination, and maintaining social cohesion, to name just a few. The scientific-minded theorist who hopes to identify a single order underlying all these functions is, Harris contends, simply in denial about the layman's common-sense understanding of language's irreducible heterogeneity. There is, he concludes, no acontextual, independent object that corresponds to the word *language,* and all scientific thinking about language must therefore be considered to be founded upon a "myth."

Science, in the view of Harris, Milner, and many others, is concerned with observation, inference, and hypothesis (not necessarily in that order), with falsifiable propositions; and language as such does not afford a purchase for scientific method. Chomsky, for one, might protest that his structures and rules represent an idealization from available data, and is no less scientific than other fields in that respect; indeed, he regards his explorations of "context-free grammar" as a super-scientific quest for the similarities between observable patterns in natural languages, an inquiry that might yield a description of a deeper or more fundamental property than anything available to the empirical method. One of Harris's many responses, detailed in *The Language Machine,* is that Chomsky's account of grammar as a self-regulating device for generating sentences independent of context is far from ideal, and in fact constitutes one of many attempts in the past century to describe language as a "machine." Harris ventures a number of explanations for this curious and unprecedented phenomenon, all having to do with the preoccupations and anxieties of cultural modernism in the twentieth century, and none of them having anything to do with the real nature of language—which, he says, cannot be determined because it does not exist. "Modern linguistics," he concludes, "for all its academic prestige, has never had theoretical foundations except the very shakiest" (1987a: 139; see also Harris 1981: 32–53).

According to Harris, "the language myth" arises from two interconnected and deep-rooted fallacies. According to the first, linguistic knowledge is a matter of knowing which words stand for which ideas on the premise that language accomplishes the transfer of thoughts between minds. When the Chomskyan linguist Ray Jackendoff says that "the language faculty is at bottom a device for externalizing and communicating meaning" from one mind to another, he commits what Harris calls the "telementational fallacy" (Jackendoff 1996: 7). The "determinacy fallacy" provides the explanation of how telementation works. We communicate with each other, determinism states, by agreeing on the use of the "same words" to express the "same ideas" and to refer to the "same things." The consequence of these two fallacies—the language myth itself—is expressed through "the conduit metaphor," a pervasive, indeed virtually inescapable, way of thinking about language as a way of transferring or conveying thoughts from one person to another.

This metaphor is inescapable as long as we hold *language* to be a kind of common denominator of languages (in which thoughts are indeed conveyed, albeit with a good deal of slippage), so that an understanding of language could be extrapolated from an understanding of languages. But this, Harris argues, is a grave mistake, and he pursues with diligence and ingenuity the confusions sown by it, and by related theoretical fantasies. These include the well-known argument of the philosopher Gilbert Ryle about "systematically misleading expressions," which Harris attacks at the root by challenging the notion that any expression could ever *fail* to mislead, at least potentially. They also include the belief, exemplified by the Wittgensteinian account of a "picture" theory of language, that language mimes or mirrors reality, a belief that is difficult to sustain in light of such linguistic features as the gender distinctions in nouns and the different conjugational forms of verbs. In light of these simple facts, and of the phenomenal variety of actual language use, there is, Harris insists, simply no way of establishing a systematic correspondence between the order of language and the order of reality. "It is entirely obscure," Harris concludes, "how we are to make sense of the notion that reality has structures which are comparable to structures of the kind relevant to verbal analysis" (1981: 27).

Harris devotes most of *The Language Myth* to posing, with an almost cruel patience, a series of embarrassing questions to each of the main tendencies of contemporary linguistics in turn, concluding with two that he addresses to one and all:

(i)   How is it possible to recover determinate linguistic forms from the heterogeneous mass of phonetic signals present in actual speech?

(ii) How is it possible to identify fixed linguistic meanings among the apparently varied and inconsistent verbal usage which speech behaviour in practice presents? (1981: 199)

No postmodernist skeptic about the possibility of scientific truth, Harris sympathizes with the linguist who pursues the hidden rules of language, rules that seem so tantalizingly close at hand, so immanent in every utterance. But he notes that such rules evaporate the moment an attempt is made to grasp them, and is skeptical that any binding rules can ever be recovered or deduced from the immense mass of available evidence. The evolution of Chomsky's own thinking over the past half-century, as he works through a series of hypotheses, seems to suggest that the empirically available "facts" of language can be enlisted to support a variety of discrete explanations of the fundament, or fundaments. "The enigma of rational speaker-hearers," Harris says, "is that although they apparently require some fixed linguistic framework which would enable them to exercise their rationality, the moment we try seriously to identify and inspect that framework, it vanishes before our eyes" (1981: 203).

The consequences of this vanishing for the project of general theoretical linguistics are serious. As frameworks disappear in succession, new paradigms in linguistics take the form not of refined descriptions of a constant object, but of new objects. At the end of her illuminating survey of the long history of linguistic thought, Julia Kristeva notes that, unlike other fields, in which descriptions of a given object or set of objects are progressively refined, "the representations and theories of language we have just summarily run through approach through the name 'language' an object that is noticeably different each time" (1989a: 325). The word *language* (and its translations) may be the same in the discourses of Plato, Augustine, Port-Royal, Condillac, Rousseau, Herder, von Humboldt, Saussure, Chomsky, Rorty, and Derrida, but the thing named by that word is not. General or theoretical linguistics has never established a consensus about the empirical base of its studies, the linguistic thing itself; and without such a consensus, the entire project of a scientific study of language itself is, Harris says, "basically mistaken: that is, one must conclude that modern linguistics has proved to be no science at all" (1981: 44). Academic attempts to segregate language from questions of human creativity, human responsibility, and human intelligence generally have produced only accounts of sadly maimed entities or pseudo-entities that cannot possibly claim to represent the essence, much less the totality, of language. "The plain fact is," he concludes, "that no rule-based model of any kind so far proposed can come to terms with the real-life flexibility of communication situations and communicational models" (1990: 135).

Harris sometimes overstates his case by minimizing or failing to provide any account of the source of the regularities, structures, and conventions most linguists study. So hostile is he to any approach that treats rules as primary and context as secondary that he occasionally permits himself the misleading implication that language is an ongoing and spontaneous social invention, something that we "create . . . as we go, both as individuals and as communities" (1990: 149). Not only does he deny the existence of language as such, he even denies the existence of languages—at least as objects of scientific investigation. For obvious reasons, then, most professional linguists reject Harris as an iconoclastic loner, a rogue scholar with an agenda. He is commonly depicted within the linguistics community as a man so obsessed with great philosophical issues he can't grasp the valuable empirical work going on in the field, a man who can't see the trees for the forest—to which he might respond by saying that he simply can't agree to call this inconstant mass of stuff a forest in the first place. For most theoretical linguists, their discipline is not yet a fully mature science; for Harris, it is not now, and will never be a science.

For over twenty years, Harris has been arguing for an "integrationist" account of communication that would erase the boundaries between, on one side, speech and writing and their interpretation, and, on the other, the general ability to navigate around in the world. In the integrationist view, what academics call language is simply one dimension of the countless ways in which we make sense to and of other people. Such an expanded account, Harris insists, should replace the numerous "segregationist" accounts that do little more than establish the basis for academic departments with a specific, limited research program (see Harris 1996). Needless to say, this recommendation, if adopted, would only make things worse; for linguistics, now faced with a different and far larger task than it had supposed, would suddenly find itself even more immature than it had thought. Very recent attempts to preserve the possibility of a science of language in the face of Harris's strictures are—as one would expect—in their very early stages, and they make so many concessions to "uncertainty," especially with respect to the contexts and circumstances that surround and determine communicative behavior, that many linguists might feel the attempt not worth making (see Weigand).

The shunning by linguists of Harris is therefore understandable. Less so is the subtler but even more effective rejection of him by those philosophers and literary theorists for whom *language* serves as the password for theoretical sophistication. One might think that such thinkers would regard Harris, with his vast knowledge of linguistics and his philosophical and historical interests, as an authority on the question that has dominated intellectual culture of the hundred years, "the language century." In fact, however, Harris is virtually unread in these circles. Why?

The reason is difficult to accept, but not, perhaps, to explain. If Harris had deconstructed genetics or molecular biology with the same authority he brought to linguistics, his name might be mentioned in the same breath as, say, Paul Feyerabend or T. S. Kuhn. But in the community of intellectuals for whom the distant and shadowy Saussure stands as the fountainhead of modern thought—the man who inaugurated the project of relativizing meaning and unraveling identity, who established the fact that language was a construction, who made it possible to see how something called "language" stood between the individual and the world by furnishing categories not dictated by reality, who articulated the principle of a system of social meaning, who discovered revolutionary new possibilities for agency in the principle of arbitrariness—in this community, the idea that the truth of language has been, in its essentials, scientifically determined is not a myth but a scholarly conviction. For such thinkers, nothing good could come of a deep and informed skepticism about the possibility of a science of language; for them, Harris's argument is a complete nonstarter.

Why has language played such a dominant role in intellectual culture over the past century? When one considers the large-scale forms of violence that have characterized this period, a preoccupation with language on the part of intellectuals hardly seems an adequate response—certainly not when many other intellectuals have been hard at work promoting the values of excess, randomness, minimalism, formalism, or other forms of nonverbal expression, so that language itself has come, in certain quarters, to seem a nostalgic holdover from the premodern era, like three-decker novels and family readings from the Bible. Harold Segal argues that the most characteristic features of the twentieth century worked to subordinate "the virtues of the mind to those of the body," and contributed to a general "dethroning of language." But the very mass and intensity of antilinguistic energy in the cultural history of the past century might actually provide one clue to the tenacity with which some intellectuals have clung to language as the problem of problems, and the solution to many of those problems. Placed at risk by what Segal calls the era's "physical imperative," language might still, some feel, provide a response and a counterweight that intellectuals could respect, if only the theory of language could be made powerful enough, if only the thought of language could be placed on a firm footing.

But an even deeper and more compelling argument for the dominance of language—and the one to which the rest of this book will be devoted—is that language, or the partially focused thought of language, has served as a proxy for other issues that resist resolution on their own terms. If the question Müller asked in 1861—"What is language?"—remains unanswered, that has not inhibited, and has in fact encouraged, the recourse to language as a way of thinking other thoughts and answering other questions. In the following chapters, I will examine the ways in which language has been conscripted as a repository of evidence for hypotheses for which there is little or no direct evidence, and a reply to challenges for which there is no immediate response.

We want, it seems, to believe that we are not simply an agglomeration of atomized individuals, but a family of man; we look for evidence that human beings constitute a society in the fullest sense, a polity united by common understanding and a common means of expression; and we would like to believe that we possess some universal species-endowment that is more meaningful than mere anatomy. We want, too, to believe that moral rules and principles have some anchor in the nature of humanity, and are not simply inventions. Oppressed by conventions and restraints, we want to believe that something in our nature commands respect as a site of unconquered freedom and the possibility for significant agency. Confused by the rapid pace of change, we want to feel that we can understand our world, that we know where ideas come from and how they influence us; we want to feel that the social realm can be systematically studied because it is organized systematically. Shocked by our singular capacity for evil and destruction, we seek not only to disavow our agency, but to reassure ourselves that we are not isolated in an otherwise languageless world, "alienated," as Harris says, "by the mysterious gift of tongues from all other living creatures" (1980: 187). The thought of language has been deployed by thinkers in a number of fields as a response to all these concerns.

Thus language is the "critical fetish of modernity." In its original sixteenth-century context, William Pietz reports, a fetish was an object to which West African peoples attributed magical or animating powers. This primitive belief in the power of objects distressed European Protestants, who associated fetishes with idolatry, even with Catholicism (1987: 5; see also Pietz 1993). In modern usage, the fetish is held to be a function of the subject's displaced fears and anxieties. According to Freudian theory, a fetish is something—for example, a woman's shoe or foot—that you (presumptively a badly confused male) look at when you don't want to look at something else. You are afraid not of what you'll see, but of what you might not see—for example, the "castration" of the mother, a distressing lack that suggests that you, too, might be castrated. On this definition, the fascinating fetish-object is constituted by the subject as a means of protection not from illness or the evil eye, but from an unpleasant sight and thus a from a painful thought. In both original and modern usages, the concept of the fetish involves, then, an attribution or misattribution of energy and power to an object that, from another point of view, does not contain or manifest them at all.

The thought of language, as entertained by thinkers over the past century, is in this sense an exemplary fetish. From a "protestant" point of view, language has been illegitimately invested with powers that are properly reserved for human beings—that is, creatures capable of intentional agency. Throughout the past century, the theoretical construction of the "concrete object" of language has grown in force, dimension, and purposiveness as the scope for human, and *a fortiori* divine agency has been, in the world of theory, reduced. In this way, language has "protected" human beings from full self-recognition and shielded us from the consequences of our own behavior. We—and especially the reflective portion of "we"—have "looked at" language as a way of refusing to look at humanity "itself." Freud might suggest that, in directing our regard at language, we are refusing to confront not just the human capacity for rapacity, destruction, or cruelty, but also the disturbing possibility that there is "nothing" there, that there is no special human being or character, no divine species dispensation, no metaphysical difference between human nature and the rest of nature. We focus on language, in this analysis, as a way of reassuring ourselves, albeit indirectly, of our special place in the order of things, our singular endowments and high destiny. In one sense, then, language-as-fetish takes into itself a capacity for agency that relieves human beings of a certain measure of responsibility for their actions; but in the other, the fetish-object of language stands as the most brilliant evidence of human uniqueness.

I fully understand that the argument for the fetishistic character of language solicits a certain kind of resistance. Asked to entertain the absurd-sounding propositions that "there is no such thing as language" or that "language does not exist," many will suspect another "Sokal's Hoax," a parody of facile postmodern antirealism advanced as a serious proposition. A layman might respond by saying that language exists everywhere, in the form of words, sentences, books, speeches, conversations, and (with a vague waving motion) things like that. With no theoretical problems that require solution and no theoretical fears that must be allayed, this hypothetical layman does not have a fetishistic relation to language. For this we must look to scholars and intellectuals in the human sciences.

The theorist might respond to the suggestion that "language does not exist" by saying such things as, "I know very well that language is disorderly, multiple, mutable, and blurred around the edges, with no clear boundaries separating it from cries, thoughts, marks, gestures, and so forth; I know that attempts to determine the essence of language as grammatical structures, words, human capacities, expression, writing, communication, and cultural systems are all tendentious. I know that communication is always context-specific and that rules and principles are very hard to grasp in their purity; I know that language is a kind of action and cannot be reduced to a reflection of thought, much less a mimesis of the real; I know all that—but still. . . ." This more sophisticated response reveals the true nature of the fetish, for it conforms precisely to the Freudian formula of "fetishistic disavowal": "I know very well that mother has no phallus, but still. . . ."

If language "does not exist" as a determined object of knowledge, it is not for that reason altogether unreal, for the thought of it has produced countless effects. For the past century, the thought of language has been immensely useful in enabling us to bring within the orbit of rational inquiry a number of subjects that would otherwise resist satisfactory articulation. Language may be a nonobject, or the object of nonknowledge, but if we knew that we did not know language, we could scarcely claim to know anything at all; feeling that we know language, on the other hand, we experience the optimism of the rational mind confronting an object that responds to its methods. We can believe that the secrets of the universe and our place in it are nearly within our grasp, and even if this confidence is misplaced, such buoyant spirits can often serve as their own justification.

Two

Ideology and the Form of Language

There is no ideology and never has been.

—Gilles Deleuze and Félix Guattari,
A Thousand Plateaus

1. Ideology and Theory

What is ideology? This simple question, often advanced as the title of the opening chapter if not the opening sentence in books on the subject, tends to linger at the end. The sheer number of scholarly accounts of ideology might suggest that a good deal of progress has been made in this inquiry, and in some respects it has: over the past two hundred years, ideology's numerous aspects, uses, forms, and functions have been discovered, assessed, and described by scholars, theoreticians, and even historians—a phenomenal proliferation of theory, accompanied by heroic efforts of semiotic containment. The Italian Marxist Feruccio Rossi-Landi begins his 1982 work on *Marxism and Ideology* by listing "eleven distinct conceptions" of ideology, which he presents as an unsparing reduction from the "several hundred meanings of 'ideology', divisible into tribes, sects, families, and special alliances" current in the world (18). Terry Eagleton begins chapter 1 ("What Is Ideology?") of his book *Ideology: An Introduction* (1991) with a list of sixteen definitions now in circulation, before settling on "roughly six different ways" of approaching the concept (28). The recurrence of the preliminary question even in recent and sophisticated discussions suggests, however, that despite all the analytical work done on the subject, ideology remains not merely an open-ended field, but a field that has yet to make a beginning or determine its object. What is ideology? The precise and formal inquiry announces the possibility of scholarly advance; the repetition of the question announces the fact of its failure.

In what follows, I will not attempt a fresh approach to ideology, as if others have simply fallen short in their attempts to describe it; nor, however, will I assume, with Deleuze and Guattari, that ideology is a mere phantasm. Rather, my focus will be on the unusually intimate, even constitutive relationship between ideology "itself" and the theory of ideology, the way in which each new theory brings into focus or even into being a new ideological "thing." If we can grasp the complex nature of the relationship between thing and theory, we may be able to understand why the inquiry into ideology has been on the one hand exceptionally dynamic and productive, and on the other hand stalled, even paralyzed. My overarching thesis is that those who have tried to think rigorously about ideology have encountered mysterious obstacles, and have, in their attempts to get a grip on the problem and to move the theory forward, turned first to economic and material explanations, and then, decisively, to language. These turns have created more than an illusion of progress; they have in fact constituted progress itself, the only kind of progress possible in the study of ideology.

By spontaneous scholarly consensus, the theory of ideology is represented as a living thing with a narratable history in which theoretical advances or refinements mark moments of growth and maturation. Thus ideology is, in the first instance, routinely described as a "child" of the French Enlightenment, part of the general revolutionary critique of religious dogma and political authoritarianism. This critique was intended by its inventors, known as "ideologues," to serve as the cornerstone of a new system of empiricist education designed to clear the public mind of false idols, and to emancipate people so they could begin to think for themselves. In the work of Marx and Engels, this elementary idea began to "mature," eventually entering into a kind of adolescence, an early promise of adulthood mixed with residual elements of theoretical juvenility. Marx and Engels detached the study of ideology from the critique of religion, and redefined ideology as the ideas to be studied rather than the study of ideas. But they furthered the ideologues' spirit of disenchanted rationalism through an account of thinking that stressed the determining power of economic factors. Ideology, they argued, was the highly determined conceptual reflex of certain socio-economic conditions; it was a way of thinking that appeared to be abstract, ahistorical, and politically neutral, but actually served the worldly interests of the dominant class, the always-rising bourgeoisie.

Like many adolescents, however, Marx and Engels were both doctrinaire and indecisive, and they left a theoretical mess that had to be cleaned up by their successors. These were the more sober and systematic thinkers of the twentieth century, especially those associated with "Western Marxism," who put the study of ideology at last on a firm footing by ridding the term of its pejorative connotations and shedding the "vulgar" concept of the economic determination of thought. Most importantly, the Western Marxists extended the domain of ideology to include such aspects of cultural life as customs, habits, norms, prejudices, and assumptions.

The theory of ideology having reached, by mid-century, this point of ripened maturity, a number of liberal-pluralist thinkers were in a position to contemplate the "end of ideology," in which large regulating ideas or cultural master-narratives were at last generally considered as superannuated relics of a fractious and unsettled epoch. The new, post-Marxist belief was that ideology had itself been outgrown by people too sophisticated to require its consolations, too insightful to tolerate its illusions. In the work of Talcott Parsons, Edward Shils, Seymour Lipset, and especially Daniel Bell, ideology was depicted as yesterday's news, its rigid categories relegated to the past by a general consensus on the value of a Western-style democracy.

Despite a republication of this obituary notice by conservative thinkers in the wake of the collapse of the U.S.S.R., reports of the death of ideology have, it now appears, been greatly exaggerated. In the work of such diverse thinkers as Slavoj Žižek, Clifford Geertz, Stuart Hall, Terry Eagleton, Claude Lefort, Ernesto Laclau, and others, ideology has been granted a second childhood. What these thinkers contend is that ideology functions not just as a retrograde force of determination in a postmodern world devoted to maximizing freedoms of all kinds, but also as an indispensable conceptual instrument for the study of cultural life, and even, for some, as a politically progressive force.

Among the other things it teaches us, history invariably reassures us of its own adequacy as a way of organizing complex materials into knowable form. But history and ideology have never made a good match. As Louis Althusser said, ideology "has no history" (1984: 33). In this famous pronouncement, Althusser was drawing a distinction between particular ideologies such as Marxism or liberalism, which might have a history, and ideology "in general," which was constant and ubiquitous, as "eternal" as the Freudian unconscious, "immutable in form throughout the extent of history" (35).

But in one sense, particular ideologies, too, "have no history." As Marx and Engels were the first to recognize, ideologies work incessantly to obscure or efface history by bestowing on certain ideas or attitudes the powerful appearance of universal truth. Mere inversions or negations of reality with no substance of their own, ideologies in the Marxian sense work to foster the process Nietzsche called "forgetting." The memorable example Nietzsche gives, in *On the Genealogy of Morals*, is the very gradual sublimation of eons of punishment, vengeance, and torture into that form of internalized threat called "conscience," which supposedly instructs us in the unchanging dictates of the moral law. Marxian ideology also seems to have a good deal in common with what Roland Barthes described as "myth": a purging of history from a given representation so that it seems a function of nature, a truism that goes without saying, and is indeed resistant to logical articulation. What the unconscious, conscience, and myth have in common with ideology is a manner of representation that renders inaccessible to immediate perception the contingent process, the historically determined agency, by which a judgment, an attitude, an idea, an image was formed, and so discourages the kind of activist critical thinking that might eventuate in a demand for change.

Thus, for people in the grip of the ideology of anti-Semitism, "the Jewish problem" can seem to have the same irreducibility as "the gravity problem" for high jumpers; for others, the political and economic dominance of the West can seem as predetermined as the sun rising in the east. Though thoroughly embedded in history and culture, ideology invariably masks, recodes, or represses this embeddedness so that people—ideological subjects—may think their routine thoughts and even exercise what they are convinced is their free critical intelligence. While time marches on, ruthlessly changing everything, ideology is busily at work assuring people that common sense, reason, and direct observation are yielding accurate information, and that what we hold as the truth would be evident to any reasonable person able to climb out of his or her prejudices and view the matter objectively. To grasp ideology historically, then, we must think against the grain, giving it something it refuses to have—in effect, claiming to have thought *of* ideology without having thought ideologically, even though the claim to such neutral thought is, in a number of the many definitions available, the very symptom of ideology.

As we can already see, one difficulty in thinking clearly about ideology is that the discourse about ideology cannot quite get clear of ideology itself. Even in the preceding paragraphs, the word *ideology* has referred both to a particular kind of force or phenomenon and to the study of this force or phenomenon. Sometimes this entanglement seems a point of mere imprecision, but at other times, it seems to suggest a deeper fact. Why is it, for example, that the era sometimes referred to as the "age of ideology" begins at the same historical moment that the term *ideology* itself was coined? In a brilliantly original and compact account, David Hawkes develops a prehistory of ideology, which he defines as a false consciousness resulting from the belief in the self-validating autonomy of representation. This belief extends back to Biblical times, and includes not only various forms of idolatry but also the medieval practice of indulgences ("a certificate denoting a specific amount of human activity . . . fetishized labour"), and, for Protestants at least, the institution of the Papacy (27–28). But as Hawkes understands, although ideology might be ubiquitous in advanced societies today, the premodern world was also a preideological world. There are no true ideologies before the advent of the term *ideology*, and nothing but ideologies ever since. It almost seems that the inquiry into the genesis of ideas, or ideology, germinated the kind of ideas it required for its object.

In his useful introduction, Eagleton notes that all "-ology" terms tend to become mixed up with their objects, so that *biology*, for example, refers to the physical, organic system rather than to the study of it, and *methodology* means not ideas about method but method itself. But the problem is especially acute in the case of ideology, since the object of study is the same kind of thing as the study itself: the study of ideology consists of the production of ideas about ideas, thinking about thinking. As thoughts can affect, interfere with, or become confused with each other, it becomes hard to know, at any given moment, whether one is thinking about thinking, or just thinking. Thus to speak at any length about ideology is to risk producing such contorted statements as the following, in which one meaning of the term is joined at the hip with another, quite different one: "For the Enlightenment," Eagleton says, "the enemy of ideology was, paradoxically, ideology. Ideology in the sense of a science of ideas would combat ideology in the sense of dogma, prejudice and mindless traditionalism" (1991: 159). But—he continues—the ideologues were themselves ideologically mystified, and so "ideology was born as a thoroughly ideological critique of ideology" (64). Paul Ricoeur says the same, in the oracular rather than the accusatory mode, commenting that, "only ideology may speak about ideology" (140). Others assert that ideology actually produces ideology: some of the most sophisticated thinkers today conceive of ideology not as a reflection of material relations of production, but as a "relation" itself, with the capacity to articulate and rearticulate itself independent of any other worldly factors (see Lefort 184, and 181–236 passim). So: ideology is the enemy of ideology, it can speak about ideology, it can criticize ideology, and it can create ideology.

But perhaps all these maddening mirror-effects in the study of ideology reflect not the true nature of ideology but only the self-regarding subtlety of the contemporary academy. Perhaps contemporary thinkers have simply lost sight of the original meaning of the term and have become more interested in their own theories than in the thing they are supposed to be theorizing. Perhaps, in other words, we might make real progress by rolling back the last century or two and returning to the first "childhood" of the concept in the French Enlightenment, of which the invention of ideology is perhaps the most characteristic, and certainly the most ambitious task.

This task was entrusted to Destutt de Tracy, the leader of the "ideologues" in the Section of Analysis of Sensations and Ideas, in the Moral and Political Sciences Division of the revolutionary *Institut Nationale*. As he conceived the project, ideology was to be a materialist, skeptical, antimetaphysical, and thoroughly demystified science—a branch of zoology, he said, that might ultimately become the science of sciences. Ideologists would study the genesis of ideas in material sensations in order to discover the true nature of thought. As a "science of ideas," ideology offered to save people from prejudice and prepare them for the sovereignty of secular reason functioning in the service of truth. Armed with new understanding, people could rid themselves of the distorting effects of tradition, prejudice, authority, metaphysics, faith, and passion. (One of de Tracy's most devoted students was the young Stendahl, whose rational distrust of the distortions produced by passion reflects his apprenticeship; another was Thomas Jefferson, whose translation of de Tracy's *Elements of Ideology* appeared in 1817.) A pedagogy, or, in Flaubert's ironic phrase, a "sentimental education," could then be developed that would enable the final eradication of illusion and passivity, a total reformation of human character ending in a complete transformation of society. A revolutionary spirit infused an inquiry that was, in its guiding presumptions, a descendant of Baconian science and Lockean empiricism. How bracing is this project, how bold in conception, how optimistic in spirit—and how far from the abysses of contemporary theorizing!

And yet one of the leading theorists of ideology in recent years has described the entire enterprise as an exercise in naïve self-delusion, an instance of "the pathos of the Enlightenment" (Lichtheim 8). And even in their own time, the ideologues encountered nothing but resistance. Reactionaries, Romantics, and Cartesians, all accustomed to metaphysical or subjectivist explanations of consciousness, accused the ideologues of insulting rather than explaining intelligence by describing the mind as a mere machine, an aspect of animal functioning rather than a quasi-divine power of reflection.

The most formidable opposition came from a one-time member of the *Institut* during the Directorate (1795–99), Napoleon, whose antipathy grew as his power increased. Making peace with the Church, Napoleon turned on the ideologues, charging that they sought to deprive citizens not just of their false beliefs, but of some "illusions" (pertaining to the historical destiny of the nation) necessary to keep society functioning smoothly, replacing them only with other illusions (concerning the capacity of secular-rationalist intellectuals to guide leaders) that caused nothing but trouble. Napoleon well understood the basic premises of ideology, that ideas arise from sensations, and that they affect and are affected by material conditions in the world; but he regarded the ideologues' tendency to abstraction and formalism at the expense of "the lessons of history" as a threat to his own preeminence. He understood above all that France could not change the world in two ways at once; and so ideology was replaced in the *écoles centrales* by a course on military instruction. Following the French defeat in 1812, the Emperor attacked the ideologues directly as proponents of a "diffuse metaphysics" that was more responsible than his own miscalculations or the Russian winter for "all the misfortunes which have befallen our beloved France" (cited in Naess et al. 151; see also Emmett Kennedy).

This assault must have been as intellectually bewildering to de Tracy and his colleagues as it was immediately and materially damaging. For them, ideology was a philosophical project designed to free the world from the mystifications of dogma and metaphysics—and yet they were being accused of being hot-blooded and frivolous, even "dreamers" and "windbags." While they had anticipated a program of progressive education that would consolidate a grand social totality, they were now being charged with causing suffering, division, and even national humiliation. Having undertaken a skeptical scientific materialism, they now stood accused of having indulged in abstract fantasizing.

At the very beginning of the history of ideology, then, we see preliminary enactments of many of the features that would come to characterize the study of ideology in later, and vastly changed times. Perhaps the most perplexing feature of ideology—both the study and the thing itself—is a tendency to contain its own opposites. There is, it seems, no statement about ideology that cannot be turned inside out. Was the initial impulse behind the study of ideology to provide a scientific counterweight to romanticism? It was; but it was also a kind of romanticism itself, characterized by naïve positivist optimism and utopian social aspirations. Did the ideologues try to promote a concrete understanding of the material facts about ideas? They did; and yet as history has shown, the study of ideology tends to thin out, dissipating into abstract accounts of -isms and -ologies. Does ideology operate "unconsciously"? Clearly; and yet it is also said to structure philosophical systems such as Hegel's or Kant's. Does ideology concern ideas? Of course; but Nazism was disseminated in the form of highly charged images organized as a racial mythology. Is ideology group-specific? Yes; but every group has its own ideology, and so the fact of ideology is universal. Is ideology a secular phenomenon? Undoubtedly; but Protestant fundamentalism and Islam may be considered ideologies. Does ideology arise amid the confusions of quotidian life? It does; but it is also engineered by self-interested rulers.

One could in fact argue that the very essence of ideology is just this peculiar ("zoological") tendency to mitosis, dividing and multiplying in such a way as to disarm critical analysis and create confusion about itself, its goals, its direction, its character. Žižek has noted a curious feature of thinking about ideology, that it invariably involves a "privileged place, somehow exempted from the turmoil of social life, which enables some subject-agent to perceive the very hidden mechanism that regulates social visibility and nonvisibility"; and yet, as he points out and as we have already noted, the theory of ideology generally insists that there is no such place, and that the feeling that one is in such a place is an ideologically generated illusion (Žižek 1994: 3). Thus, "when some procedure is denounced as 'ideological' . . . one can be sure that its inversion is no less ideological" (4).

When, for example, such contingent events as natural disasters, the spread of AIDS, or a hole in the ozone are interpreted as sure signs of the wrath of God, we could say that such an investment of contingent events with large-scale meaning is an "ideological" gesture. On the other hand, however, the failure to grasp any pattern in the flow of existence can also be characterized as an "ideological" distortion of vision induced by some unrecognized force. In the first case, ideology generates a sense of the necessity of the merely contingent; in the second, ideology dissimulates necessities and produces a sense of endless contingency. Without losing its edge as a critical concept, the category of ideology spreads itself over everything, so that the critique, the analysis, the neutralization of ideology are all, in Žižek's recurring phrases, "ideological *par excellence*," "thoroughly ideological," the very "ideological as such."

It is easy to accept the proposition that there is no escape from ideology. The far more difficult fact is that, while there is no escape from ideology, there is also no escape from the sense that we have, our principles and convictions notwithstanding, escaped. Ideology remains a problem because the solutions to it constitute more problems, and we are constantly returned to square one. Theorists in search of square two have sought to explain ideology in terms of other disciplines, other discourses that do not have this same recursivity. For the past century, that discourse has been language. But to understand why, we need to pass through the era of classical theory, as far as ideology is concerned—the era of Marx and his successors, when the key to ideology was economics.

2. Marxism and the Economic Specter

Unlike de Tracy, whose flailing and desperate career took him from aristocratic origins, to the barricades, to a prison cell (where he first conceived of a science of ideas), to the *Institut*, to the Senate, and finally, in 1830, to the barricades once again, Marx and Engels were dedicated intellectuals. They write, in *The German Ideology*, not against the archaic power of priests and kings, but against a style of philosophizing, a neo-Hegelian ("German") idealism, or "ideology," which they accuse of overestimating, in a manner at once inconsequential and sinister, thought at the expense of action. "Life," they write in a famous aphorism that sought to reverse an ancient philosophical hierarchy, "is not determined by consciousness, but consciousness by life" (1983b: 170).

A spirit of theoretical optimism informs their work from the start. One could not, they argue, learn about life by imagining abstractions or essences, but only by making concrete observations of "existing social relations" as lived by "real, active men" (1983b: 175). Philosophers, they point out, are naturally inclined to overrate speculative or "separated" thought. By promoting the value of consciousness and of thinking about thinking, they implicitly advance the view that, since the basic project of existence is knowledge, philosophers stand on the highest rung of the human ladder. But philosophers are deluded if they think that they will reap the rewards of a successful campaign on behalf of the contemplative life, for the real beneficiaries are those in the dominant class, the bourgeoisie, who have the highest stake in the status quo. A widespread conviction that human beings are essentially creatures of thought will produce the impression that people are free, as thoughts are said to be free; people under this impression might believe that their own lives, with their grinding inequities and injustices, do not deserve their full attention, not to mention their outrage. Their lives are the way they are, people might reflect, just because the world is the way it is, and all anyone can do about this condition is try to understand the laws of its higher necessity. The German ideology "naturalized" its own activity—thinking—and the bourgeois social order from which it emerged, and discouraged a specifically critical reflection on, much less revolutionary action against, the actual circumstances of life.

For Marx and Engels, ideology was a systematic form of distraction and illusion. It was not a method, as it had been for the ideologues, but an object of critique, as it was for Napoleon. But the goal was the same, to study the origin of ideas in order to rid oneself of confusion and prejudice and think clearly at last. Thought, grown ever more abstract, self-reflexive, and attenuated during the period of bourgeois ascendancy, could renew itself by plunging, in a spirit of scientific materialism, into the realities of existence. Confident that they had grasped the problem by the throat, Marx and Engels promised solutions. They were equally definite on what the critique of ideology would finally yield. They sought to understand the subtle ways by which the ruling class legitimated its dominance by making it appear to be inevitable or justified. Armed with insight into the strategies and methods of the powerful, ordinary people could begin to think differently—nonideologically and scientifically—and could prepare themselves for action. Marx and Engels presumed that clear-thinking people would not rest with a mere understanding of the world; infuriated at what they saw, the populace would be moved to change it. By disclosing the true origins of ideas and ideals in privilege and force, ideology critique could impel the revolution. Marx and Engels preserved the messianic thrust of the French ideologues, but redirected it: instead of trying to inculcate the discipline of ideology as a form of critique, they sought to expose the machinations of ideology as a form of mystification.

Despite this emphasis on clarity, the dominant feature of Marx and Engels's account is confusion at every level. In the first instance, ideology is *produced* by confusion. The opportunity and need for ideology arise at that stage in economic development when a division of labor (between classes, between town and country, between industry and agriculture) creates the potential for a conflict of interests, a conflict that is deeply unwelcome to those who profit most from the division. With a division between, for example, intellectual and material forms of labor, thoughts themselves, once organically inmixed with and directly determined by actual existence, become the specialty or even the private property of the intellectual class, which assumes responsibility for thinking as such. As privileged members of the bourgeois ruling class, intellectuals naturally devote themselves to "negating" the fact and necessity of class conflict, and to defending or trying to neutralize the division of labor that enables them to think while others work. It is, then, class division and class conflict that produce the apparent self-sufficiency of theory, which in turn works to the advantage of the theorizing class, the bourgeoisie. In much the same way, nation-states generate imaginary differences between each other in order to mask or deny the real internal conflicts within each one. Marx and Engels call "ideology" all those thoughts that naturalize and universalize sectoral conflicts within society, sowing concord in places where, "objectively," there should be discord.

In this respect, ideology *is* a species of engineered confusion. Those who are "in" it think wrongly about their circumstances and interests, and even think about the wrong things altogether. They are, as Engels would put it in a famous 1893 letter, trapped in an ideology-induced state of "false consciousness" (766). In a notoriously problematic analogy, Marx and Engels compared ideology, which inverted the natural hierarchy of life and thought, to the effect of a *camera obscura*, an optical device in which images appeared "upside down." Commentators have worried over the aptness of this comparison of ideology's distortions to a mechanism for discerning proportions that was, for Locke and others, a model of the production, by scientific means, of an exact reflection of reality. But the basic intention is clear, to depict ideology as a wrong-way-round understanding of the world that leads people to mistake their own interests.

An even clearer indication of this intention is the repeated deployment of a rhetoric of "spectres," "ghosts," "illusions," "chimeras," "fantasies," "imaginary beings," and "phantoms" that runs like a trail of smoke through this and other Marxian texts (see Eagleton 1991: 63–92; Mitchell, 172–78; and Derrida 1994). Thought becomes spectral or chimerical, according to Marx and Engels, when it cuts loose from the real conditions of life and assumes an unreal autonomy. When we believe, for example, that the boss deserves our unquestioning loyalty, that the criminal justice system dispenses fair and impartial judgments, that the race will surely go to the swiftest, that conscience gives us access to the unchanging moral law, or that capitalism is the natural economic system of free people, we are, a Marxist might charge, thinking ideologically, since a close and disinterested observation will simply not yield those conclusions. All these beliefs, the Marxist might say, are simply phantoms, products of an intimidated and confused brain, evidence of ideology's effectiveness.

At this point, it will come as no surprise, however, that the confusions specific *to* ideology seem to have taken root in Marxian thoughts *about* ideology. The characteristically declarative and uncompromising phrasings of Marx and Engels cannot conceal the fact that two very different cases struggle for dominance in their text. Consciousness, they assert, is organically related to material conditions, "directly interwoven with the material activity and the material intercourse of men. . . . Consciousness can never be anything else than conscious existence, and the existence of men is their actual life-process" (1983b: 169). Ideology is a particular kind of consciousness; and yet it is—they also assert, without hesitation—separated from actual life in that the illusions it generates, while favorable to a particular class, apparently float free of any class interests, so that ideological thought does not seem to be directly determined by a given "life-process." This contradiction is what led Althusser to say that *The German Ideology* offers "an explicit theory of ideology, but . . . it is not Marxist" (1984: 32).

However incoherent their combination, both "organicist" and "separatist" claims are necessary to the overall project. Consciousness must be grounded in material conditions so the priority of "existence" can be maintained; and yet by an equally powerful necessity, Marx and Engels must concede that ideological consciousness cuts loose, or appears to cut loose, from those conditions. Their explanations of this phenomenon are, as a consequence of this concession, tentative and unpersuasive. They suggest, for example, that at an early stage of cultural development—"at first"—consciousness was interwoven with material life, only to split off at a later date when the "division of labor" had progressed to a certain point, after which—"from now on"—consciousness could "flatter" itself that it was independent and self-grounding. This is, of course, no good. How could the division of labor occur unless consciousness had already become separated from life? And how, precisely, does consciousness go about deluding itself through self-flattery? Marx and Engels are trying to formulate a general account of the relation of thoughts to material conditions, but seem unable to square their overarching materialism with the specific indictment of ideology. They seem unable, that is, to say how it is that some (ideological) thoughts serve specific material interests by cutting loose from them, unable to reconcile the idea of a separated theory with the claim that ideology serves bourgeois interests as the practical consciousness of the middle class. Their problem is that they must find a way of criticizing bourgeois consciousness without criticizing consciousness itself; the problem many later thinkers have with them is that they scarcely seem aware of their problem.

They were not, however, doctrinaire in advancing their analysis. In fact, Marx himself lacked confidence in *The German Ideology*, and after an initial failure to publish the manuscript, consigned it to "the mice," never to be published in his lifetime. But at virtually the same time that he and Engels were struggling with their text, Marx was developing the critique of "alienation" that achieved its definitive statement in the Preface to *A Contribution to the Critique of Political Economy* (1859). Here Marx engaged the problem of consciousness in more concrete terms by articulating the notion of a legal, political, aesthetic, or philosophical "superstructure" that is "conditioned" or "determined" by an economic-material "base." These terms seem inherently sounder and more concrete than the discourse of phantoms, specters, and illusions filtering through *The German Ideology;* and even the term *ideology* is placed on a surer footing when Marx describes the superstructure as a set of "ideological forms in which men become conscious of this (economic) conflict and fight it out" (1983c: 160). Materialism is preserved here as a methodological premise, but it is supplemented by an account of a dimension of social life in which class conflict comes to consciousness in the form of ideas, disputes, propositions, judgments.

But these clarifications have themselves proven to be immensely problematic. If ideology is reconceived in this general and nonpejorative way, the bracing specificity and provocative spirit of challenge that energize *The German Ideology* are lost. Class conflict becomes a mere characteristic feature of social life, and does not tend in any particular direction, least of all to its own abolition. Even more troublesome is the fact that Marx does not provide a test for deciding whether something is part of the base or part of the superstructure. The position of many practices and institutions is, as more recent commentators have noted, uncertain. Where, for example, do popular films, professional sporting events, the media, political campaigns, or even universities belong? Lastly, and most bedeviling of all, the meaning of the terms "condition" and "determine" is crucially imprecise. The final result of the effort to distinguish economic base from reflective superstructure is, it seems, to nullify the distinction itself.

Marx's restless mind continued, however, to worry the difficulties he had committed himself to exploring, and soon after the publication of *A Contribution to the Critique of Political Economy*, he began work on what would eventually become *Capital*. Although this work apparently abandons the subject of ideology, it in fact represents an intriguing new development in his thinking on this subject, in which the same problems reappear under another name: commodity. The emergence of this term in *Capital* constitutes a moment of high conceptual tension in which the doctrine of materialism confronts its other, its own particular kind of unreality and confusion. For as Marx unravels the mysteries of the commodity, it becomes clear that the commodity represents the explicit confounding of both the distinctions between "organic" and "separate" thinking, and between base and superstructure.

A thing becomes a commodity, Marx says, when it becomes an object of exchange, when it acquires a general value that can be compared to that of other such things. A table, for instance, has a certain "use-value" that I recognize when I tuck into dinner; but it is not a commodity until it is exchanged for something else—a certain amount of money, a wheelbarrow, a bicycle, a service performed. How is this "exchange-value" determined? Marx argues that an object's exchange-value actually represents the quantity of "congealed" human labor expended to produce it. The value of labor is not, of course, a constant, and so "congealment" remains a mere figure for what must be a shifting and relative fixity. Still, it can still be posited that in a "perfect" system, if the table costs the same as a wheelbarrow, that must be because the same amount of work went into their making. The alienated form of money masks the fact of labor, and thus obscures the social and economic reality of the "relations of production," and by this means enables the untroubled sequence of exchanges that constitutes the capitalist "system."

To this point, the outlines of the argument are clear enough. But then Marx, with his keen sensitivity to the immaterial, the fantastic, and the aberrant, notes that although the humble table might appear a "trivial" and "easily understood" thing, it is actually "a very queer thing, abounding in metaphysical subtleties and theological niceties" (1983a: 444). The instant a useful table becomes a commodity, "it is changed into something transcendent. It not only stands with its feet on the ground, but, in relation to all other commodities, it stands on its head, and evolves out of its wooden brain grotesque ideas, far more wonderful than if it were to start dancing of its own accord" (445). What bizarre thoughts does the leaping table "think"—what ideas does its position in the system of exchange embody? According to Marx, the table "thinks" that its value is an objective property that constitutes a "social relation" between itself and other items of exchange, when its value is really determined by the labor that produced it.

Under the spell of the commodity, we, too, think that a table costing $100 really possesses that precise value and is equivalent to other things that cost that much. Value, which is in fact a function of a social relation between men—actually, a series of relations between laborers and capitalists, and laborers and other laborers—takes on "the fantastic form of a relation between things" (Marx 1983a: 447). Things become subjects, endowed with a peculiar kind of mental life and even social structure; the commodity becomes a "fetish," and people who live in this system—or more precisely, people who *are lived* by this system, whose lives are instances of it—easily and unconsciously equate all kinds of different labor that go into the production of things. We are deluded not because the ruling class has a stake in fantasy, but because we have collectively ceded the function of thought to our commodities, which are poorly equipped for the task. "We are not aware of this," Marx says in a famous comment, "nevertheless, we do it" (449). Clearly, Marx is revisiting the problems associated with ideology (and anticipating the problems developed by psychoanalysis) without knowing it—that is, without using the term itself—and doing so with greater boldness and penetration than he had when he did use the term.

One of the most dramatically prescient features of this rethinking is that the irrationality and unreality that had, in *The German Ideology*, marked the alienation of consciousness from material existence has migrated, in *Capital*, from the superstructure to the base. Whereas *The German Ideology* situated illusions and chimeras in the bourgeois misconception of reality, *Capital* places them in the very heart of social and material reality itself. In the later text, a factor of spectrality has penetrated economics, creating an "unconscious" in the core of capital, a ghostliness in the very wood of the table (see Balibar 168; Eagleton 1991: 85; and Žižek 1989: passim). As Derrida puts it in a lively deconstruction of what might be called the "physics of presence" in Marx's discourse, "the wood comes alive and is peopled with spirits: credulity, occultism, obscurantism, lack of maturity before Enlightenment, childish or primitive humanity . . . *Capital* contradiction" (1994: 152).

Some post-Marxist thinkers have found Marx's later account exciting, but the thrills are cheap, being proper to lower-order fictions of the uncanny, while the theoretical and even political costs are high (see Sprinker). The theory of the commodity fetish removes the false fronts of bourgeois ideology, only to replace them with a far more obdurate confusion in things, a distortion that cannot be neutralized by ideology critique. The commodity's power to produce conceptual distortion and false consciousness cannot be undone short of a wholesale reconstruction of the entire system, but the confusion sown by the commodity itself makes such a reconstruction difficult if not impossible. When thinking is done by things, or arises in the relations between things, ideology cannot be "unmasked," nor can it be opposed to a more objective "science." No longer relegated to fantasy or unreality, ideology has now installed itself in the fabric of the everyday. While this new account certainly represents a change in Marx's thinking, it does not represent theoretical progress, for ideology has become more inaccessible to thought than ever—less recognizable, more impervious to coherent articulation, less a feature of the political and even of the perceptible. Indeed, Derrida concludes that Marx effectively, if unintentionally, reconceptualizes materiality as such, and does so in a radically antimaterialist and really anti-Marxian spirit by recasting it according to an archaic "religious model," in which ghosts, secrets, mystiques, enigmas, fetishes—and ideology—form an immaterial but powerful chain (Derrida 1994: 148).

Nor were those who came after Marx more successful in formulating a progressive, noncontradictory understanding of ideology. By the end of the nineteenth century, socialist theorists were prepared to surrender Marx's most fundamental premise, that ideology was "unconscious"; and some were even speaking, in an approving manner that would have astonished Marx, of "the Communist ideology" or the "proletarian ideology." Lenin explicitly promoted "socialist ideology" and defended its scientific integrity (383–84). At this point, Eagleton says, "the situation is now thoroughly confused" (1991: 90).

Confusion does appear to be reaching a kind of maximum. But in fact the study of ideology was about to be reinvigorated by the arrival of new data, not about ideology "itself," whatever that might have meant, but about language. In the twentieth century, ideology was saved for empiricism and scholarly inquiry—saved, that is, from its own crippling or discouraging contradictions and incoherences—because thinkers found that while the direct gaze trained on ideology may have yielded only a blur, a peripheral-vision view of language could illuminate ideology from the side. Thinkers have, in other words, turned away from the chimerical or fantastical thing, ideology itself, and toward the empirically "solved" entity of language as the ultimate ground or medium of ideology, a determining "base" in relation to which ideology could function as superstructure.

If we return to Marx and Engels with this subsequent history in mind, we can see that the seeds of the linguistic turn had already been sown in *The German Ideology*. The few and almost furtive gestures toward language in *The German Ideology* are, as one might expect, undeveloped, but their very inadequacy calls attention to the need for a more thoroughgoing emphasis on language. At certain stressed or troubled points in *The German Ideology*, language emerges as a possible site of analysis, only to be dismissed with, one feels, a false assurance. This, at least, is how one might read the following passage, parts of which have already been quoted:

> The production of ideas, of conceptions, of consciousness, is at first directly interwoven with the material activity and the material intercourse of men, the language of real life. Conceiving, thinking, the mental intercourse of men, appear at this stage as the direct efflux of their material behaviour. The same applies to mental production as expressed in the language of the politics, laws, morality, religion, metaphysics, of a people. Men are the producers of their conceptions, ideas, etc.—real, active men, as they are conditioned by a definite development of their productive forces . . . we do not set out from what men say, imagine, conceive, nor from men as narrated,

thought of, imagined, conceived, in order to arrive at men in the flesh. (1983b: 169)

The passage omitted in this quotation introduces the image of the *camera obscura* that turns reality upside down, a device that functions as the governing mechanism not just of ideology but of the passage itself. For Marx and Engels begin this meditation by according language serious attention as the "direct efflux" of "real life," but conclude, in a gesture that Raymond Williams dismisses as an "objectivist fantasy," with an expression of disdain for "men as narrated" (1977: 60). Narration, they imply at the end of this passage, could not possibly produce any "positive" knowledge, but only an alienated, secondary, superstructural—in a word, ideological—distortion. Still, just a page later, Marx and Engels try to redeem certain uses of language by distinguishing between "empty talk about consciousness" and language in which "reality is depicted" (1983b: 170). They seem, in short, uncertain about whether all representations are false, or only false ones.

Perhaps at this point the most provocative comment one could make about the Marxian account of ideology is that it is *not* hopelessly confused. But such a case can be argued by beginning with the premise that only an "incoherent" account could register, as well as describe, the actual properties of ideology. The second most provocative thing one could say about this text is that it has not been effectively superseded by subsequent work. But once again, Marx and Engels can be defended by suggesting that they partially intuited the theoretical conflation of ideology and language that has since been trumpeted as the salvation of Marxism itself, a liberation of Marxism from Marx's own limitations.

To be sure, this intuition takes curious and fugitive forms. But consider the passage in which Marx and Engels advance the claim that, "from the start the 'spirit' is afflicted with the curse of being 'burdened' with matter, which here makes its appearance in the form of agitated layers of air, sounds, in short, of language. Language is as old as consciousness, language is practical consciousness, as it exists for other men, and for that reason is really beginning to exist for me personally as well; for language, like consciousness, only arises from the need, the necessity, of intercourse with other men" (1983b: 173). The division of labor that marks bourgeois alienation is here tracked to its source in the fragile distinction between spirit or matter, a distinction that immediately becomes a distinction without a difference. The burden of "matter," it turns out, is borne by air, or rather by the "agitation" in the "layers" of air that constitutes language. Language, at one moment in Marxian thinking a source of ideological distortion, is at another moment materiality itself. Both fundamental and ambivalent, language disallows at the outset any clear distinction between real materiality and unreal conceptions, which is to say, between truth and ideology.

What Marx and Engels all but say is that the world is as inconceivable without ideology as it is without language. Post-Marxists and non-Marxists alike have made an often unacknowledged return to Marx by triumphantly "discovering" this argument as if on their own, while in fact they are merely working out the implications of a few tentative and conflicted comments in *The German Ideology*. Marx has proven to be a poor prognosticator in the fields that he cared deeply about, history and political economics; but in a field for which he would have had nothing but contempt, the academic inquiry into the theory of ideology, he has been uncannily prescient.

Marx's half-turn to language brings into sudden focus an unstressed element in de Tracy and some of his successors. A polymath, de Tracy based his work on ideology in part on Condillac's theories of language, and was working on a *Grammar* at the same time as he was producing his four-volume *Projet d'éléments d'idéologie* (1801–15). In this latter work, de Tracy tried to establish "a grammar and language modeled after mathematics . . . in which each idea was assigned its corresponding linguistic sign" (Barth 4; see also Hawkes 195 n). The context for such a project had been established by what Foucault calls "Classical" thought generally, and by the *Logique de Port-Royal* in particular. Classical thought cleared a space for signs whose meaning was established by the human linguistic community, not by God or nature (Foucault 1970: 58–67). As Foucault points out, the functioning of signs in the Classical era is not exhausted by the task of representation, for the sign, in addition to representing, also establishes relations with other signs. As an account of ideas that stressed the contingent ways in which ideas become assigned to positions in an interlocking system of signs, de Tracy's "ideology" constituted a general theory of representation consistent with Classical thinking on language, a grammar and a logic, as Foucault puts it, "of all possible science" (240).

But it is with respect to the future of ideology and the theory of language that de Tracy's work is most interesting. In his *Projet*, he outlines the course of linguistic development from simple actions and imitative pantomime, all the way to a fully elaborated language that contains the genius of a culture, the very form of a people's experience. The intention animating this vast scheme is clearly to demolish the notion of an original or a universal tongue, and to replace it with the idea of a cultural-linguistic "habitude" shared by speakers of each individual language. The idea of a defining energy or inner form within each language, supported on other grounds by von Humboldt and Herder, could be understood by later thinkers (who thought of ideology as an object of knowledge rather than a modality of thinking) as a repository and engine of each culture's "ideology." An unbroken line can thus be drawn from Malebranche, Condillac, and Port-Royal through de Tracy to von Humboldt, Herder, and then to Taine. What all these thinkers shared was an understanding of a socially determined system of meanings, a collective invention that informed the consciousness of the individual without ever, itself, *being* fully conscious in any individual. When Saussure took over this concept from Taine, he added to it the notion of a signified, a concept to which the signifier refers, providing a modest component of individual consciousness to what had been considered up to that point as a collective phenomenon, the production of signs.

Saussure founded the modern discipline of linguistics, but as the perhaps unwitting heir of de Tracy, he also gave a decisively modern turn to the evolving theory of ideology. Although he never used the word, Saussure defined language *as* ideology; or rather, he renamed as "linguistics" what had, until then, been an inquiry into the relation between ideology and representation. After Saussure, it became all but impossible to think of ideology without thinking of language, and of language as Saussure defined it.

3. From Post-Marxism to Postmodernism; or, It's *Not* the Economy, Stupid

The assimilation of ideology to language as part of a general rejection of mechanical causality and class and economic reductionism is the most characteristic gesture of "post-Marxism." Latent or incipient in Marx's texts, this gesture is "post" in that it makes fully articulate a possibility Marx only allowed for. From its beginnings in the work of V. N. Vološinov and Antonio Gramsci, post-Marxism has taken the form of a delicate process of engagement and disengagement, fidelity and autonomy, repetition and revolution.

Vološinov and Gramsci have much in common: both professed Communist political commitments; both suffered grievously at the hands of their respective governments, Stalinist in the first case and Italian Fascist in the second; and both were decisively post-Marxist in the sense just given. They have, moreover, a postmortem affinity. Politically suspect because of certain of his convictions about language, Vološinov was exiled, a likely victim of the brutal purges of the 1930s, and his work—if it *is* his; Mikhail Bakhtin may well have written the two books for which Vološinov is known—was suppressed for decades; no substantial English translation of his work appeared until 1973. Gramsci, a leader of the Italian Communist Party, was incarcerated by Mussolini in 1926, and spent the remaining eleven years of his life in prison, where he produced, without books and under the watchful eye of the prison censor, over 2,800 pages of what eventually became known as *The Prison Notebooks*, which remained unpublished in Italian until after the war and did not become widely available in English until a selection appeared at about the same time, in 1971.

Thus, while both—following in the tradition of de Tracy—worked in embattled circumstances, their work became influential in the West in the theory-infatuated academic scene of the 1970s, which was eager to hear the discourse of real Marxists, as long as it could not be accused of "vulgarity." Between the moment of production and the moment of reception, almost everything had changed, and much of what Vološinov and Gramsci said was, to their Western audiences, dated, obscure, or irrelevant. But on one subject—the relation of ideology and language—they found themselves on the cutting edge.

Indeed, the impulse to cut—to prune, to reduce to slivers, to make the first incision—is everywhere visible in Vološinov's *Marxism and the Philosophy of Language*. One of the very first Marxist thinkers to write without direct reference to the works of Marx himself, Vološinov presents his work in the spirit of the pioneer who sweeps away persistent misconceptions, sets essential definitions and principles, and maps the territory in which others will find their way. An enemy of vulgar or mechanistic Marxism, especially of the belief that certain ideas necessarily originated in the experience of a given class, Vološinov is even more hostile to vulgar Freudianism. The presumptive author of a 1927 anti-Freudian treatise (*Freudianism*), Vološinov regarded the "psyche" as little more than a theoretical fantasy, a pseudo-scientific abstraction, a motivated misnomer.

The only reality he recognized as pertinent was the "social milieu" and the communicative system that reflected, supported, and structured it. What we seem to experience as the psyche, he argued, is simply a nodal point or even an effect of this larger system, a "tenant lodging in the social edifice of ideological signs" (1973: 13). Private thoughts, for Vološinov, are as illusory as a private language. Cries of pain, infant's babbling, silent ruminations—all these are still oriented toward others, and take what form they have from the necessity of communicating. Hence, "*the organizing center of any utterance, of any experience is not within but outside—in the social milieu surrounding the individual being*" (93). Vološinov's modernity is founded, then, on the antipsychologistic belief that the subject is determined by the communicative structure, the sign system, rather than the other way around—the very position taken by postmodernist thinkers, many of whom, ironically enough, cite as an authority Lacan and his "return to Freud."

While these oppositional gestures occupy the background of Vološinov's text, the foreground is concerned with battles within linguistics, a field that, he says, has been dominated by two kinds of mistake. The first, represented by the work of von Humboldt, can be characterized as a species of "romanticism," an overvaluation of the "creative" powers of the individual speaker who continually generates fresh language. The second mistake, represented by Saussure, consisted of an excessive "rationalism," an overemphasis on the received message, the sign, and especially the autonomous *system* of signs. Like many others in Leningrad in the 1920s, Vološinov was deeply impressed by Saussure's definition of the sign as the essential element in language, and retained the fundamental categories of the sign and the system of signs in his own work. Still, he believed that Saussure, like the romantics, missed the real key to language and communication, and to identity and subjectivity as well. This key was provided by the living current of social energy—which he called "ideology"—that informs and structures the entire socio-linguistic complex. To Saussure's formalism, Vološinov wanted to contribute just one small additional factor—"human relationships."

Furnished by the socio-linguistic system but used by the individual, the sign—or, as Vološinov generally put it, the "word"—mediated between the two, serving as the means by which the individual was structured "internally" and gently positioned within the communicative loop. Vološinov held controversial—even, perhaps, fatal—views on the word, which he described as ideologically neutral, constantly offering itself to diverse purposes as it was "imprinted" with values and notions that circulated in society. For Vološinov, the word is a kind of Poland, essentially independent but washed over by all manner of energies and attitudes that seek to claim it as their own and deploy it for their purposes. The word is, as he put it, "multi-accentual," and while it can, in theory, bear any kind of message, it belongs to no class or group.

This assertion of the ideal autonomy of the word did not agree with the ideological climate in Russia at the time, in which any assertion of "neutrality" was suspect; but it had the strictly theoretical advantage of focusing attention on the word itself, which Vološinov described, in perhaps the most intriguing formulation in the book, as "an arena of the class struggle" (1973: 23). For Vološinov, classes struggle not for material resources alone, but also for power, including the power to determine social meanings and evaluations. With all classes trying to appropriate signs for their own purposes, the sign is *the ideological phenomenon par excellence*," a "little arena for the clash and criss-crossing of differently oriented social accents," the very point at which the social milieu, with all its discordant energies and competing forces, becomes articulate and legible (13, 41).

Vološinov sought to effect a sweeping reorientation of the study of the sign, the psyche, and ideology. Ideology, he argued, is not just a mass of prejudice blocking real thought or accurate perception, a death force inhibiting change or social transformation. Existing in the space between the economic base and language, ideology is always both transforming and in transformation. In this ambiguous mid-region, ideology lives and mutates in a condition of constant, complex, and interdependent flux, a merging of currents. We are, in Vološinov, very much farther downstream than Marx ever reached, and have actually begun to imagine the social world as a kind of fluid, through which ideological waves pass. So liquid are Vološinov's conceptions, however, that the classical Marxian concepts of base and superstructure have begun to quiver, to lose their form, and even to flow into each other. In one branch of the stream, ideology takes the form of the "immediate superstructure"; but in another, ideology determines the sign, thereby assuming the function of the base (1973: 13). The sign, in response, becomes part of the determined superstructure—and yet,

Vološinov insists, signs are not just reflections or shadows of reality, but "particular, material things," "material [segments] of that very reality," and must therefore be part of the determining base (10, 11). In short, both ideology and the sign are both base and superstructure.

Perhaps we could say that, for Vološinov, ideology exists in a third space— superstructure with respect to relations of production, but base with respect to the sign and the individual psyche. But even this ingenious solution, which recalls recent theoretical modifications by Raymond Williams and Terry Eagleton, is too rigid. For Vološinov does not draw a clean line between the psyche, language, ideology, and the social milieu, but prefers to describe these as phases, facets, or moments of a constant dialectical interpenetration. In his system—which is no system at all—the psyche *is* the signs it uses, signs *are* ideology, ideology *is* the social milieu. There is, he says in this deliquescing vein, "*no basic division between the psyche and ideology*," because "*the psyche effaces itself, or is obliterated, in the process of becoming ideology, and ideology effaces itself in the process of becoming the psyche*" (1973: 33, 39).

For Vološinov, everything in the mind is a sign and every sign is completely ideological. This willed, even principled indiscrimination is so striking in a work ostensibly devoted to scientific rigor that some have felt that it must be motivated by some extra-scientific factor. "It is easy," Rossi-Landi says, "to have a nagging suspicion that [Vološinov] deliberately confused the ideological and the linguistic so as to make it impossible for any simplistic dichotomy to be invoked in refutation of [his] position, in particular the . . . distinction between revolutionary science and reactionary ideology . . . one gets the distinct impression while reading the book that [he] might have deliberately contrived a way of jumbling up everything higgledy-piggledy in the hope that in more enlightened days the correct distinctions could be drawn once more, and that it would no longer be dangerous to draw them" (245).

Whatever the reason, Vološinov seems determined to make it hard to know what's what, much less what's causing what. By very nearly identifying ideology and language, he has liberated Marxian theory from a primary source of vulgarity, the idea of ideology as "false consciousness," and has also begun to imagine a more nuanced account of the nature of "determination." But he has sacrificed the tonic materialism, the bracing empirical clarity that had always characterized Marxian thought, or at least Marxian aspirations. He has radicalized and raised to the level of theory the cross-purposes and cross-currents that, in Marx, were mere contradictions. With everything "effacing" itself in the act of becoming something else, the entire scene of analysis is merely provisional, in transit. More damaging still, Vološinov has bought into a version of language that has a disastrous if largely unrecognized political downside. This, at least, is the argument of Raymond Williams, whose programmatic text *Marxism and Literature* (1977) contains the decisive, indeed terminal, post-Marxist critique of Saussure and the entire idea of language as a formal system of signs.

Williams credits Vološinov with having cut through all sorts of theoretically primitive notions, including the idea of language as a direct reflection of class or national character, as a verbal equivalent of things or qualities, as a neutral instrument of expression, and as a medium of unimpeded creativity. Vološinov avoided all these errors, Williams says, by recognizing from the outset that language is essentially a *material social practice*. As we have seen, this discovery immediately enables remarkable advances in the study of both language and the social system, which become, at a stroke, permeable to the other in a way that makes each more interesting. Culture is seen as the determining force behind a network of meanings, while the sign gains weight and force by being placed in a social context. Appreciative of these genuine contributions, Williams still finds much to criticize about Vološinov's "(incomplete) revaluation of the concept of 'sign,'" and it is this criticism that truly defines Williams's own position (1977: 36).

The criticism is both explicit and implicit. Explicitly, Williams marks as the chief limitation of Vološinov's work his retention of the Saussurean sign-system as the general character of language despite the virtually acrobatic moves he must make to accommodate it to his overall social and socialist orientation. Vološinov's commitment to dialectical materialism resulted quite properly, Williams says, in an account of the sign as dynamic, a function not just of a fixed factor of "sociality" but one element among many in an evolving and self-transforming society. Still, Vološinov's account was "limited by its perspective of determinate systems within an 'evolutionary' category"—systems, that is, of relative stability—"and still requires amendment by the full emphasis of social process" (Williams 1977: 42).

This "full emphasis" would yield not just a modified picture of the sign but a fundamental reconceptualization that places social processes at the heart of signification itself. Anything less, any "isolation of 'the sign', whether in Saussure or Vološinov, is at best an analytical procedure, at worst an evasion" (Williams 1977: 42). To isolate or even to emphasize the sign itself is, for Williams, to evade—probably for politically suspect reasons—a true understanding of language's constitutive agency as a social and material force, one that contributes vitally to the changing practical consciousness of human beings. And worse: if we meditate continually on the "products" of signification rather than the "process," Williams says, we may well be led to an overestimation of the role of law, rule, and systematicity generally that could only be called reactionary.

Here as elsewhere, Williams tries to unhinge the progressive tradition of Marxism from the gloomy stasis of Stalinism and "actually existing social-ism" by identifying Marxism with ongoing social transformation. His dis-course is both more theoretically sophisticated than that of Vološinov—which cannot, after all, be surprising—and more supple and differentiated. In fact, Williams describes language in terms so apositional, relational, and unfixed that they refer to no thing, no fixed or formalizable entity at all, but only to a principle of mobility and otherness, a general relatedness and in-betweenness. Language, he says in this spirit, is a matter of complex reciprocal influences, mediations, "a socially shared and reciprocal activity, already embedded in active relationships, within which every move is an activation of what is already shared and reciprocal or may become so" (1977: 166). So wavering and murky in itself, this characterization of language had, however, a certain necessity for Williams as a key principle in his attempt to refashion Marxism. What Williams was trying to do was to reinvent the general theory of his-torical materialism in such a way that bourgeois individuals, persuaded (by ideology) of their own autonomy and ideal freedom and more committed to language than to labor, could find their place in it, could recognize them-selves in a Marxian mirror.

This was, as Williams well knew, delicate business, because an overly generous accommodation to bourgeois thinking could easily be taken as a sign of surrender or co-optation. And so Williams's second general correction of Vološinov took the form of a consistent but relatively unstressed rehabilitation of the concept of the individual, especially the unregulated, uncensored, lib-eral individual. "At the very centre of Marxism," he writes in the conclusion to *Marxism and Literature*, "is an extraordinary emphasis on human creativity and self-creation" (1977: 206). Altogether absent from Williams is the antipathy found in Vološinov and in many other Marxian thinkers to the concept of individual agency. Instead, Williams speaks of "a continuing social process, into which individuals are born and within which they are shaped, but to which they then also actively contribute" (37). Williams even enlists Vološinov himself in support of the view that society "realizes" individuality: "Meanwhile, following Vološinov, we can see that just as all social process is activity between real individuals, so individuality, by the fully social fact of language . . . is the active constitution . . . of the social capacity which is the means of realization of any individual life" (41). In the plainest possible statement of this position, he writes that society "can never . . . be categorically abstracted from 'individuals' and 'individual wills' " (87). Collective life is, in Williams's brand of Marxism, the proper home in which individuals can live in security and comfort. And "social process" does not mean the danger and turbulence of class warfare, much less the iron laws of economic determinism, but rather a nondetermining context for individual activity and aspiration.

This emphasis on language is where ideology comes in, and where it leaks out. If language is a primary social process in which individuals and groups exercise their creativity and realize their potentialities, it must also be the medium of ideology. This is in fact the burden of Williams's chapter on ideology, the longest in the book, where he labors, with the assistance of Vološinov, to define ideology in terms of "signification," by which Williams means all those aspects of the total social process by which meaning is generated and disseminated. This inflation of the term makes ideology as difficult to place as language, and indeed difficult to separate from language; but it enables Williams to claim that ideology, *like language*, is a medium of "creativity." In fact, the final chapter of *Marxism and Literature*, entitled "Creative Practice," concludes with the synthetic statement that "creative practice"—a term he had already applied to language—"is already, and actively, our practical consciousness," which is Williams's favored term for ideology (1977: 43, 212).

At such moments, language and ideology seem to be melting into each other. But the situation is aggravated, for those who prize clarity, by a further overlap between both these terms and Williams's most celebrated phrase, the "structure of feeling," which is, like language and ideology, defined as a social-material form of practical consciousness (see 1977: 130ff.). As we read on in Williams, we can see that all the key words are defined as "processes" rather than as "products," and that all the processes feed into each other in a kind of conceptual entropy, a puddling as indiscriminate as Vološinov's. At the end, it is difficult to say what anything is, even "creativity." As Williams defines it, creativity is not exemplified by Shakespeare's plays, the discovery of the structure of DNA, or Gothic cathedrals, but is rather best described as—of course—an ongoing, emergent, collective social process. Creativity, which, in the tradition of von Humboldt was assigned to the individual, is assigned to the collective—or, in Saussure's terms, to the *langue* rather than to the *parole*. In fact, the individual, for whom Williams has so carefully prepared a rhetorical space, is never accorded the privileges one normally associates with individuality, such as autonomy, intention, and consciousness. As far as the individual is concerned, Williams's emphasis on creativity is a decidedly mixed blessing. Williams describes it strangely as a "struggle at the roots of the mind" as one confronts "a hegemony in the fibres of the self and in the hard practical substance of effective and continuing relationships" (212). The individual mind, it seems, can only experience creativity as a subrational struggle against dark and stubborn forces, with an uncertain outcome.

In short, Williams reinvents Marxism by accommodating the individual—but defines the individual as a nexus of hegemony and relationships.

The negative theoretical consequences of Williams's identification (inspired by Vološinov) of ideology with the processes of signification itself are, then, numerous and far-reaching. They include, first, a general inability to distinguish ideology from any emergence of meaning whatsoever. Second is the inability to specify, much less to advocate, a particular ideological direction, a particular agency of change, an *ought*. (The disadvantage of such reticence on the part of the political left was demonstrated in dramatic fashion when, shortly after *Marxism and Literature* was published, Margaret Thatcher, who had no such reluctance to prescribe, was swept into office by a public hungry for leadership.) And third, while the identification of ideology with language-as-social-process avoids the "rationalism" Vološinov identifies in Saussure, it constitutes a species of "romanticism" through its promotion of the creative and self-determining "society." Not only, then, has Williams inherited from Vološinov an inability to advance by offering a productively concrete account of ideology, but he has actually regressed by committing the one theoretical error that Vološinov had not.

Williams commits other errors as well, ones that Vološinov hadn't imagined. He accuses Marx of a clumsy and profoundly confused effort to devalue mind at the expense of matter by using a "deliberately degrading vocabulary" to represent ideas and consciousness (1977: 59). But, somewhat like Marx, who explains how matter first becomes "confused" with consciousness in the agitation in the air that constitutes speech, Williams argues that consciousness is "accessible only in unarguably physical and material ways: in voices, sounds," and so forth (62). On the basis of this original confusion of matter and consciousness in language, Williams proceeds straight to the assertion that thoughts—some thoughts—are virtually, or "unarguably," material or quasi-material things; and this enables him to discuss, as if they were concrete and observable entities, such things as "direct class consciousness" and "direct systems" (66–67). He complains about Marx's confusion, but his quarrel is really with Marx's clarity, which unequivocally promotes matter over mind. He fully endorses Marx's confusion of matter with mind. For both thinkers, the crucial idea, the one that solves all problems, is the concept, crystallized by Saussure, of language as a concrete entity, a material instance of consciousness.

The other traceable post-Marxist influence on *Marxism and Literature* is Gramsci, whose concept of *hegemony* is perhaps the immediate ancestor of Williams's "structure of feeling." Gramsci has been far more influential than Vološinov for several reasons. First, Gramsci's work, which is diffuse and disorderly owing largely to the conditions under which it was written, lends itself to free appropriation by thinkers in diverse fields, while Vološinov is primarily a linguist. Second, Gramsci's work, in its emphasis on the unconscious dimension of the ideas that structure social life, is able to make its peace with psychoanalytic thinking about the mind in a way that Vološinov angrily refuses to do. Perhaps the most significant contributing factor to Gramsci's postmortem success as a general theorist, however, is his insistence on the overlapping, internally divided, and variable character of the forces that circulate in society. Whether from conviction or from the fact that he wrote always under the censor's shadow, Gramsci—who never mentions "Marx" or "class struggle"—paints a much more recognizable picture of modern society than Vološinov. While Vološinov speaks of the "multi-accentuality" of the sign as an "arena of class struggle," as though the sign were complicated but classes were not, Gramsci understands that the ruling class in "civil society" does not dominate or even seek to dominate with perfect effectiveness. Indeed, for Gramsci, the very concept of domination is complex. He lends no support to the notion that there is a consistent or pure class subject; not even the ruling class truly knows itself or its interests. While, for Vološinov, those on top always seek stability while those on the bottom invariably prefer volatility, a Gramscian society is variable and relational, all its structures fissured and in transformation.

These differences are what hegemony—all the ways in which a dominant power obtains the consent and cooperation of those it dominates—is all about. Much of the analytical or theoretical work associated with hegemony is performed by the term itself, and Gramsci clearly saw the "development" of the concept of hegemony as a means of "carrying on the struggle" (Gramsci: 165). *Hegemony* is, if not an altogether new word in Marxian social theory, at least a newly prominent word that, as Gramsci uses it, picks out and grasps as a unity a set of functions that had never before been seen in this way. Williams notes immediate analytical advances over the terms *culture* and *ideology*. In contrast to *culture*, *hegemony* suggests that society is conflictual, structured by relations of dominance and subordination; the term is, as Eagleton comments, "inseparable from overtones of struggle" (1991: 115). Where *culture* focuses on the encompassing social totality, *hegemony* directs attention to specific instances and particular "distributions of power and influence," as Williams calls them, within that totality (1977: 108).

But conflict and particularity notwithstanding, *hegemony* also refers to the forces that hold an entire society together, and this recognition of unity distinguishes hegemony from ideology, which generally refers to a class-specific system of beliefs, values, or practices. Gramsci himself occasionally uses *ideology* in just this way, as the relatively consistent system coercively imposed by the ruling class. But *hegemony* does not indicate a conscious understanding—hence Williams's reference to a "hegemony in the fibres of the self"—nor does it make such a sharp distinction between the dominant and subordinate classes. A hegemonic circumstance is not a stark binary but a complex unity in which a whole body of practices, assumptions, values, convictions, orientations, perceptions, and judgments structures the sense of reality experienced by an entire culture.

If Gramsci breaks with classical Marxian notions of economic determination, he stands firmly in the Marxian tradition as a thinker who makes his greatest contribution to the study of ideology by focusing on something else. One of the problems created by the Marxian conviction that ideology springs from and serves the ruling class is that, especially in modern civil society, even oppressed or marginalized people often feel "free." They do not always or even often feel that their thoughts are "determined in the last instance" by their economic circumstances, or imposed from above by their betters. For those who regard their participation in the system as spontaneous and voluntary, *hegemony* is just the right term, for a hegemonic society is one in which a general social consensus and cooperation, while undoubtedly sought by those who hold power, also serves at least the perceived interests of many of those who do not.

Hegemony is an advanced version of *ideology* in another respect as well. If, in some of its more retrograde formulations, *ideology* seems relatively inert, *hegemony* describes a manifestly living thing, one that must be constantly renewed, defended, and renegotiated, with considerable scope allowed for agency and purposeful change. In this respect, Gramsci's thought is actually more dynamic, fluid, and post-Marxist than Williams's. For what *hegemony*, in a secondary meaning that occasionally emerges in *The Prison Notebooks*, really describes is not just the total sense of social reality that prevails in times of relative calm, but rather the unstable condition in which a new or different sense of reality has cracked off from the dominant one and is beginning to develop itself independently in response to the actual experience of a particular group. In the crucial section of *The Prison Notebooks* on "The Study of Philosophy," *hegemony* refers in particular to the dynamic and reciprocal relation between intellectuals—not just the party elite, but those who, like Williams and Gramsci, are specialists in theoretical reflection, as well as lawyers, labor leaders, political activists, and opinion-makers—and the class that nurtured them and whose interests they represent.

On these relations, Gramsci is quite specific. All men, he says in one of the often-cited passages in the text, are intellectuals capable of self-transformation and self-awareness, but only a few take this project as their primary task. Those who do must never lose contact with their own group, the "mass." If they cease to be "organic intellectuals" with a firm base in their group's experience, they become irrelevant to the struggle. One measure of the intellectual's integrity is therefore the degree of "adhesion" between the intellectual and the group. The intellectual must try to lead not by offering astonishing new concepts, new dreams, new hopes, but rather by "making critical" an existing practice in order to clarify a certain disjunction or contradiction between "official" conceptions and experienced reality. Intellectuals serve, in other words, not as beacons for the mass, but as the "whalebone in the corset," helping people understand how they can effect their own transformation (340). Appealing at first to "common sense," intellectuals try to help people see how some aspect of the "structure," the economic or institutional base, does not match up with the "superstructure" of established beliefs and evaluations. Once this disjunction is clarified, people become aware of a fissure in their knowledge between what they have believed, on official testimony, and what really is. At this point, they can begin to act as an "organic totality" to agitate for real change in some particular direction (330–34).

This secondary, and yet more active meaning of *hegemony* thus refers to an intellectual unity, a concept joined to an ethic, that has detached itself from common sense in order to criticize it, with the goal of transforming society to bring it more closely into alignment with its own shibboleths, creating a new social formation that is genuinely unified from base to superstructure. *Ideology*, by contrast, remains for Gramsci a limited, provincial, particular enterprise, a product of inorganic intellectualism with little or no true adhesion between the elite and the mass, and therefore incapable of a genuine transformation of social thinking. In this as in other respects, it is possible to read all of Gramsci's work on hegemony as an attempt to reimagine ideology from the point of view of a modern society.

The clearest sign of this attempt is Gramsci's reluctance to surrender the term *ideology* altogether. In a lucid passage, he notes that the reason *ideology* had acquired a negative connotation for many Marxists was that the term actually refers to two things, the "historically organic" systems of thought and feeling "necessary to a given structure," and the "arbitrary elucubrations of particular individuals" (376). The articulation of hegemony is intended, we might infer, to provide a separate term to cover the first meaning alone. Liberated from its withered and degraded other, hegemony could be seen to "have a validity which is 'psychological'" and social at once; it could assume its proper status as a force capable of organizing mass movements on behalf of "historical blocs," not just political campaigns or parties (377). In short, *hegemony* refers to nothing other than a purified, modernized, and "historically organic" mode of ideology.

But Gramsci can only liberate hegemony from the dark disorder of ideology by affiliating it with some powerful and stable concept. That large friend is language. Like many embattled intellectuals embroiled in local struggles,

Gramsci saw the category of the universal as the goal of critical thought. The task of the organic intellectual was to cultivate those particles of the universal embedded in the sensibilities of every small group, and use them gradually to orient the group toward its own maximal potentiality, without, of course, abandoning the grounds of the group's identity. The best, because most commonsensical, model for this abstract-sounding process was, he thought, to be found in the experience of language. Drawing on a distinction that is partially effaced in English, Gramsci differentiated between *lingua*, a particular natural language, and *linguaggio*, or language in general, the entire linguistic system or faculty. Each particular language, he argued, "contains the elements of a conception of the world and of a culture," and so within every language are all the resources needed for its own self-transformation from a provincial to a universal way of knowing. You could speak Italian, or Armenian, or Tagalog, or English, and still address, and be addressed by, the world because your particular language represented a legitimate fragment of the general human language faculty (325).

This containment of the universal within the local models the relation between hegemony and ideology, and sets the intellectual a precise task: to work to facilitate the passage from the latter to the former, from the lesser to the greater. Moreover, this intuited if unmarked homology between mankind's social and linguistic conditions confirms another passage Gramsci implicitly but constantly advocates, from "economism" or reductionist materialism, to a "philosophy of praxis" that acknowledges the immaterial aspects of society as well. Traditional Marxian notions of ideology—those, for example, found in a few, but not in all passages of *The German Ideology*—leave unstressed the proper universalism, the idealism, the active generation of thought that characterizes hegemony and links it with the "natural" and global phenomenon of language.

But here's the rub. If the concept of hegemony makes its peace with idealism as well as psychologism, and yet seeks to maintain a connection with the materialist tradition, if it articulates a view of society as being both unified and conflicted, if it places the intellectual elite both inside and outside of the mass, if it values both common sense and intellectual daring, then it might well be accused of trying to explain everything and succeeding in explaining nothing. To assimilate one vague and diffuse concept, ideology, to an even vaster and more undefined one, language, in order to produce a third term, hegemony, may be to gain an immense power for the new term, but to do so at the expense of all incisiveness or precision. *Hegemony* is in danger of becoming not a set of arguments or claims, not a true concept and not even a proper word, but simply a magic name for a series of circumstances one wants, for political reasons, to group together conceptually—a name, that is, for an idea one wishes one could have, but cannot because all true ideas have narrower limits, more well defined boundaries, more edge, a greater power of exclusion.

One index of *hegemony*'s indiscriminate inclusiveness is the conservative reading to which it has been periodically subjected. A radical Communist activist and a martyr to his convictions, Gramsci would not have thought of himself as a theorist of capitalist consumer culture. But that is exactly how Edward Said takes him, in a recent essay on intellectuals in society. "Today's advertising or public relations expert," Said writes, "who devises techniques for winning a detergent or airline company a larger share of the market, would be considered an organic intellectual according to Gramsci, someone who in a democratic society tries to gain the consent of potential customers, win approval, marshal consumer or voter opinion" (1994: 4). Said compares this tepid conception with Julian Benda's more sharply delineated image of the "gifted and morally endowed philosopher-kings who constitute the conscience of mankind," and notes that while there are plenty of Gramscian intellectuals about these days, busily filling their roles, performing their functions, Benda's sort, representing the true, heroic strain of the intellectual vocation, remains a rarity. Gramsci, of course, would have protested that he was outlining the conditions of such heroism in civil society, that he was describing effective intellectuals and not prophets, that one could only be heroic if one was organic, and so on. But the fact that Gramsci could be read this way, not perversely but literally, suggests that a dimension of his text has escaped his own intentions or control, and has done so not for the usual reason, that all texts are subjected to variant readings, but because he fails to delineate a specific theoretical, much less a political position.

Suggesting an active and transformative role for the intellectual, Gramsci's work has proven to be highly attractive and even inspiring to many thinkers, if not to Said. But the failure of *The Prison Notebooks* to exclude legitimate conservative readings, its inability to secure itself against its own perversions, suggests a limitation in the capacity of his text to theorize anything at all. For this reason, we may predict, all those who explore the concept of hegemony will at some point encounter a theoretical dead end, an empty pot at the end of the rainbow. Perhaps the most influential and original thinker to fit this description is Stuart Hall, the leading figure in British Cultural Studies and a thinker who has freely acknowledged his indebtedness to both Vološinov and Gramsci.

In Hall's work, the insights of these early post-Marxist pioneers are carefully selected, elegantly presented, and burnished into contemporary high theory. Deeply respectful of the materialist premises of Marxism, Hall has also been productively responsive to a postmodernist emphasis on language. Indeed, the distinctive feel, both cosmopolitan and activist, worldly and theoretical, capacious and incisive, of Hall's work derives directly from his efforts to negotiate the claims of cultural materiality and the "signifying systems" in which that materiality comes to countenance and consciousness. Like other post-Marxists, Hall recognizes the dangers of economic determinism, class reductionism, the easy equation of ruling class and ruling ideas, and the base-superstructure model; and he has, accordingly, advocated and practiced a more supple, nuanced, and sophisticated critical discourse. Unlike some other post-Marxists, however, Hall has also insisted that the resources for this more advanced discourse are contained or at least implied in the Marxian texts themselves. He has, therefore, been engaged in a sustained and vigorous rearticulation of Marx's insights as the most direct and reliable route to a sound understanding of, and a critical purchase on, the present.

Take, for example, Hall's treatment of Marx's assertion that the determination of social ideas is "economic in the last instance." This, Hall argues, is a characteristic Marxian near-miss. What Marx almost said was that, while economic factors alone cannot determine the specific thoughts of a given social class, or fix which ideas will be made use of by which classes, material constraints provide the "conditions of existence" for practical thought, setting limits to what is thought and by whom (Hall 1986b: 42). Because—as Marx said—history is open to struggle and change, political developments have a "real indeterminacy" that is strictly Marxian, even though Marx is commonly thought to have believed in the economic determination of consciousness. In short, Hall urges, the authentic message of Marx should be read not as a closed but as an open horizon of theorizing and action; thoughts are determined, Hall says, "by the economic in the *first* instance" (43). Materialism and determinism are preserved as essential arguments against abstraction and idealism, but only in inverted form.

Perhaps because of its *camera obscura* investment in "inversion," Marxian ideology provides Hall with the perfect pretext for his reclamation project. For just as *language* has come to represent a privileged instance of the volatility, multiplicity, and indeterminacy of a capitalist world in a state of "perpetual revolution," a world of conflicting, temporary, and mobile meanings, so ideology theory has come to stand, for Hall and others, for the point at which Marxian materialism confronts language. And so, in search of the hidden contemporaneity, the quick buried in Marx's moribund formulations, Hall turns to Marx's somewhat informal and ad hoc thoughts on ideology. He notes two general tendencies: in the first, Marx commonly equates ideology with false consciousness and bourgeois mystification; but in the second, he takes ideology as a term for "*all* organized forms of social thinking," the practical as well as theoretical ways in which people "figure out" society (1986b: 30). These two clearly don't rhyme, and the dissonance may have led some embarrassed post-Marxists to abandon the term *ideology* altogether, thereby collaborating unwittingly in the conservative "end of ideology" movement. But the original radical thrust of Marx's thinking can be restored, Hall argues, if we try to discover what Marx would have said if he had attended to his subject in a more systematic, or even in a more rigorously Marxian way.

If we begin with only the fundamental premises that ideas are concretely related to certain material conditions, and that there is some kind of correspondence between the ruling class and ruling ideas, we can, Hall suggests, modify the rest to accord with the current state of knowledge and society. While Marx declares that ideology "distorts" the truth by "eternalizing" and "universalizing" contingent ideas that in fact arise from and support bourgeois dominance, we should understand "distortion" to refer not just to the ways in which the truth is warped or misrepresented, but to all the forms of *partial* or *inadequate* knowledge that prevent people from having a full and empowering understanding of their circumstances. If, for example, workers experience only freedom and consent in the way in which they sell their labor, receive wages, and spend their money, this sense of freedom cannot be denied, but it can be supplemented by pointing out to the worker that exploitation is involved both in the procurement of labor and in excessive profiteering. The deeply ingrained habit of focusing on the point of exchange rather than the points of production or profit-taking obscures, Hall would explain to the workers, these forms of exploitation; if we expand our vision to take in the entire process, we get a more comprehensive and accurate image of the truth. So, Hall would conclude, even if Marx had not spelled all this out, he had given us the conceptual means of doing so.

What, in general, Hall adds to Marx is a thorough working-out of the way in which certain definite ideas structure people's commonsense and "automatic" processing of the system, providing the categories and habits by which people understand the world. Just as important, he adds an emphasis on the agency of language in providing these categories and habits as the ground of a "break" with rigid economic determinism. "Modern theorists," Hall says,

> have tended to arrive at this break with a simple notion of economic determinacy over ideology through their borrowing from recent work on the nature of language and discourse. Language is the medium *par excellence* through which things are "represented" in thought and thus the medium in which ideology is generated and transformed. But in language, the same social relation can be *differently* represented and construed. And this is so, they would argue, because language by its nature is *not fixed* in a one-to-one relation to its referent but is "multi-referential": it can construct different meanings around what is apparently the same social relation or phenomenon. (1986b: 36)

In this crucial passage, Hall marks out his own position, a refinement of Marx enabled by "recent work on the nature of language." This "work"—Saussure's 1906 announcement of the "arbitrary" nature of the sign, especially as appropriated by Lévi-Strauss—enables Hall to apprehend both the dynamism preserved in the amber of Marx's thought and an emancipatory "arbitrariness" sleeping in apparently impacted social formations.

As "we" now understand it, the nature of language is not a rigid formal system, not a hardwired "capacity," not a mere instrument of individual expression, but a thoroughly socialized and volatilized medium of thought and expression that is necessarily implicated in the various forces that sweep through the social world. And it is in the arena of force that language meets ideology. For ideology, Hall argues, is at its purest and most effective not in the form of particular identifiable messages, but as a "system of coding," a way of structuring messages in general (1982: 71). This coding, this fixing of connections between sign and "associations" or "field of reference," can only occur as the consequence of some force or agency. If we accept the premise that meanings are "arbitrary" rather then "natural," we must, Hall says, conclude that the world "has to be *made to mean*," and somebody or something has to do the making (67). Hence Hall's preference for the term *representation*, with its suggestion of purposive activity, over terms such as *reflection* or *reference*. Indeed, Hall's most favored term for the process of meaning-making is the even more virile *articulation*, by which he means the whole business of determining social understandings by winning acceptance for some codings and excluding others. *The nation, black, feminist, profit, queer,* and many other such terms can be coded as positive or negative, progressive or conservative; but they are always coded somehow and their coding is always the consequence of a struggle. "The power to signify," he says, "is not a neutral force in society," but a work, an accomplishment (70).

While Saussure may have been a necessary reference, the more immediate ancestors are clearly Vološinov and Gramsci. From the former, Hall appropriates the notion that the sign is the arena of class struggle, the object of contestation, the prize to be won. The real point of Vološinov's work, Hall argues, is that no group has any legitimate or permanent ownership of a sign or a chain of signs: the class struggle is constant, the sign is always (in theory at least) up for grabs, and the control of meaning is always provisional and temporary. From this point, Hall can argue that what Saussure called the "life of signs in society" entails social struggle. For, as Vološinov argues and Hall reaffirms, a sign that has been "withdrawn from the pressures of the social struggle . . . loses force, degenerates into allegory, becoming the object not of a live social intelligibility but of a philological comprehension" (Vološinov 1973: 23; see Hall 1986b: 38–42). For Hall, Vološinov's "philology" aligns with what Marx and Engels described as an ideology-induced sense of "eternality," an inertial condition of uni-accentuality that reflects the real but temporary dominance of some force in the ongoing contest. As a linguist, Vološinov illuminates and modifies Marx's economic reductionism, and creates a theoretical space in which Hall can work to liberate Marx's formulations from their own authority, so they may be reintroduced, in properly multi-accentual form, into a dynamic, fluid, and recognizably contemporary setting.

The debt to Gramsci is different in kind, and may actually constitute a debt owed by Gramsci to Hall. Hall is primarily interested in Gramsci's account of the routine operation of ideology in a well-ordered or hegemonically effective civil society. The real arbitrariness of the governing ideas in such a society is repressed, inaccessible to criticism and thus to reform or rejection, a fact that might appear to discourage progressive optimism. Why—Said and others might demand—should we have any confidence that a given hegemonic worldview could be transformed from a passive structure of perception to an active instrument for change? On what grounds should we believe Gramsci's promise that a particular practice can somehow become "critical"? For answer, Hall points to one element of the nature of language, contributing an argument for hegemony that Gramsci himself never contemplated. For the most part, Hall says, we simply use our language, and can do so with perfect competence even if we cannot explain the syntactical rules that govern the production of meaning. "In the same way," he argues, people making statements "may be unconsciously drawing on the ideological frameworks and classifying schemes of a society and reproducing them—so that they appear ideologically 'grammatical'—without those making them being aware of so doing" (1982: 72).

As with grammar, so with ideology: both function best when they function unconsciously. The fact that one can learn grammar, acquiring a critical understanding and thus a certain power over one's use of language without sacrificing competence, suggests that ideology need not remain unconscious, that people need not only reproduce without understanding the anodyne formulae of received wisdom, the clichés of common sense. With a new confidence provided by the model of language, Hall argues, we could grasp social struggle as a process by which the Gramscian intellectual seeks to make signs problematic to those who use them, to disclose to the general public the rules for generating meanings so that they might feel empowered to generate their own, authentic meanings rather than simply reiterating the messages that surround them. "The nature of language" thus enables Hall to characterize Gramsci as both an optimist and a realist.

As responsive as Hall has been to the power of the idea of language to illuminate otherwise insurmountable problems surrounding the concept of ideology, he has always been wary of what he considers extremism or puritanism. He has, for example, little interest in the structuralist approach to "language without speakers," which, he maintains, makes it difficult to conceive of effective, much less transformative individual agency. For Hall, one of the primary benefits of the linguistic turn in the study of ideology has been the reintroduction of the individual subject, which had been a fragile and uncertain presence in Marxian discourse. Committed to the subject, Hall has been actively hostile to the work of Althusser, or at least to "Althusserianism," which constitutes, he says, an orthodoxy and ultimately a kind of "intellectual terrorism" (1981: 380). But Hall is also suspicious of other thinkers who go too far down the linguistic road. While he gratefully acknowledges a debt to Ernesto Laclau, his enthusiasm is limited to one book, *Politics and Ideology in Marxist Theory* (Hall 1986a: 53). In Laclau's later and better-known *Hegemony and Socialist Strategy* (1985), co-authored with Chantal Mouffe, Halls feels that the linguistic turn is taken all the way around the bend, so that, as Hall says, "there is nothing to practice but its discursive aspect" (1986a: 56). And at this point, things have gone disastrously wrong.

"The discursive aspect" must, it seems, be measured out in moderation, as if it were a hot sauce that, poured too liberally, would overwhelm the flavors it was intended to enhance and complicate, resulting in what Hall calls a "reductionism," an "analytical slippage" that is "theoretically wrong" (1986a: 57). Interestingly, however, Hall does not specify a theoretical error; instead, he points to the insufficient "political inflection" of *Hegemony and Socialist Strategy*, a dissipation of worldliness as a consequence of an excessive reliance on language as an explanatory category. The question to be posed here is whether, having acknowledged and accepted the "massive political consequences" of thinking linguistically, Hall can legitimately moderate the force of such thinking when he feels Marxian materialism to be threatened.

One can—as Hall does—distinguish between the thought that social formations and practices *are* language and the thought that they are *like* a language, for there certainly is a difference. Under the second account, we could, for example, think of language as a kind of structural metaphor while still insisting on the ultimate primacy of such classically Marxist categories as "material relations," "historical necessity," and "social formations." But while this might, for a post-Marxist thinker, be preferable, we must ask whether it is *theoretically* necessary. If, following Gramsci and Vološinov— with Hall's approval—we understand language as a social, material, and historical fact, then on what basis can we distinguish between language and "properly" social, material, and historical facts? If *articulation* refers not just to speech but also to the ways in which ideological elements cohere and impose themselves on people, then what's the difference—the theoretical difference—between language and any other kind of social force? If the effect of introducing language into the analysis of social formations and transformations is to make a space for individual and group agency, then how can we distinguish language from such agency without reverting to some notion of language without speakers? How can we tell where language ends and the rest of the world begins?

In response to Hall, who raises these questions but cannot answer them, I would argue that the totality of language cannot be reduced, isolated, or contained by any legitimate means, and certainly not merely because it interferes with prior commitments or produces unappealing consequences. The profound conceptual power and vast conceptual reach of "language itself" cannot be enlisted on behalf of specific values or ends; neither can language be fenced off from politics or practice. Language does not stand alone, it does not have an independent existence apart from those who use it or the ends it serves, it cannot be deployed as a theoretical much less as a practical lever, and any effort to conjure it into being as a limited whole—an effort that defines the post-Marxist account of ideology—constitutes an "analytical slippage" of the kind that Hall rightly deplores.

If he feared the consequences of such slippage, Hall was right to draw the line at Laclau, whose work exemplifies the slide from politics to language. Like Gramsci, Laclau and his collaborator Chantal Mouffe make a genuine and original contribution to the theory of ideology without mentioning the word, about which they have what can only be called ideological reservations. Far superior, from their point of view, is Gramsci's *hegemony*, which they take to describe not just the means by which social consensus is achieved, but, more specifically, the principles that govern a world saturated with language through and through, a world that can in fact best be understood as a form of language, or, to recall Wittgenstein, a "language-game."

The importance of language in Laclau and Mouffe's *Hegemony and Socialist Strategy* is underscored by the fact that much of their theoretical work is performed by the substitution of terms. Whereas traditional Marxism speaks of the class struggle, Laclau and Mouffe would substitute *antagonism;* for *polit-*

ical classes, they would insert, *pace* Gramsci, *collective wills;* for *practice, discourse;* for *communism, democracy;* for *identity, position;* for *society, discourse;* for *positivity, negativity;* and, most importantly, for *politics, articulation.* In making these substitutions, Laclau and Mouffe see themselves as the successors to Gramsci, who first enunciated a principle of politics as a matter of articulation—that is, of contingent acts of meaning-making. For Laclau and Mouffe, the silences of Gramsci's text concerning the Marxian questions of class struggle and the laws of economic determinism represent theoretical achievements of the highest order, for they force us to conceptualize society and politics without the crutch of economic determinism. Freed, with Gramsci's help, from material necessity, we can now, they say, begin at last to think from a democratic rather than a communistic point of view; following the "fall of this last redoubt of class reductionism," we can think of classes themselves as relational positions rather than essences (Laclau and Mouffe 85).

The key to the new conception of democracy, or "populism" as they sometimes call it, is representation. Revisionary Marxists, Laclau and Mouffe also intervene in, even as they reproduce, an older way of thinking about representation that directly inflects the theory of ideology. It is, of course, no accident that the term *ideology* was invented at just the historical moment that representational government came into being. For government by representation is only possible after the departure of the charismatic sovereign, when ideas begin to flow more freely through society, their source less certain than before. At this revolutionary moment, ideology, as an inquiry into the origin and nature of ideas, becomes both possible and necessary. And with the sudden expansion of print journalism at this time, language assumed a new prominence as the medium of social ideas. By this linkage, the governmental and linguistic senses of representation became partially identified.

Representation establishes a connection between the vehicle or medium of representation and the thing represented, but it also institutes a distance between these two, a space that under a perfectly effective sovereign, or signifier, would be reduced to zero. Theoretically secured by language, this space is the arena of negotiation, the forum in which men, as Marx said, become conscious of conflict and fight it out. Seen under the template of representation, society is open to intervention, volatile, contingent, unfixed, and incomplete. Perhaps the preeminent theorist of this incompleteness is Claude Lefort, who in *L'invention démocratique* (1981) first claimed that in modern, democratic societies the place of power was "empty"; and then, in *The Polit-ical Forms of Modern Society* (1986), added that the space of invention and democratic negotiation was language, or "discourse." Marx, Lefort claimed in a complex and detailed argument, had a strong sense of the difference between knowledge and ideology, but an insufficient sense of the difference between ideology and reality, and failed to grasp the "productive" power of discourse. If Marx had understood the symbolic dimension of the social domain, the way in which power in a modern society is inseparable from its representa-tion, Lefort argued, he might have been able to escape the determinism that was his theory's greatest weakness. The fact that even ideological language is not directly determined by reality, or what Marx called "relations of pro-duction," meant that a measure of the "imaginary" and thus of the "hidden" and even "creative" was installed in all social representations, especially ideological representations.

Laclau and Mouffe made this argument much more specific by insisting that the zone of creative socio-historical agency that Lefort called *discourse* had to be understood as the system of signs as articulated by Saussure. Thus the Swiss linguist became the master-theorist of modern society, for it was his principles of arbitrariness, systematicity, negativity, and the fissured sign that modeled the immanent norms of the democratic social order. Down with the real, and the royal; and up with the sign.

As long as we are thinking about representation, however, the revolution is incomplete, for *representation* retains as a kind of aftertaste the notion of the proper, fully adequate, or necessary representation, and so actually recalls the deposed sovereign. Laclau and Mouffe are activist theorists for whom the "role of theory is not to elaborate intellectually the observable ten-dencies of fragmentation and dispersion [of advanced capitalism], but to ensure that such tendencies have a transitory character" (14). And so, to move things along, they seek to replace *representation* by the term that so captivates Hall, *articulation*. In the work Hall most admires, Laclau's *Politics and Ideology in Marxist Theory* (1977), this term had emerged—suddenly, as if startled by its own aptness—alongside *discourse* in the declaration that linguistic units *"have no necessary class connotation, and that this connota-tion is only the result of the articulation of those elements in a concrete ideo-logical discourse"* (99).

One can infer from this that *articulation* denotes something more than a linguistic gesture, a "concrete" deployment of language in a given set of social-material circumstances, a "discourse" in which the linguistic and the extra-linguistic are fused. As Laclau developed the concept, however, *articulation* referred primarily to acts rather than to the consequences of acts, and so suggested a higher degree of agency and unpredictability than did *representation*. This augmented sense of historical pliability was congenial to Hall, who also appreciated the frequent references to specific facts about fascism in Italy and Germany, Peronism, and the history of the Marxian struggle with class reductionism, all accompanied (to the astonishment of many of Laclau's readers) by complaints about overtheorization and abstraction in the work of other thinkers. These bracing particulars and complaints were, however, to disappear from Laclau's work over the next twenty years as he became more invested in the concept of language.

Articulation truly comes into its own as a fully linguistic concept only in *Hegemony and Socialist Strategy*, where it assumes a central role in an ambitious theoretical labor whose end is nothing less than a populist revolution in theory that would be (distantly) analogous to the French and Russian Revolutions in politics. Here a further difference between *representation* and *articulation* becomes immediately evident in that, while the linguistic meaning of representation derives from its political meaning, the sequence and priorities are reversed in the case of articulation. Clearly, what Laclau and Mouffe aspire to is a wholesale renovation of all the terms and concepts of Marxian political theory by imposing the "laws" of language on politics and society. They argue, for example, that the crucial Gramscian concept of hegemony is best understood as a principle of articulation. Hegemony presupposes the contingent, incomplete, and open character of society in a field crossed by "antagonisms" that block all movements toward closure, all forms of positivity, all self-identity. And what, Laclau and Mouffe ask, could this be but a social version of Saussure—the "split" between signifier and signified, the relational character of all meaning, the arbitrariness at the heart of the sign?

Not that Saussure realized what he'd stumbled upon. In fact, according to Laclau and Mouffe, Saussure conspicuously failed to grasp the true force of his own discovery: he claimed, for example, that the meaning of a given term is determined in a closed and systematic field, a claim that represses the very thing—the open, incomplete, and "unsutured" character of the sign—that had constituted his originality. Informed by deconstruction, with its notions of "freeplay," "dissemination," and semiotic infinity, Laclau and Mouffe restore to Saussure the full dimensions of his thinking about "the life of signs in society," and extend the resultant concept of hegemony to cover the entire field of social, cultural, and even personal identity, which are now seen to have the same "floating character" as the Saussurean sign (113).

This newly renovated and purified Saussure is then put to work as the key to Gramsci, who had also failed to realize the true potential of his discovery because he was ignorant of Saussure's ideas on language. Laclau and Mouffe attempt to redeem Gramsci from his retrograde insistence on "fundamental classes," class experience, and the necessity of a hegemonic "center." They also try to save Althusser from his own tendency to theoretical rigidity by refashioning his concept of "overdetermination" as a loose synonym for polysemy, and by simply dropping his insistence on a monolithic and self-obsessed state, which, they feel, is inconsistent with the nature of articulation. Thus they move directly from the scientific severity of Saussure, with his stern denial of "positive" meaning and his insistence on abstraction and system, to a politically motivated advocacy and a celebration of carnivalesque performativity as the rule, or misrule, of society as a whole.

As we can see, Laclau and Mouffe fully expect to realize enormous political consequences from their inquiries; for by interrogating Marxian theory from the point of view of Saussure, they want to inscribe as a law of all identity the properties Saussure discovered in language. If every subject, and every *kind* of subject, is no more than nodes in a social sign system, relational elements in a Gramscian "war of position," then innovation and turbulence are the norms, and the only unalterable law is antagonism. If the laws of language can be shown to be the laws of society, they suggest, then *in fact* the only possible "natural" political circumstance is one of radical and plural democracy, with "democracy" referring not to any particular political organization, but rather to a permanent openness to change or "hegemonic rearticulation." The "materiality" attributed to language suggests, to them, that the principles of language have a concreteness that cannot properly or legitimately be denied, although they may be repressed or violated (see Laclau and Mouffe 108).

While Hall derives a critique of economic determinism from a reading of Marx's articulations, Laclau and Mouffe achieve the same end from a reading of articulation itself. All notions of objectivity, "naturalism," "reductionism," essence, necessity, linear development, material or nondiscursive conditions, totalities, a party vanguard—all these elements of a "Jacobin imaginary"—are revealed to be in violation of their own ground-conditions, nothing more than aggressively persuasive illusions (2). What *appears*, in theory as in society, is out of synch with what really *is*, and the duty of those who believe that practice should follow from principle, and appearances from reality, is first to think straight, to bring all concepts into alignment with the law; and second to act to remove the contradictions that remain between theoretical truth and social practice.

Of course, everything hangs upon the success of the effort to establish a law of language that holds good in the world, a feature of language that compels people to think or act in a particular way. How do Laclau and Mouffe establish such a law in a work devoted to nonnecessity? We can watch it happen: "Here"—deep in the third chapter—"we arrive at a decisive point in our argument," when "the incomplete character of every totality necessarily leads us to abandon, as a terrain of analysis, the premise of '*society*' as a sutured and self-defined totality." Does this mean that we should abandon all terrains? Without a terrain to stand on, how could we analyze at all? Lucky for us, "on this point, our analysis meets up with a number of contemporary currents of thought," including those of Heidegger, Wittgenstein, and especially Derrida, to whom falls the task of laying down the law of language (111). "It became necessary," as they quote Derrida, "to think both the law which somehow governed the desire for a centre in the constitution of structure, and the process of signification which orders the displacements and substitutions for this law of central presence—but a central presence which has never been itself. . . . Henceforth, it was necessary to begin thinking that there was no centre . . . that the centre had no natural site. . . . This was the moment when language invaded the universal problematic, the moment when, in the absence of a centre or origin, everything became discourse" (Derrida 1978b: 280; Laclau and Mouffe 112). Authorized by "contemporary" currents—ultimately, Saussure, the same source as the "recent work" cited by Hall—and the considerable prestige of already-canonical Derrida, the law is decreed. "Henceforth," since we are dealing with a world newly become linguistic, it is not just possible but necessary to declare that "all identity is relational," that "every subject position is a discursive position" that "partakes of the open character of every discourse," and so on.

It also becomes possible and even necessary to treat language, the crowbar that pries up the massive rock of fixity and discloses the swarming life beneath, as itself fixed, with a definable nature, properties, and limits. "If language is a system of differences," Laclau and Mouffe begin one sentence, "then antagonism is the failure of difference; in that sense, it situates itself within the limits of language." So language *has* limits; and it has a defined function as well: "language only exists as an attempt to fix that which antagonism subverts" (125). The most prominent such fixity is "the subject," which, in a characteristic postmodern assertion, they describe as "constructed through language" (126). In brief, language is an unsubverted, unconstructed, intelligible object that produces a wide range of specific and concrete effects. The limitations they occasionally place on language only confirm its identity. Whenever, for example, they speak of the "exteriority" of the "articulated elements" to the act of articulation, they imply that something resists the laws of language, and so defines language's boundaries and nature. We can see their dilemma clearly: in order to unravel all determined identities, they must subject identity as such to the disintegrative force of language; but this gesture creates, in a world of antagonistic relations, one shining, fully integrated thing—language alone.

In his more recent work, Laclau has gone even farther toward imposing the law of language as the law of the social. In "Why Do Empty Signifiers Matter to Politics?" a 1994 essay published in *Emancipations*, Laclau drops his use of the term "discourse" and reverts to the split Saussurean sign, particularly the "floating signifier," as the bedrock of an emancipatory social theory. "We know, from Saussure," he begins, "that language . . . is a system of differences, [and] that linguistic identities—values—are purely relational" (Laclau 1996b: 37). And on the rock of this certain knowledge, Laclau constructs a complex, state-of-the-art argument about the "empty signifier" that interrupts the smooth process of signification and by this means manages to "signify" the relational system itself. In political terms, this system might be called "community" or "society." No subgroup, he points out, naturally stands for community as such, but in the course of social struggle, some group—the bourgeoisie, the working class, women—might acquire the temporary power to represent itself as the one sector of society whose interests are identical to those of society as a whole. In acquiring this power, a social group lays claim, he says, to the status of the empty signifier. If, for example, society finds itself in a state of radical disorder such that order itself is "present as that which is absent," then some group may emerge through competition as the one whose particular objectives represent order as such, whose goals are not only its own, but those of the totality as well (44). The real emptiness of the signifier will not only make such a claim possible but will also ensure that it will not be permanent, thus preserving society's essential openness.

The deeply paradoxical effect of supplementing Marx with Saussure is, then, not just to volatilize the old fixities, the relations of production and the laws of economic history, but to replace them with new ones—the laws of language—that are every bit as fixed as the old ones. So, while the "post-Marxist" movement in which Laclau and Mouffe are major players has rejected Marx's most central ideas, it has also exposed itself to the very same critique that they have directed against Marx. Rather than holding on to what is most valuable in Marx, the critique of capitalism and the utopian promise of social justice, they have retained that which is most dubious, most reactionary, most theoretically naïve. And by proposing *hegemony* as a replacement for *ideology*, they have substituted a nonconcept, which they describe as a "game" and a "discursive surface," for what was at least affirmed by Marx as a concept (3; see also McGee). Taking one step forward, post-Marxism takes many steps backward: Marx plus Saussure equals something very like zero, an "empty signifier" indeed.

Identifying politics with language, Laclau crystallizes a certain tendency that had been present in the theory of ideology from the very beginning, the attempt to solve problems associated with the project of developing a theory of social ideas by effectively changing the subject and speaking instead of language. Laclau is just one of the most powerful recent exponents of a tradition in which the greatest contributions to the theory of ideology are made by those, including Marx and Gramsci, who make no mention of the word (see Laclau 1996a). Thinking of ideology without the word—which is guilty by association with such retrograde vulgar-Marxist terms as "economic determinism," "superstructure," "ruling class," and "class identity"—Laclau registers a widespread intuition that something about ideology both provokes and resists description, and that, in order for the provocations to succeed and the resistance to fail, some adjustment in the discussion is required. Since Saussure, this adjustment has taken a single dominant form: the replacement of *ideology* as the subject of discussion by *language*, on the premise that language is a solved problem, a known entity with fixed properties.

The most powerful counter-argument is not that Saussure was wrong, or that the sign is not split, or meaning not relational, but simply that the sign is but a part of the limitless mass of stuff that constitutes language, and that Laclau, like so many others, selects his facts about language from a stupendously, even infinitely large set of possibilities. The immense conceptual power and resonance of "language" cannot legitimately pass to the mere socially constructed, instrumental system of signs. I would add, in fact, that the principle of selection by which a scant few facts are plucked from the totality must be, in a classical Marxian sense, ideological. What, other than ideological commitments, would motivate the selection of Saussure as the linguistic scientist of choice rather than, say, Chomsky? Why would a socialist libertarian such as Laclau whose subject is scientific knowledge about language ignore the work of the most eminent linguist, not to mention the most eminent socialist libertarian, in the world? The answer is disturbingly self-evident: Chomsky believes that language defines and even constitutes human nature, and Laclau cannot allow or even entertain such claims as long as he regards "unfixity" as "the condition of every social identity" (Laclau and Mouffe 85).

Indeed, Chomsky has explicitly stated his scientific and even political opposition to accounts of identity based on the infinite susceptibility of all identities to rearticulation. "If in fact humans are indefinitely malleable," Chomsky writes in direct contradiction of Laclau, "with no innate structures of mind and no intrinsic needs of a cultural or social character, then they are fit subjects for the 'shaping of behavior' by the state authority, the corporate manager, the technocrat, or the central committee" (1987a: 154). A stiff challenge—too stiff, apparently, for Laclau to consider replying to. His failure to consider or even to mention Chomsky underscores the tendentiousness of the theory of ideology as it has developed since Marx, a theory that refers to language as a field conquered by science, but only science circa 1906.

Some who position themselves on the political left regard the linguistic turn in the theory of ideology as a characteristic bourgeois-academic evasion of the truth. In his large book on ideology, Eagleton, for example, attempts to make a "political intervention" by stressing ideology's direct derivation not from the mechanisms of language but from "lived relations" (1991: xiii). A study of ideology's "contradictions," Eagleton says hopefully, will disclose cracks in the surface of power by which "a ruling order may come to grief" (xv). But can the linguistic turn be so easily sidestepped? Eagleton makes no attempt to account for the repetition of what he considers a reactionary theoretical misstep by those who should have been savvy enough to avoid it. Nor can one escape the impression that he has made things easy on himself by giving minimal accounts of those linguistic thinkers of ideology who are not easily dismissed or refuted, including Vološinov, Pecheux, Lefort, and Laclau and Mouffe, and by omitting *all* mention of one of the most powerful leftist exponents of the linguistic argument, Stuart Hall. Eagleton's failure really to engage the linguistic argument may reflect his intuition that ideology itself is really inaccessible to analysis except on linguistic terms, no matter how inadequate or indecisive these may be. Ruling classes, he must understand, do not tremble when the chattering classes decide to discuss lived relations rather than language.

All the thinkers discussed in this section retain the primacy of the concept of society as an analytical category. For that reason, their version of the linguistic turn typically pivots on the work of Saussure, for whom language was a social construction. They generally ignore the work of Chomsky, which discounts the role of society and awakens the slumbering, or anesthetized giant of biologically determined human nature. Those who come to ideology by way of psychoanalysis are in a far better position to construct a subject-centered account of ideology. One might think that the work of Chomsky, a linguist who is also a critic of ideology—the preeminent linguist and the most famous and committed critic of ideology in the world—would interest them. In fact, however, these thinkers, too, are committed to Saussure; moreover, they are not just indifferent to Chomsky, but *aggressively* indifferent, for reasons that may be both ideological and psychological.

4. Language and the Psycho-Ideological Subject

The station at which many post-Marxists get off the linguistic train is marked "Althusser," which is, they recognize, but one last stop before the dreaded destination of "Lacan." The crimes of Althusser, theoretical and otherwise, have been exhaustively documented by many, including Althusser himself. His work has always excited a violent reaction from thinkers such as Williams,

Eagleton, Hall, Anthony Easthope, E. J. Hobsbawm, Cora Kaplan, and others. Paul Ricoeur devotes more pages—three long chapters—to Althusser than to any thinker other than Marx in his *Lectures on Ideology and Utopia;* and Eagleton does the same in his book on ideology. Books with such titles as *Althusser: A Critical Reader* and *The Althusserian Legacy* are filled with extended reflections on Althusser's account of ideology (see Elliott, and Kaplan and Sprinker). In fact, commentaries on this subject quite frequently outrun the word count of Althusser's own brief statements, giving the impression that there is more to be said about Althusser's account of ideology than Althusser found it necessary to say about ideology itself. And this despite, or perhaps because of, the fact that Althusser's comments on the subject are contradictory, cryptic, and fragmentary. Much of this commentary is devoted to establishing what Althusser almost or ought to have said, but one of the primary reasons for the explosion *of* language surrounding Althusser's account of ideology is surely the prominence given in that account *to* language.

First among the reasons for the intense but conflicted response provoked by Althusser's work is the fact that his long membership in the French Communist Party gave his work credentials of a kind that could not be ignored by Left intellectuals. While the Marxist historian E. P. Thompson might dismiss Althusser's work as a signal example of the "poverty of theory," many others on the Left felt obligated to devote themselves to a patient if uneasy detailing of theoretical innovations and errors. Second, Althusser's doctrinaire insistence on the scientific "break" with ideology and on the primacy of theory put humanistic Marxists on the defensive, and required them to respond, generally at length. And third, Althusser's work on ideology—his most famous work of theorization, but also "his most ambiguous theoretical venture," according to one critic—was difficult and strikingly idiosyncratic in its psychoanalytic orientation (Mulhern 169). For despite Althusser's dutiful Marxian claims that ideology was to be located in concrete practices, his emphasis on the subject and on processes of "subjectification" represented a significant departure from classical Marxian materialism. For many theorists, the relation between Althusser and Marx, mind and matter, was a crisis that had to be met, a problem that had to be worked out.

In fact, Althusser's deviation from doctrine was only superficial, for "the subject" turns out to be a screen for the most traditional detour of all, to language. Before pursuing this detour, however, we must be specific about the precise connection Althusser draws between psychoanalysis and ideology. Engels had described ideology as "false consciousness"; Althusser accounts for this falseness by locating ideology in a place unknown to Engels in 1893, the unconscious. Ideology was "false" because its motive, origin, and true character were unknown and unknowable, on an inaccessible plane of mental activity. And yet—as Freud said of the unconscious—ideology was "eternal"; as Marx said, it had "no history." Althusser stands near the front of a line of thinkers who have tried to translate ideology into psychoanalytic terms, or the psyche into ideological terms (see Eagleton 1991: 131–36). But before we can proceed any farther, we must distinguish between two distinct accounts that fade in and out of focus in Althusser's provocatively ambivalent formulations.

The first account is articulated in a brief section of *For Marx* (1965), in which ideology is described as a "system of representations" endowed with "a historical existence and role within a given society." Emphatically unscientific, this system stresses the "practico-social function" over the "theoretical function" (Althusser 1970: 231). Ideology is described as a "relay" from scientific or theoretical understanding to the unconscious level of individual action, and back again (236). Ideology is necessary for even the most preliminary comprehension of reality, Althusser says, for social processes themselves are so difficult to apprehend that the eye unaided by ideology would be powerless to grasp them. Without ideological "overdetermination," even science itself would remain merely speculative. Representing the fusion of reality and illusions, ideology is, as Paul Ricoeur glosses this strand of Althusser's thinking, both lived and "imaginary"; "it is the lived *as* imaginary" (Ricoeur 136). There can be no question, at this point, of ideological "distortion," nor, *a fortiori*, of an "end to ideology," because the scientific awareness of reality must, like all other knowledge, be saturated with ideology.

We must be sensitive to the tone of generous and humane appreciation with which Althusser here treats ideology, which is said to enable people to live worthwhile lives in conditions that might otherwise be bewildering or dehumanizing. Intervening between people and the hard truths of class inequities and exploitation, ideology provides a kind of layer within the mind in which one can negotiate one's way by imagining that one lives by voluntary agreement in a beneficent world. Ideology adjusts people to their social roles, informing them as to appropriate values, judgments, motivations; it transforms men's consciousness, "so as to raise them to the levels of their tasks and the conditions of their existence" (Althusser 1970: 235). So fundamental a role does ideology play in the mind that Althusser can scarcely, at this point, imagine what a human society would look like, or how human beings could survive without it. Althusser's discourse is as a consequence consistently humanistic, invoking "conditions of existence," "attitudes and behavior," and "consciousness," and declaring that ideology serves as a kind of node in which "the relation between men and their conditions of existence is lived to the profit of all men" (see Ricoeur 139; Althusser 1970: 236).

For Marx provides an account of how particular ideologies, specific systems of representation (humanism, liberalism, Protestantism . . .), accommodate people to their conditions of existence. Four years later, in 1969, when he writes his famous essay "Ideology and Ideological State Apparatuses," Althusser is far more interested than before in policing the compromised boundary between science and ideology. And he has changed his emphasis, speaking not about how ideology makes life bearable for everyone, but rather about the role of government in promulgating the ideas of the ruling class. In both respects, he is now concerned to provide greater theoretical clarity and a sharper conceptual edge than he had achieved in *For Marx*. The question we must pose is whether the second account clarifies and complements the first account or simply contradicts it.

Difficult, even tangled and contradictory, the 1969 text is primarily known for its occasional epigrammatic pronouncements, such as that ideology represents not a distortion of reality, but the "imaginary relationship of individuals to their real conditions of existence" (Althusser 1984: 36). It is, in other words, not the system of real relations of production or real class relations that constitutes ideology, but our "imagined" relations to those relations. Ideology involves a functional "misrecognition," a term Althusser forcibly extracts from Lacan. Thinking ideologically, we do not misrecognize the truth, believing, for example, that our employees are grateful, our spouses and children adore us, and all's well with our black brothers and sisters, when in fact plots are hatching, lifelong hatreds are being nurtured, and blood is flowing through the streets. Instead, we misrecognize our relation to those conflicts, our place in the system. Ultimately, we misrecognize ourselves.

To the question of who or what is responsible for this misrecognition, Althusser returns a shockingly succinct answer: the state. The state, he argues, labors always to maintain and reproduce itself, both by force (the police and army) and by ideology. Unlike the former, the latter is not administered directly by agents of the state, but by "ideological state apparatuses," or ISAs, including the school and the family, whose silently efficient functioning adapts individuals to the dominant culture. The bourgeois mind is shocked by the thought that the home and school are obedient extensions of the state; but Althusser administers another, apparently gratuitous blow, this time to his own theory, by deconstructing the distinction he had just drawn between repressive force and ideology. The famous example of how ideology works—"hailing," as when a policeman calls out in the street, and the ideologically constructed guilty party turns around, certain that he is the one being summoned—is drawn from the repertoire of the "repressive state apparatuses" rather than the presumably less immediately threatening practices of the ISAs. (It is, after all, not guilt alone that turns you around, but the knowledge that, if you try to run, it will be worse for you.) So Althusser at once identifies ideology as an indirect, mediated, and ambient pressure, and describes its operations in terms of the shouting policeman on the street. But perhaps the most immediate source of disorientation, to those accustomed to thinking of ideology as a socio-political phenomenon, is the site at which Althusser locates it: the deepest psychological constitution of the subject.

Althusser seems to be drawing out the logic of a pun between "subjection" in the sense of "being subject to," and "the subject" of experience, the "I." But he also seems to be defending himself against obvious questions: how do people respond to ideological hailing unless they are already the "guilty party," already thinking ideologically; and, why don't people revolt, why don't they want to be free? His answer is that people are "always already" caught in the grip of ideology, thinking they are free when they are not. Structured from the outset by imaginary misrecognition, their confusion runs deep. A function of the state, ideology subjects people to the master-subject, but it does not do so by simply teaching people to admire their leaders, a teaching easily shrugged off when evidence of their perfidy, stupidity, or venality accumulates. The role of ideology in our mental life is far more fundamental and intimate. The real functioning of ideology, Althusser says, is to "interpellate" people as subjects, inducting them into the "rituals" and "practices" that regulate and structure human existence. Indeed, in a real sense, this interpellation predates birth, inasmuch as neonates simply assume positions in a socio-familial structure that awaits them.

At this point, the homonymic slippage between kinds of "subject" has enabled and concealed a break in Althusser's thinking. For with the concept of the interpellation of subjects, he is no longer providing a theoretical account of the tactics of a self-interested governmental machinery, but something radically different. While the state may be altered or overthrown, ideology in this sense cannot. You cannot get beneath ideology-as-interpellation, cannot reach back to a time when ideology was not. Reinforcing one wall of the fort, explaining that people do not overthrow the state because they are utterly and thoroughly ideologized on all sides, Althusser has left another exposed, for he has worked himself into the position of asserting that ideology precedes individual consciousness. Althusser seems, at this moment, to be cogitating some other pun, such that *ideology* refers both to something that we can grasp and understand, and to something that we cannot, some different kind of thing altogether. It is hard even for the most sophisticated students of critical discourse to imagine ideology before ideas, hard to understand why a general context deserves the name of ideology, hard to comprehend the "moment" of a process of interpellation that is "eternal," hard to see how the state can infiltrate the uterus.

Althusser refers many such questions to Lacan, a thinker not known as a penetrating analyst of social or cultural issues, and so unlikely to carry much authority with those who regard themselves as experts on the subject of ideology. But Lacan is crucial to Althusser because of his great, if Delphic, authority on difficult questions, and, more particularly, his charting of the formal structures of subjectivization. Althusser discovers in Lacan a theory of misrecognition, an emphasis on the "subjection to the Subject" (which Althusser identifies as the state), and, most important, a scientific account of psychoanalytic processes based on the nature of language (1984: 55). In a 1964 essay on "Freud and Lacan," Althusser described Lacan as a heroic figure who had finally realized the properly scientific nature of Freud's discovery by applying the discipline of linguistics to the study of the subject, its pathologies, and its cure.

What truly distinguishes Lacan as scientist, as far as Althusser is concerned, is Lacan's prescient recognition that the Saussurean sign could serve as a graph of the unconscious, and, more generally, Lacan's insistence on the "*primacy* of the formal structure of language and its 'mechanisms'" as these illuminate the "forced 'humanization' of the small human animal into a *man* or a *woman*" (Althusser 1984: 160). This process occurs, Althusser says in a moment of inspiration, during the passage from what Lacan calls the order of the "Imaginary" to that of the "Symbolic," from the purely biological law of nature to the law of culture, a law that "is confounded in its *formal* essence with the order of language" (161). The entire complex argument is crystallized by Michel Pecheux in a single formulation: "*unconscious repression and ideological subjection* are materially linked . . . inside what could be called *the process of the Signifier in interpellation and identification*" (92; see also Thompson 205–31). Although the "always-already" aspect of Althusser's thinking on ideology a few years later is not yet evident in "Freud and Lacan," the direction of his thinking is clearly set at this moment, when he discovers in Lacan's appropriation of Saussure a way and a warrant for undoing the traditional humanistic subject by emphasizing form, structure, mechanism—or, as he will eventually put it, "apparatus."

Althusserian antihumanism crystallizes in this alien word, which defeats all by itself the implicit humanism of "the subject." Ideology, he says, always works through an apparatus—a structure of pressures and inducements that recruits subjects to various practices or rituals consistent with the order of the law or culture—that is strictly indifferent to individual identity, strictly "material" in its nature, strictly mechanical in its procedures. The subject is not just overwhelmed but determined in its unconscious nucleus by the autonomous, illusion-generating, ideological apparatus. While the ideological apparatus could be characterized as a "process without subjects," that process works exclusively to produce subjects. To put it another way, we could say that the illusions the apparatus generates concern chiefly itself. For what the ideological subject thinks is that it is *not* thinking ideologically, but freely, according to its own will, transcending material constraints through an act of pure and unforced inwardness. Such thoughts, Althusser says, are the very form of our subjection. We become free and autonomous subjects by first submitting ourselves (unconsciously) to the ideological law; once we have done that—and we cannot help but do it—the law reproduces itself in us "spontaneously." Ideological thoughts produce a constant sense of pleasure, power, and freedom; and this accounts for the striking fact that ideological subjects, as Althusser says, work "all by themselves" (1984: 55).

The Lacanian ancestor of the apparatus is the mirror, in which the infant, according to Lacan's primal scene, "recognizes" himself as a whole body with all the parts he sees in others, and thus as a unified subject, like them. Applying this model as a template, Althusser is able to explain ideology as a species of narcissistic illusion that extends, as it does not in Lacan or Freud, indefinitely in time: one outgrows the mirror stage or primary narcissism, but one can never surmount the apparatus, which remains an indispensable condition of subjectivity from the cradle—and even long before that—to the grave.

Althusser's debt to Lacan is immense, but also profoundly inaccurate. Althusser provides dubious, partial, or sharply slanted accounts of Lacan's thinking, ignoring Lacan's debt to such thinkers as Hegel and Kojève, and misrepresenting in demonstrable ways the meaning of crucial Lacanian terms such as the Imaginary (which he conceives as Marxist "illusion"), the Real (which he conceives in Marxist terms as "concrete reality"), and the Other (which he conceives as the State); he recenters the decentered Lacanian subject, and, in short, misrecognizes misrecognition (see Eagleton 1991: 143–45; Ricoeur 148–51; Macey 149–51). But for the purposes of the present argument, none of these errors is as significant as his seemingly instinctive embrace of Lacan as a scientific thinker who made psychoanalysis whole and sound by assimilating it to linguistics. With this gesture, Althusser locks in the "Triple Alliance" of French theory in the 1960s: Althusser-Lacan-Saussure. For Saussure provides Lacan what Lacan provided for Althusser: a formal structure that could be substituted for the humanistic discourse of the subject and intersubjectivity. That structure was language, especially the bifurcated sign.

The unusual warmth with which Althusser stresses the "*primacy* of the formal structure in language and its 'mechanisms'" in Lacan suggests the importance of linguistic mechanism for Althusser as well. In fact, given the slippages between Althusser, Lacan, and Saussure, it is tempting to speculate that when Althusser talks about ideology, he is really talking about language. What else could account for the specific contradictions between and within Althusser's accounts of ideology? Consider the antinomies of Althusserian ideology that we have discerned so far:

1. Ideology is one thing; ideologies are another.
2. Ideology has no history; and it reproduces the current system as determined by the state.
3. Ideology is a system of social representations; and it is a psycho-social apparatus.

4. Ideology is material-concrete; and it is ideal-illusory.
5. Ideology is exemplified by humanism; and it is the cornerstone of theoretical antihumanism.
6. Ideology is a process without subjects; and its only function is to produce subjects.
7. Ideology produces specific meanings available to consciousness; and it operates at the level of the unconscious, in response to concrete conditions of existence.
8. Ideology works by misrecognition; and, through "hailing," it produces recognitions.

Simply bewildering when considered in themselves, these contradictions (or overdeterminations) make somewhat more sense if we consider them not a muddled account of ideology, but as a faithful if distanced reproduction of the Saussurean account of language. Thus, we could say, it is language that is both universal (*langue*) and local (*parole*); that has no history and yet functions in particular historical circumstances; that is both material and ideal; that expresses human consciousness and yet remains "unconscious" in the individual; that is both "human" and has a formal structure. We understand the Althusserian discourse on ideology when we grasp it as a specific version or continuation of the discourse on language.

What I am contending is that the right way to read Althusser on ideology is to begin by abandoning the notion that Althusser is making a good-faith attempt at theoretical or descriptive adequacy, or that he has made a "major breakthrough" in thinking about ideology, as Eagleton assures us (1991: 146). Such approaches proceed on the positivist assumption that there is a thing, ideology, about which true or false statements may be made; and the "history of ideology"—of the theory of ideology—does not inspire confidence on that score. We should begin, rather, with the presumption that Althusser has in fact misrecognized his own subject, which is not ideology at all, but language. Speaking of ideology, Althusser is in fact reproducing Saussurean clichés about language as a self-contained system of signs that merely seems to mime the structures of reality. This presumption can be tested by inserting *language* or *linguistic* into the Althusserian text wherever the terms *ideology* or *ideological* occur, as in the following passage: "what thus seems to take place outside [language] in reality takes place in [language]. What really takes place in [language] seems therefore to take place outside it . . . one of the effects of [language] is the practical *denegation* of the [linguistic] effects of [language] by [language]: [language] never says, 'I am [language]'. . . . Which amounts to saying that [language] *has no outside* (for itself), but at the same time *that it is nothing but outside* (for science and reality)" (1984: 49). The passage as rewritten is, to be sure, cryptic, but it is not altogether opaque, certainly not more so than the original.

But statements about language at this level of generality tend to be cryptic, for the reason that, as I argued at the end of the first chapter, language alone or language as such never takes determinate form, and cannot be observed in itself. And so a second hypothesis, more profound than the first, concerning Althusser on ideology would be that "language itself" is a misrecognition, a screen for something else. In his effort to give a name and thus a concrete ontological form to the unnameable, the ultimate condition of human existence, Althusser has been led to the edge of thought itself. With immense intellectual ambition, he has tried to imagine a single principle that would unite the antinomies of human life. Perhaps mistakenly, he has called that principle *ideology*. But if it is a mistake, it is one with a particular genealogy, and not a dishonorable one. It is immensely tempting but finally impossible to provide a fully adequate description of ideology or language; these must remain lexical phantoms, objects of infinite description. The necessary conclusion must be that what we actually *see* in Althusser is that *language* and *ideology* are *both* misnomers for each other, and that there is *nothing*, no concrete object, in play at all. The two terms face each other like two mirrors of infinite dimensions, reflecting only each other, so that the image in each is only the image of the other, which is, of course, only itself once again.

If there is a thinker even more heavily invested in mirrors than Althusser, it is Žižek, the Slovenian wizard who, with a spectacular burst of productivity beginning in the late 1980s, has rapidly established himself as a *sui generis* intellectual-of-all-trades, with a claim to eminence, even preeminence, in several distinct disciplines. Remarkably versatile, he has also run for, and narrowly missed winning, the presidency of Slovenia—which would surely have made him the only dedicated Lacanian in a position of political power. This would have been ironic, given the understanding of power that Žižek derives from Lacan; but it would have been altogether, even ominously fitting, given the authority that Lacan exercises over Žižek's wayward thought.

So volatile and various, Žižek is in the first instance an apostle of Lacan whose commitment determines—albeit in an unpredictable way—his position on every issue. It informs, for example, his understanding of Althusser, which I shall discuss in a moment, and inflects his analytical habits generally, as he indicates with such comments as, "our Lacanian standpoint compels us to here to insist . . . ," or, "from the Lacanian point of view, we must see that . . ." Žižek accords Lacan a theoretical authority that is well-nigh "totalitarian" in character. And this is in a sense appropriate, because, according to Žižek, Lacan provides the best theoretical account of the kind of unsymbolizable trauma whose social or political form is totalitarianism. Lacan appeals, in short, to a residual Stalinism in Žižek, who sees in totalitarianism a laying-bare of certain psychic and political energies that liberal democracy blithely dissimulates and denies (see Žižek 2001).

But as a citizen of newly independent Slovenia, Žižek also has commitments to a cosmopolitan and progressive liberalism that represents the best future for his and other nations. While Žižek was studying in the Lacanian milieu of Paris in the early and mid-1980s (and being analyzed by Jacques-Alain Miller, Lacan's son-in-law), he met Laclau, who was working on *Hegemony and Socialist Strategy*, the book that would secure his position as one of the preeminent theorists of "radical democracy." Žižek formed an affinity with Laclau that was both personal and theoretical, and Laclau contributed a preface to the first book of Žižek's to reach an English-speaking audience, *The Sublime Object of Ideology* (1989). In it, Laclau records Žižek's visits to "our research programme on Ideology and Discourse Analysis at the Department of Government at the University of Essex on many occasions," from which issued "a number of joint research projects" (1989: xii). In this and subsequent works, Žižek refers to Laclau and Mouffe with appreciation and respect, crediting them with the decisive post-Gramscian articulations of the principle of antagonism, and of the political implications of the sign's "emptiness." Stitching together Lacan and Laclau, totalitarianism and democracy, provides Žižek with a project of considerable urgency and complexity. But we can already see that he has been provided with a firm foundation for this project in the common commitment of Laclau and Lacan to the Saussurean sign as the point of theoretical origin. The "isolation of the sign" from its social matrix that Williams criticizes in Vološinov is, for Laclau, Lacan, and thus for Žižek, the necessary precondition of genuine understanding. Together, these three thinkers demonstrate once again the strange persistence of the antiquated Saussure, who serves as the reliable base of even the most theoretically sophisticated superstructures.

This point of agreement still leaves much unsettled, however, for, true to its nature, the sign can mean many things. To Laclau, as we have seen, the cleft in the sign between signifier and signified means that all identity—including such large-scale formations as political parties and even national identity—is similarly fissured or dis-integrated. As a formal structure that holds the key to human identity and essence, the sign serves as a principle of principles, a quasi-material support for a normative ethics and a politics in which conflict is constant and appropriate and the place of power is theoretically open. If we begin with the sign, Laclau (and Mouffe, whose ambiguous agency in *Hegemony and Socialist Strategy* represents an intriguing "division in the subject") suggests, we will be led to the conclusion that all representatives of authority are mere provisional place-holders, and that democracy is therefore the form of social organization that accords most closely with the ground-conditions of our being.

Žižek agrees with this account, and never fails to indicate his indebtedness. The general antagonism derived from language (the sign) is for him a fundamental principle, and clearly underlies his promotion of democratic institutions in which volatility, instability, and openness to change are the norms, as opposed to "totalitarianism," with its ideological fictions of coherence, wholeness, or permanence. But even as Žižek defers to Laclau as the pioneer in the articulation of antagonism, he is moving in another direction altogether. He is, to begin with, much more aggressive than Laclau in arguing that the sign constitutes a law that human beings cannot evade, no matter how they may try. For Žižek, language represents a rigid determinism in human existence that makes it impossible to sustain the notion that human beings are autonomous and free. The sign is, in fact, an intolerable interference in the humanist conception of life, a traumatic break or cut that does not just resemble or evoke castration but is a direct form of castration, in the psychoanalytic sense. We are forever prevented from achieving integration and wholeness because the signs we use are themselves divided; and because we are constituted as linguistic creatures, our very natures are determined by an arbitrary social mechanism, an inert and intrinsically "stupid" system. To make this case, Žižek characteristically refers not to Laclau but to Lacan, for whom the sign is not an inspiriting source of freedom and openness, not the form, medium, and model for human emancipation, but the primary point of access of the subject to the death instinct, a dark and resistant *"object in subject"* (1989: 180).

Responsive at a much deeper level to Lacan than to Laclau, the highly resourceful Žižek is capable of discovering little docking-points for Laclau in the theoretical arguments that he takes as the untranscendable horizon of reflection. Taking up a passage in Hegel's *Phenomenology of Spirit* concerning language as the "very medium of the 'journey of consciousness,'" Žižek notes, in characteristically witty fashion, that this journey is exemplified by the act of "flattering the Monarch," in which what we say disavows our convictions, but does so in a way that is in a sense truer than our convictions, for we do in fact wish to flatter, and to be seen to flatter, the Monarch. In fact, he adds perversely, flattery can actually constitute "an ethical act: by pronouncing empty phrases which disavow our innermost convictions, we submit ourselves to a compulsive disrupting of our narcissistic homeostasis . . . we renounce heroically what is most precious in us, our 'sense of honour,' our moral consistency, our self-respect" (1989: 211). With every phrase, Žižek moves farther from Laclau; and yet at precisely this moment, Laclau—in the form of a rather heedless witticism, perhaps a mere pleasantry, recalled from "a private conversation"—is invoked. Flattery is an extreme but revealing instance of what Lacan would call *"an alienation proper to language as such,"* the way in which language use itself constitutes a point of alienation; and since such alienation is also seen in the self-accusatory atmosphere of totalitarianism, whose most revealing instance was the show-trial "confessions" of innocent people who held the purposes of the Party to be higher than their own fates, "Ernesto Laclau was quite right to remark that *it is language which is, in an unheard-of sense, a 'Stalinist phenomenon'*" (212). By such ingenious means, the democratic optimist Laclau becomes stapled to an argument that runs through Hegel and Lacan, all the way to Stalin.

The terrain on which Žižek becomes (almost) conscious of the conflict between his master-spirits, and fights it out, is ideology, Žižek's most general term for all the ways in which antagonism is denied. Class conflict, for example, is an ideological project whose root cause is not economic inequality but the sign: we fight with each other because we cannot confront the fact that we are internally conflicted. Thus, Žižek insists, in a formulation that manages to include elements from Laclau and Lacan, ideology is properly understood as a recoil from the trauma of antagonism. On one occasion, we can actually observe Žižek in the act of suturing the two discourses to produce a single continuous argument. Ideology, Žižek says in the crucial passage,

> is not a dreamlike illusion that we build to escape insupportable reality; in its basic dimension it is a fantasy-construction which serves as a support for our "reality" itself: an "illusion" which structures our effective, real social relations and thereby masks some insupportable, real, impossible kernel (conceptualized by Ernesto Laclau and Chantal Mouffe as "antagonism": a traumatic social division which cannot be symbolized). The function of ideology is not to offer us a point of escape from our reality but to offer us the social reality itself as an escape from some traumatic, real kernel. To explain this logic, let us refer again to the *Four Fundamental Concepts of Psycho-analysis.* . . . (1989: 45)

To judge from the flow of this passage, Laclau and Lacan collaborate in a rich account of ideology (although neither uses the term), with Laclau contributing the concept of an antagonism that cannot be directly symbolized and Lacan explaining that the unsymbolizable element constitutes a "traumatic kernel." Laclau explains, that is, why no ideology can be perfectly or permanently effective, and Lacan explains why we need ideologies in the first place.

But this appearance of theoretical amity cannot conceal an underlying network of discord. In *Tarrying with the Negative* (1993), Žižek attacks the contemporary infatuation with "openness" and "the elated 'deconstructionist' logomachy focused on 'essentialism' and 'fixed identities'" as a deluded if not hypocritical promotion of precisely the style of dispersed subjectivity that most closely corresponds to late capitalism, which seeks the "unbridled commodification of everyday life" (217). In other words, he rejects with extreme prejudice Laclau's position but not Laclau himself. Nor does Laclau feel properly flattered by all of Žižek's attentions. In *Contingency, Hegemony, Universality* (2000), Laclau accuses Žižek of a gross misreading of the entire tradition and especially of Lacan's place in it. From start to finish, Laclau declares, his erstwhile protégé has "Lacanianized the tradition of modernity, most visibly in the case of Hegel, in a way which I see as hardly legitimate" (75). If Lacan were alive, he, too, might protest Žižek's appropriation of his arguments and authority for an endorsement of liberal politics, no matter how "radical." Thus, to express this curious situation with maximum epigrammatic efficiency, we may say that Lacan marks an antagonism between Žižek and Laclau, and Laclau signals a traumatic interruption in the otherwise untroubled relation between Žižek and Lacan.

This can only be called confusion, but it is a confusion Žižek himself helps us to understand. For by concealing the antagonism between his two authorities, Žižek has contrived an illusion of wholeness and integration that brilliantly clarifies his arguments on ideology. In a discourse conspicuously rich with clarifying instances, Žižek is, in this case, his own best example. He is, moreover, one of the very best examples of my overall argument, that the theory of ideology has for the past century made "progress" by turning away from its presumed object and toward language.

5. Conclusion: Inversions

With such massive evidence of a tendency to define ideology in relation to language, we cannot be surprised at the existence of a symmetrical tendency to define language in relation to ideology. This tendency takes two forms, which I will only sketch. In the first, language is bluntly identified not as the secret mechanism of ideology but as itself an ideology that structures the world in particular ways. Studies of the "manipulation" of language by those in a position to control the flow of information have proliferated in recent years in the wake of Robert Hodge and Gunther Kress's pathbreaking *Language as Ideology* (1979). Hodge and Kress see themselves as participating in a wider discourse of social-linguistic theory whose intellectual masters are Derrida, Foucault, Herbert Marcuse, Lacan, Pierre Bourdieu, Jean Baudrillard, Kristeva, and Edward Said; but their project reaches more directly back to Whorf, whose pioneering study of the "construction of reality" in the Hopi language they consider a precursor to their own more sophisticated approach, which tries to identify the "ideology" implicit in classification, representations of movement, time, tense, and number, modes of negation, and so forth (Hodge and Kress 4–14).

Within the general field opened by Hodge and Kress, other more specific studies of language as the vehicle of particular ideologies have emerged. This field is dominated by studies of gender; the field of gender and language is dominated by those who argue that "male" and "female" designate distinct ways of being in the world; and among these, the most prolific seem to believe that language works tirelessly on behalf of men. A recent book on *Language and Masculinity* explores the ways in which manhood is represented or constructed in language, with special attention to the ways in which men exercise "ideology power" by linguistic means.

Men, it appears from the literature, are amazingly devious and effective in this respect. Not only do they speak a language of power, but they use language in powerful ways, dominating conversations, speaking loudly or coarsely, failing to listen, insisting on their point of view. Their subtlest stratagem—indeed, their only subtlety—is finally to cloak themselves in reason. "What better way is there to exercise power," Jack Sattel asks, or perhaps declares, "than *to make it appear* that *all* one's behaviour seems to be the result of unemotional rationality? Being impersonal and inexpressive lends to one's decisions and position an apparent autonomy and 'rightness'" (quoted in Johnson and Meinhof 17). In this context, Chomsky's principle of the "autonomy of syntax" is seen to be vulnerable to a deep inquiry that discerns in Chomsky's "scientific" pretensions an exemplary masculinist project that effectively furthers a covert sex agenda by proposing that language is, like a gentlemen's club, "a totally closed system" whose only content is its own system of rules (Johnson and Meinhof 14; see also Thorne and Henley; and Thorne et al.).

While some, following an influential 1973 study by Robin Lakoff, note that women tend to speak a "powerless language," others argue that language makes women powerless by inflicting on them an ideology derived from masculine dominance. According to Nancy M. Henley, "language ignores, it defines, and it deprecates women. As a result, women and girls are hurt both psychologically and materially by it" (3). The "generic masculine" in particular makes women a kind of afterthought of language, reinforcing society's sexism. The adoption of sex-neutral pronouns, Henley argues, would raise people's consciousness about sexism in language and in society at large by making people think about the reasons why these terms seemed so strange and incongruous. One of the most influential figures in this emergent discourse is Dale Spender, who argues that the "English lexicon" is "a structure designed to glorify maleness and ignore, trivialize or derogate femaleness" (42). English in particular, Spender charges, is "literally man made" and, by such means as the coding of "motherhood" as an exclusively positive term, has become "one of the means by which (English-speaking) males have ensured their own primacy" (12). Her work is supported by Deborah Cameron, who has disclosed, in the presumptively "genderless" English language, an entire system of relegation and exclusion that literally goes without saying, operating largely in the dark, as in the sentence, "Fourteen people, three of them women, were arrested," a sentence that would seem decidedly askew if the three were men (1985b: 23).

The prevailing presumption in this school of thought is that language—both the currently dominant discourse and language as such—enforces a particular ideology, that differential power relations are not merely expressed in but constructed by language. They offer hope, however, that the linguistically disempowered may refashion language by various means—not just lexical reform, but hyphens, portmanteau words, neologisms, and unconventional syntactic structures—and produce a language more intimate with various desiderata: the body, desire, social upheaval, community, or aesthetic value. As Henley puts it, a change in the language might "express the ideology, and later, the reality, of equality" (16).

Informing this argument is an unexpressed and complex set of beliefs about language. First, it is believed that language is a tool that people use, and can shape or fashion as they will. Moreover, language is a social construction rather than a biological or a natural given, and since it has evidently changed over time, it can be changed here and now, by directed effort. By "language" is meant individual words, chiefly nouns and pronouns, not grammar or communicative action in general. In fact, "language" in such contexts actually refers primarily to writing; generally excluded from consideration are contextual factors, including the identity and relationship of the speakers and hearers.

The reason language is so reduced in this discourse is that the desire driving the entire project is the furthering of justice by means of specific alterations in linguistic practice; and for this project to be plausible, language must be considered as a thing apart from human being in general—a tool one can use, a screen beyond which one can, through determined effort, glimpse reality. For only if language is isolated in this way as a determined thing distinct from people and the infinite variety of communicative transactions in which they engage can the prescriptivist project of altering or modifying it make any sense. But the next move in the argument depends upon the opposite premise, that the structures of language constitute, for the language-users, the very structures of reality. In the final analysis, these thinkers feel, language tricks us, but if we make a special effort, we can make it trick us in a good way. In order to convince ourselves that language might be changed, we must conceive of language as a limited, specific, and malleable thing, but in order to feel that our interventions have really accomplished something profound and structural, we must believe that language provides an untran-scendable horizon of perception and thought.

Given that such arguments seem to arrive at an impasse or contradiction, we may wish to consider another way altogether of thinking the relationship between language and ideology. A number of thinkers have adopted a posi-tion that inverts the language-is-ideology argument, contending that language provides a kind of antidote to ideology. In a passage from his late essay on "The Resistance to Theory" that has been read as a sign of an incipient turn to social issues, Paul de Man suggested that deconstruction properly applied would equip people to shrug off the mystifications of ideology. "What we call ideology," he wrote, "is precisely the confusion of linguistic with natural reality. . . . It follows that, more than any other mode of inquiry, including economics, the linguistics of literariness is a powerful and indispensable tool in the unmasking of ideological aberrations" (1986: 11). One could, by read-ing rigorously—that is, by focusing on the language itself, bracketing the referent, and suspending any "aesthetic" effect—avoid mystifications and perceive aright. Of course, all you would perceive would be language, but at least you would be clear about what you perceive, and to that extent, you would escape ideology.

It sounds simple, but it is not. To "see" or "hear" language is necessarily to grasp what it refers to, describes, picks out, indicates, suggests, brings into being, or causes to emerge in a given context. It is also, therefore, to be affected in various ways. If one has no reaction to the sentence, "There's a cen-tipede on your neck," other than to appreciate the assonance, one has not truly "heard" the sentence at all. In treating language as what philosophers might call a "natural kind," de Man has not avoided confusion but has redoubled it, fleeing from nature straight to—more nature. As we saw in the previous chap-ter, much of de Man's later career consisted of the drawing of marvelously refined distinctions between such humanistic categories as judgment or cogni-tion and the "merely figural," "tropological," or grammatical features of a strictly inhuman language that rebuffed all humanist yearnings. For the late de

Man, ideology was aligned with humanism, and on this basis his admirers claimed that his career constituted a "flight from ideology." His detractors argued, by contrast, that he had in fact fled *to* ideology, especially the very "aesthetic ideology" he deplored (see Norris). With emotions on both sides running high, the possibility that de Man's account of language constitutes a bidirectional flight *from-to* ideology is rarely raised.

The conviction that language provides a counter-force to ideology brings de Man into unexpected proximity to a thinker with whom he otherwise has little in common, Jürgen Habermas. The difference between these two lies, first, in the particular linguistic act that each stresses—reading for de Man and speech for Habermas. If we can keep clear the distinction between texts and nontexts, de Man suggests, if we can devote ourselves to a technical and purified act of *reading* in which we perceive not real referents but the mechanisms of reference itself, then we will be able to run by the nets of ideology. As we will see in the next chapter, de Man professes little interest in such concepts as morality, which he treats as a kind of linguistic mirage, but his whole approach has a solid moral foundation, and this allies him with Habermas, who argues that language combats ideology on the ground of morality. Unlike the (ideological) world, Habermas argues, language has a moral ideal built into it, and to use language properly is a moral, as opposed to an ideological, act.

Perhaps Habermas's most controversial claim—one that has provoked the charge that he has not exposed himself sufficiently to the currents of postmodernism's discoveries about language—is that all language is inherently oriented toward rationality and communicative transparency, and bears within it the germ of an "ideal speech situation" free from domination, a political as well as a linguistic condition of equality, mutual comprehension, and respect. As rationality is buried deep within language, so is language buried within the "lifeworld," serving as a gentle but relentless guide to the right, even when misused for purposes of distortion or manipulation. The task of ideology criticism—the interrogation of language for elements of "distortion"—thus becomes a practice of discerning, in various utterances or texts, those elements that are consistent with the fundamental purposes and forms of language, and segregating them from other elements that are not.

In fact, Habermas suggests, the distinction ultimately falls between the relatively degraded or imperfect present and some future condition of justice in which all participants in a socialist democracy will have equal access to the truth such that in all disputes the "unforced force of the better argument" will prevail. In seeking this condition, critique is "interested" and cannot claim to be neutral. But the interest itself is universal, for, as Habermas sees it, the very survival of the species is at stake in establishing a society in which language is actually deployed for the purposes for which it is most perfectly suited. Disturbances, slippages, points of opacity, ideological static—these represent not just affronts to sense, but insults to humanity as the linguistic species; and we act, Habermas argues, in our own most profound cultural, personal, historical, and even evolutionary best interests when we try to root them out.

Equally indifferent to the concerns of de Man and Habermas, Chomsky proposes an even more compelling account than either of the anti-ideological force of language. For Chomsky, ideology is not opposed to language, but to science, reason, and truth. His is a classical Marxist (or Engelsian) view of ideology as a system of self-interested and correctable misrepresentations disseminated by those in a position to do so. Ideology offends against a fundamental human instinct for free creative inquiry, self-expression, and work, the strongest evidence for which is the capacity to learn and use language. Endowed with a common aptitude for creating new sentences, human beings are intrinsically and instinctively nonideological; left to their own devices, as they ought to be, people would arrive at the ideas, attitudes, and values that best suited them. The human faculty of language thus constitutes, for Chomsky, an argument for a libertarian-anarchist social order as well as an argument against ideology.

Chomsky is a powerfully lucid thinker, but he does not seem to realize that there may be a problem in contending that (a) language is the most powerful and pervasive medium of ideological distortions, and (b) the language faculty is the most powerful anti-ideological weapon that exists. Nor does he entertain the possibility that his own language may not be altogether free from ideological tincture. His insistence on his own ideological purity seems a blind spot, even a determined theoretical naïveté in an otherwise massively fortified conceptual structure. Can language ever become so utterly pellucid that it implies or supports no ideology whatsoever? Some years ago, Roland Barthes gave voice to an antiscientific sentiment then widespread in the humanities by identifying the implied ideology in "the rational economy of classical language" (1967: 49). Chomsky's "unsophisticated" account of ideology has enabled him to fend off such arguments without really confronting them. It would have been interesting—and would still be interesting—to hear a sustained response from Chomsky on this issue.

. . .

As we have seen in this long chapter, ideas of language have been deployed in a wide variety of ways in the study, or pseudo-study, of ideology. In fact, it now appears an inescapable conclusion that *language* can be enlisted in support of any possible position on ideology, and that ideology is a sufficiently indeterminate thing that any possible position on it may be taken. Depending on what aspect of ideology is brought into focus, some "fact" of language may be invoked to explain it, including form, open-endedness, arbitrariness, unfixity, materiality, creativity, transparency, distinctness from the world, the union of form and concept, and so forth. There are as many aspects of language as there are possible meanings of ideology—"several hundred," each with subdivisions, according to Rossi-Landi's estimate. There is no end to facts about language, and therefore no end to arguments about the real nature or true character of ideology.

One response to this situation would be to declare the entire inquiry into the linguistic constitution of ideology to be circular or nonfalsifiable, and to take it off the agenda of scholarly and critical inquiry. That would be an unfortunate result. For one true fact that emerges from this inquiry is that even if we are no closer to a perfect understanding of ideology than we are to beholding with our eyes the concrete entity of language, an immense amount of intellectual labor has been invested in the effort to relate the two in some positive way, and this effort has been immensely productive. One cannot argue that the world would have been better off if Marx and Engels, V. N. Vološinov, Raymond Williams, Stuart Hall, and Louis Althusser had never written on this subject. *Ideology* is one of the names under which critical thought has pursued its objectives. It is a name that at least suggests the laudable desires that those objectives be productively aligned with the "lifeworld," that thinking and ideas should not become altogether detached from material existence, that we should think critically about the ways in which ideas abroad in society become lodged in the subject, and that we should cultivate a principle of resistance to thoughts we do not wish to have. Judged in this light, the study of the reciprocal determinations of ideology and language should be encouraged, on the condition that we understand that its value lies not in its direct results, which must, of course, be immediately discounted, but in its by-products.

Three

ETHICS AND THE LAW OF LANGUAGE

1. Words as Guides, from Hume to Bernard Williams

One of the most striking features of the intellectual history of the past century is the relentless convergence of the hitherto separate fields of language and ethics. In the extended context of the Western tradition, this convergence may appear shocking, for ethical philosophers since Plato have generally distrusted language, especially literary language, as a subversive distraction from the kind of worldly rigor needed to conduct sound ethical reasoning. But from another point of view, this convergence is not surprising. From the beginning—since God created the world, and man, by a word—language has been felt to be instinct with spirit and has therefore always been a tempting resource for those who have struggled to articulate the relation of man, the only linguistic animal, and the ethical law that binds man and man alone. For this reason, language and ethics have never been altogether distinct concepts, and have indeed always demonstrated a kind of magnetic attraction for each other.

This old attraction took on new life when, with the advent of Saussurean modernism, the thought of language as such, language alone, began to dominate linguistics. For, unlike particular languages, language can be said to be universal and distinctive of the entire species; like the ethical law, it binds all alike (see Heidegger 1962: 312–48; Rorty 1989: 9; and Connor 102–32). A general or theoretical linguistics that takes as its object language alone has, then, already laid the groundwork for an understanding of language that is at once scientific and ethical. As we saw in the discussion of Saussure in the first chapter, the impossibility of a literal or empirical description of language alone invites a metaphorical supplementation that reflects, in Saussure's case, particular normative concepts. In fact, it can be argued that theoretical linguistics becomes aware of itself as a fully modern and even scientific undertaking at the moment when it conceives of language as a force capable of exerting an ethical, that is, universal, influence on all human beings.

For its part, the inquiry into ethics has, for over 250 years, modernized itself by making the linguistic turn. At the dawn of the Enlightenment, it was beginning to be widely recognized that the ancient ethical questions—How ought one live? What is the good? What is the source of my sense of right and wrong? How do we know our duty? What is "imperative" in human life? Can there be ethical knowledge?—were having a difficult time finding answers that could command respect in a rationalist climate. Ethics is law; but what, and where, is the law? Why is a given principle credited with being "ethical," when others are characterized as "political," "self-interested," "pathological," or "ideological"? What mysterious warrant gives a given principle the kind of "overriding" force traditionally associated with ethics? Can ethical words be defined in nonethical terms? With so little evidence of the binding power of any principle worthy of the name of ethics, how can the legitimacy, much less the effectiveness, of the law be seriously asserted?

The specific version of these questions that challenged David Hume—with whom I will begin, in recognition of his direct influence on Kant—was, How do we know what is right if neither dogma, convention, nor reason tells us? Hume's way of addressing this imperious question announces an agenda through which ethical theory is still making its way, without yet arriving at "new business." In response, Hume attempted to construct not just a philosophy but a psychology, a sociology—and, most interestingly for our purposes, even a rudimentary linguistics. Since Hume, "progress" in the understanding of ethics has generally taken the form of disclosing an even deeper and more pervasive linguistic determination of the principles of ethics than had previously been supposed. A consensus on the intimate relation between language and ethics has not, however, produced agreement on the nature or content of the ethical law: the "ethics of language" do not crystallize in a single form. In fact, one of the most remarkable features of the linguistic turn in this field is the sheer variety of applications to which language can be put as an ethical agent. The narrowing of the search for the source of the law to the domain of language has resulted in an expansion rather than a contraction of the conception of the law itself, an expansion thoroughly in keeping with the generous and capacious spirit of Hume's thinking.

Hume was among the first to attempt to think through what had traditionally been conceived as metaphysical questions in modern, nonmetaphysical terms—the subtitle of his first book, *A Treatise of Human Nature* (1739–40) is *An attempt to introduce the experimental method of reasoning into moral subjects.* This method had no place for religious conviction, and accorded only a diminished role to reason, which Hume thought overrated. For Hume, reason was not the master of feelings or sensations, but only a diminished and moderated form of them. An understanding of morality had therefore to begin not with reason but with feelings, sentiments, and especially the primary and irreducible sensations of pain and pleasure, the true grounds of moral ideas. Such an approach—godless, atomistic, radically anti-idealist, empiricist, and utilitarian—was intended to sweep away all forms of dogmatism, piety, and intellectual mystification.

The method permitted no appeals to abstractions or idealizations. Hume was relentless in his pursuit of such theoretical fantasies, insisting in his more mature writings that our most cherished ideas, including that of a "self," are weak and ambiguous concepts, not facts, and had a tendency to blend in with other, similarly shapeless things. Impressions, on the other hand, have a bracing specificity: they are distinct from each other and distinct from ideas by virtue of their greater "vivacity." For Hume, if a thought or feeling is not grounded in an impression, it is not grounded at all. The cause-effect relation, for example, cannot actually be observed, and so must be considered a kind of cognitive-optical illusion that occurs whenever one thing regularly precedes and accompanies another, like the motion of a billiard ball that has been struck by another. Many of Hume's readers have questioned this point. Surely, they say, when we see someone open a letter from the IRS, and then see him cry out, it is difficult to say that we do not *see* the connection between the two. But Hume insists that the connection merely seems to be visible, and that the agency behind this seeming is nothing other than custom, "the great guide of human life. . . . Without the influence of custom, we should be entirely ignorant of every matter of fact beyond what is immediately present to the memory and senses" (1975: 5.1: 44–45).

Such realism had nothing to fear from contemporary science: no evidence of a "self" or a cause-effect "relation" was likely to emerge from some gentleman-scientist's laboratory. But it encountered difficulties on its own, philosophical terrain. Kant, for one, was mystified by the notion of the nonexistent self. All impressions, he said, had to belong to someone, and Hume's allowance for "unowned" impressions seemed curious. But the real problems arose in Hume's account of "moral sentiments," those feelings that captured the human sense of right and wrong.

While Hume might dismiss reason and theology with a shrug, he believed fervently in moral sentiments, which he described in the *Treatise* as natural, infallible, and automatic. He regarded as an indisputable fact that when we see a child harmed, we naturally and immediately condemn the harming action; and that if we witness an act of generosity or bravery, we automatically and rightly praise the act as virtuous. We do so not merely because the acts themselves are intrinsically worthy of blame or praise, but because of a powerful and universal feeling of "sympathy" whose spontaneous eruption within the human breast testifies to a common human moral endowment. As Hume put it, "The minds of all men are similar in their feelings and operations. . . . As in strings equally wound up the motion of one communicates itself to the rest; so all the affections readily pass from one person to another, and beget correspondent movements in every human creature" (2000: 3.3.1: 368). The pleasure we take in acts of virtue and the displeasure we experience in the presence of vice constitute, for Hume, directly observable evidence of the moral sentiments implanted by nature in the human breast, part of the original fabric and formation of the human mind.

But what about those occasions where the passage from the act to the sensation to the sentiment is interrupted, conflicted, confused, or simply erroneous? How could Hume celebrate the limitless freedom of the imagination, as he did, and still insist that it had no power to interfere with the production of appropriate moral sentiments (1975: 5.2: 47)? How is it that people of diverse characters in widely varying circumstances feel precisely the same moral sentiments? And how are people to receive any moral instruction? Is there no guide to the right other than our inconstant feelings?

These questions disturb the youthful assurance of the *Treatise*, and even motivate one of its most famous moments, a kind of tacked-on appendix to the case Hume makes against reason as the origin of moral distinctions. "I cannot," Hume remarks, "forbear adding to these reasonings an observation, which may, perhaps, be found of some importance. In every system of morality, which I have hitherto met with, I have always remark'd, that the author proceeds for some time in the ordinary way of reasoning, and establishes the being of a God, or makes observations concerning human affairs; when of a sudden, I am surpriz'd to find, that instead of the usual copulations of propositions, *is*, and *is not*, I meet with no proposition that is not connected with an *ought*, or *ought not*." The change is "imperceptible" but crucial, for since the *ought* expresses a new and different kind of relationship, "'tis necessary that it shou'd be observ'd and explain'd' and at the same time that a reason shou'd be given, for what seems altogether inconceivable, how this new relation can be a deduction from others, which are entirely different from it" (2000: 3.1.1: 302). Philosophers have always worried about this passage because it creates doubt about Hume's position on a key question, whether the passage from *is* to *ought* can ever be made by legitimate means. On one reading—the "standard interpretation"—he seems to deny that it can, but on another, he only expresses disappointment that those who make it do not spell out their reasoning more clearly (see Hudson). This is no small issue, for it reflects a larger uncertainty in the *Treatise* about the question of the *ought*, the imperative that guides us as if from above. Plainly, we feel the force of moral imperatives; but how, and why, since all moral sentiments are grounded in human nature itself?

Hume clearly felt that his treatment on this point was inadequate, because when, in 1751, he revised Book 3 of the *Treatise* ("Of Morals") by writing the *Enquiry concerning the Principles of Morals*, he introduced a new element into the discussion. He begins with a restatement of his position that the character of an action is determined by "some internal sense or feeling, which nature has made universal in the whole species" (1975: 1.1: 173). But, he adds, before instinct makes this determination, it must go through a process of establishing facts, making distinctions and comparisons, and drawing conclusions—a process, in short, of reasoning. This would seem to install reason at the heart of morality, and thereby compromise his case against reason; but in order to foreclose on this possibility, Hume asserts that "the very nature of language guides us almost infallibly" in making the crucial decisions. Since "every tongue possesses one set of words which are taken in a good sense, and another in the opposite, the least acquaintance with the idiom suffices, *without any reasoning*, to direct us in collecting and arranging the estimable or blameable qualities of men" (1975: 174; emphasis added). Since language use is natural and necessary for us, it should not be considered a rational process, and so, Hume suggests, we can receive moral guidance without benefit of reason.

With this conception of language in place, Hume can be said to have addressed his old problem, of how we pass from *is* to *ought*, a passage we make not by logical but by lexical means. The very nature of language, with its "sets" of words for vice and virtue, accomplishes the feat. To see is to think of the word, and thus to be led to the proper evaluation, and from thence to the brink of right action. If a given action elicits a "virtuous" description, then it *ought* to be performed or applauded. That little old lady *is* in need of assistance crossing the street; it would be *generous* and *kind* to assist her. Contemplating the prospect of such assistance gives us an immediately positive and pleasurable sensation. Therefore, one *ought* to give her a hand. Through the intermediate agency of language, we can tell what *ought* to be from a mere description of what *is*.

But other questions arise. Where does this "nature of language" come from? How can we say that human nature has all the answers to moral questions if, on occasion, it requires instruction and even correction by another kind of nature? The uncertain status of nature in Hume's discourse produces a pattern of equivocation that is highly uncharacteristic in this philosopher of plain common sense. He is systematically unclear, for example, on the relation between the nature of language, the nature of man, and nature in some larger sense. A typical invocation of this simplest and most elementary of principles creates insoluble logical problems, as in the following: "Had nature made no such distinction, founded on the original constitution of the mind, the words *honourable* and *shameful*, *lovely* and *odious*, *noble* and *despicable*, had never had place in any language" (2000: 5.1: 214). This seems a mere restatement of Locke, who says that "Nature, even in naming of Things, unawares suggested to Men the Originals and Principles of all their Knowledge" (Locke 1975: 3.1: 5). But Hume's point is actually far subtler, even to the point of obscurity. While Locke identifies language and nature, and places them both outside and prior to the human mind, Hume gives the human mind priority, and—vaguely, to be sure—suggests that nature and language follow on after, "founded" on the human mind. What Hume seems to be saying, unfolded to its full extent, is that the distinctions in the human mind must be made by nature, naturally, but then nature seems to take instruction from itself and create moral distinctions among qualities, which are then faithfully reflected in the nature of language, to which human beings can turn for instruction as to their own nature, which, as we know, was formed by nature.

The reason we need guidance is that human nature is naturally self-interested, and even the most amiable, sympathetic, and humane person thinks first of himself. The "natural" virtues remain properties of one's personal character and are not necessarily oriented toward the welfare of others. As a medium of social interaction, language is conformed to the general interests of mankind, as expressed in the "artificial" virtues whose systematic cultivation produces, for example, justice as opposed to benevolence. "General language," Hume says, is "formed for general use," and "must be moulded on some more general views" (1975: 5.2: 228). Still nature, but nature at its best, language guides individuals away from a limited construction of their own nature and toward a more spacious or universal conception, which, as Hume concedes in a labored passage in an appendix, is still "natural" (see 1975: Appendix 3: 307). To reinforce the "externality" of language, Hume on one occasion even says that language comes to "invent a peculiar set of terms, in order to express those universal sentiments of censure or approbation, which arise from humanity." Using these terms provided not by nature directly but invented by language, people disseminate moral concepts: "Virtue and Vice become then known; morals are recognized; certain general ideas are framed of human conduct and behaviour," and the general good is promoted (1975: 9.1: 274).

Without the support provided by language—the definitions of words in particular—Hume's argument would have little intellectual or emotional appeal, for he would have represented an essentially disjointed world in which the mind could only be guided by either instinct or etiquette. Situated between these two mighty forces, language gives the mind a legitimate role to play in determining its own nature and interpreting events in the world. But because Hume never works out a detailed theory of language, it is easy to underestimate how specific a notion of language and its operations he deploys, easy to miss the fact that he omits far more than he includes.

Hume's understanding of language anticipates Saussure's in being a means of communicating shared social knowledge. But it diverges sharply from Saussure—veers, indeed, in the direction of Chomsky—in that it claims the status of nature, and therefore of necessity, rather than being "arbitrary" and merely "conventional." Humean language is, however, distinct from both Saussure and Chomsky in that it provides explicit instruction in the moral law. But perhaps the most striking divergence of Hume from all modern linguists is that Hume never discusses sign systems, syntax, the larger semantic patternings, the social contexts of utterances, or indeed any more general or systemic characteristic of language. For Hume, the fundamental unit of language is the word, and the ethically significant aspect of the word is the "qualities" directly associated with it. Hume is actively hostile to the notion that evaluations can be confused, conflicted, combined, inconstant, misguided, or unconscious; and he is altogether insensitive to the ways in which a description can be, for example, both exact and ironic or precise and metaphorical. For Hume, it is essential that language provides people with an infallible guide, but the account of language he produces is so limited and reductive that it cannot be taken seriously today.

To his partial credit, Hume seems to understand this. Again in the spirit of Locke, who devoted a number of pages in his *Essay* to a discouraged accounting of the imperfections and abuses of language, Hume concludes his *Enquiry concerning the Principles of Morals* with yet another clarification, in which he takes up questions raised but not settled by his account of the nature of language. In a final appendix called "Of Some Verbal Disputes," he notes that the English language provides no absolutely precise way of demarcating virtues from talents, vices from defects: anything that could be described as a moral accomplishment could also, he concedes, be described as an organic condition, an aptitude, a lucky knack. From this small point a cascade of difficulties issues forth, as Hume considers the differences between social, intellectual, and moral virtues; between qualities of head and heart; between the voluntary and the involuntary. Faced with a proliferation of increasingly meaningless or misleading distinctions that suggest that language either has a mind of its own or no mind at all, Hume relinquishes the project of trying to establish the laws imprinted by nature in language. "Every one," he says, "may employ *terms* in what sense he pleases: but this, in the mean time, must be allowed, that *sentiments* are every day experienced of blame and praise." In the end, Hume resigns himself to the dispirited assertion that "it is of greater consequence to attend to things than to verbal appellations" (1975: 322).

At this point, Hume seems closer than ever to a position that could command respect in a modern context, the proposition that language is an arbitrary and artificial system of differences without positivity. But he seems miles away from himself, for he has demonstrated that a harder look at language's dizzying capacity to generate distinctions, categories, and nuances can produce confusion about key points, such as whether justice is or is not "natural." His terminal position, a dogged insistence on the primacy of "things," represents an abandonment of the revolutionary gesture with which he had begun, a completion of the linguistic turn back to the starting point.

Hume's late retraction notwithstanding, his suggestion that individual "ethical" words provide a guide to morals stands as one of his most enduring contributions, and threads together schools of thought commonly held to be widely divergent, even opposed. The demystifying presumption that words rather than abstract concepts are the key to ethical understanding governs Bentham's utilitarianism (which begins with an examination of such terms as *good, right, duty,* and *obligation*); and, in the twentieth century, it can be traced in both intuitionism as articulated by G. E. Moore (who argued that "good" was, like "yellow," an objective judgment on a nonnatural and "simple" quality) and its opposite number, emotivism, as elaborated in the work of such figures as Carnap, A. J. Ayer, and Charles Stevenson.

According to the emotivists, "moral language" constituted a special subset of words distinguished for its affective or emotional content—useful for exhortation or the expression of attitudes, but not for science or even description. The most influential emotivist at mid-century was R. M. Hare, who approached the analysis of "moral language" with a refinement Hume never imagined. Hare focused on the logic of "modal imperatives," the distinctions between beliefs and values, and the difference between prescriptive and descriptive language, in an effort to determine the nature of ethical obligation. In Hare, the empirical method yields the conclusion that all value judgments—all uses of such terms as *ought, should,* and *good*—have a prescriptive component, and seek to influence individual acts of decision. Thus Hume is relieved of his uncertainties through the addition of several supplementary arguments: that the determination of facts precedes, and is distinct from, evaluations; that evaluative decisions are always underdetermined by the arguments; and that, in a truly rigorous argument, no *ought* can possibly follow from an *is.*

In retrospect, it is apparent that Hume's hesitations, self-corrections, and ambiguities give evidence of a subtler mind than his successors. The mechanistic quality of Hare's distinction between prescriptive and evaluative words on the one hand and descriptive, nonevaluative words on the other has become all too clear. The critical reaction to Hare has taken the form of demonstrating that this distinction does not hold, and that when, for example, we call a firefighter who saves the lives of others at the risk of his own *brave*, we are stating fact and value at once (see MacIntyre 1966: 249–72). If values were distinct from facts, Hare's critics have pointed out, then any principle that answered to an individual's feeling or sentiment could claim to be "moral," even if it were silly, unfounded, or pernicious. With Hare as its leading proponent, the entire project of poring over individual words for keys to moral understanding labored under two burdens: first, by relegating moral language to the realm of the emotions, such an approach discounted the role of reason, or the giving of reasons, in ethical deliberation; and second, with respect to the rest of language, it asserted an indefensible proposition, that "nonmoral" language has no affective or emotional component, no element that might, in the right circumstances, become "prescriptive." From the standpoint of the present day, the entire episode seems to invite not a philosophical but a historico-cultural analysis, as one salient in the ongoing English battle to surround and control emotion, passion, or affect, to demarcate the space in which these can exist so the rest can be counted on for a brisk and manly disinterestedness. The fact that Hare wrote during the era of Rex Harrison's portrayal of Prof. Henry Higgins in *My Fair Lady* might not be altogether without explanatory power.

Even among those who reject emotivism, however—and, strikingly, even among those who are unpersuaded of the value of the linguistic turn in ethics—the interrogation of the ethical properties of words has remained a compelling philosophical project. Alasdair MacIntyre's long career has taken the form of a keening for the lost "moral vocabulary" of the classical era (with the difference that he seeks to promote the moral principles not of Aristotle but of Augustine), and a condemnation of the "acids of individualism," which have corroded that vocabulary and made it incoherent in today's world (MacIntyre 1966: 266; see also MacIntyre 1981, 1988). MacIntyre has little use for modern analytic philosophy, and rejects contemporary ethical theory as a symptom of philosophical and even cultural degeneracy. Still, he finds himself turning to language, and to the definitions of words, in order to measure the losses incurred by modernity.

A less doctrinal and polemical thinker than MacIntyre, Bernard Williams rejects in even more explicit terms the abstractions and simplifications of the linguistic turn. A chapter on this subject in *Ethics and the Limits of Philosophy* is unequivocally critical of the tendency to reduce an ethical inquiry that threatens to be unmanageable and profound to a more tractable set of linguistic issues. Moore, Hare, and others who take the fateful turn all reveal, to Williams's cosmopolitan eye, an academic narrow-mindedness and timidity. The attempt to segregate *is* from *ought*, prescription from description, or evaluation from fact produces, he says, both bad moral theory and bad linguistic philosophy. Things are not so neat, and in order to grasp the complexity and specificity of ethics, we must apply "social" rather than linguistic explanations.

This is an interesting argument, but far more interesting is Williams's next step, which constitutes the primary contribution of his book, to concentrate attention not directly on society, but on a set of " 'thicker' or more specific ethical notions . . . such as *treachery* and *promise* and *brutality* and *courage*, which seem to express a union of fact and value" (129). Such words seem to leap the fact-value divide because they contain in a complex unity both components, neither one of which dominates the other. The presence of such terms in a society's lexicon suggests a sediment of concrete social evaluation, and therefore an integrated society that knows what it's about and has coded that knowledge in the language it makes available to all people in the group. If, for Hare, moral words were distinguished by a prescriptive hardness that reflected the imperative quality of moral judgment, for Williams, it is the blurred or equivocal quality of words that yields the secret of ethics. While Hare proceeds by the autobahn of logic, Williams proceeds by the footpaths of social understandings.

But the most striking aspect of Williams's undertaking is that he has rejected neither the linguistic turn in general nor the focus on "the use of words" that he had specifically attacked (Williams 121). He has simply proposed another set of words than the ones other philosophers had studied. Others had proposed to study ethics by focusing on words; Williams proposes to study ethics by studying society—by focusing on words. We are, with Williams, no closer to ethics "itself" than we are in the laboratories of the emotivists. Indeed, we might be farther than ever from an understanding of the lawlike or "universal" character of ethical intuitions on which Hare had insisted. For by concentrating on "social understanding," Williams restricts himself to the implied evaluative judgments of a given linguistic culture, and discourages or distracts attention from any truly universal aspect of language, such as the fact with which Chomsky begins, that human beings are all linguistic, or the hypothesis Chomsky extracts from that fact, that human languages share some kind of universal grammar. In short, Williams continues a tradition he deplores, the concentration on definitions, and thwarts a promising area it seems he should support, the inquiry into linguistic universals.

In fact, Williams has radically undersold the case for an ethics based on language by suggesting that only a few words can claim ethical thickness, where a more capacious approach might have posited thickness as a quality of language itself. In so doing, he has ignored countless available facts about language and its use, and has projected onto what Hume called "the nature of language" a habit of thinking in terms of villages within kingdoms, islands within seas. The result, in terms of ethical theory, is an ethics without the requisite muscle to account for the common experience of difficulty in arriving at ethical decisions in cases where custom does not guide, guides in multiple directions, or guides in ways we cannot square with our deeper sense of the right. In order to understand this aspect of ethical intuition and ethical decision-making, other aspects of language must be enlisted, and for this we must return to the Enlightenment tradition, but to Kant rather than Hume.

2. Language as Law

On the Kantian "Maxim"

Kant's critique of ethical or "pure practical" reasoning has overpowered that of Hume and others in the history of ethical philosophy in part because its main concept is dominance itself. For Kant, ethics centers on the idea of law, of an overriding imperative that cannot be denied. From the Kantian point of view, the heart (or brain) of ethics is a transcendent *ought* that emerges not from any consensus produced by the disorderly processes of history or culture, and not from what Hume called nature, but from within reason. For Kant, the essence of the right was reason, which human beings could comprehend and to which they are obligated because they are rational creatures. Such an approach would seem to lead away from language, the medium of social interaction, and toward some more "inhuman" principle of law. In fact, however, language has proven to be immensely useful to thinkers who try to identify some worldly ground for the otherwise abstract and disembodied concept of the rational law. The task that now confronts us is, then, to try to articulate the implicit theory of language held by thinkers who have looked to language not for guidance on the law, but for the law itself—who have, that is, found in language the social and psychological site of the ethical imperative.

A tougher bird than Hume in every respect, Kant rejects the Humean premises that the kernel of morality was human sympathy, that morality consisted of "sentiments" or feelings, that morality derived from man's natural inclination to sociability, and that the empirical method was in any way appropriate to the study of morality. For Kant, the foundation of morals is metaphysical, and is based on the fact of human autonomy, the capacity for exercising a free will. Accordingly, his account of the operations of practical reason begins with the primacy of the rational will over psychology, theology, or what he called "anthropology." If ethical thinking becomes modern by taking the linguistic turn, then Kant's ethics are not, by this measure, fully modern. But language does play a role on the margins of Kant's ethical thinking, and attention to the margins will disclose an unexpectedly large role for language. This role, properly understood, will then help to account for the immense influence of Kant over subsequent forms of modernity.

How does the rational will become effective in the world? How do we, with our weak and confused little minds, know the dictates of reason? How does reason engage with experience and sense-perceptions? If reason is untainted by ordinary human impulses or desires, how does it communicate in a way that we, sunk in our ordinariness, can understand? How do we assess the moral quality of our actions in this contingent world? How, in short, can *pure reason* be *practical*, that is, ethical? The answer to all such questions begins with a single word: maxims.

Free from the uncontrollable or "pathological" surges that bother the other parts of the human being, the rational will is free to give itself the law, to judge freely and without external influence. Its judgments can therefore be tested by means of the categorical imperative: a given act qualifies as moral if and only if a rational person could wish that the maxim governing the action were made compulsory for all. In other words, the test of whether the rational will has given itself the law, or whether some lower or more contingent appetite or interest has intruded, is that the dictates of the rational will constitute a general law that ought to be followed by everyone who finds themselves in similar circumstances. Some practices that appear to produce good results would, if followed universally, produce disastrous consequences. If, to take the classic Kantian example, everyone lied to secure his own advantage, then all faith in utterances would be destroyed, and that would be bad for everyone, including liars. But how can we know what law we've followed, and how can we communicate this law to the others who might be guided by it? The initial formulation of the categorical imperative gives us the answer: "*Act as if the maxim of your action were to become by your will a general law of nature*" (Kant 1977: 170). We are not, in other words, concerned with actions themselves, but rather with maxims.

What is a maxim? As Kant says in a footnote, a maxim is "the subjective principle of volition" (1977: 148 n). It is distinct from the law itself, which he defines as the objective principle of volition, because it is interior to the subject. A maxim is an objectively true statement about a subjective disposition, an accurate representation of an inner motivation. A maxim is in a sense impersonal, since it represents not the individual's self-awareness but the absolute truth of the motive, the inner quality of the action itself. Maxims are essential, for they make it possible to distinguish right things done for the right reason from right things done for the wrong reason, which are, in a sense, even worse than wrong things done for the right reason. The moral character of any worthy action is, after all, determined not by the action itself but by the motive. If, for example, you conducted your business fairly, charging the same price to a child as to an experienced adult, but did so not because you cherished the ideas of honesty and fairness but merely because it would be bad for business if your cheating were made known to the public, you would rightly be judged an untrustworthy cynic. Even though your action was honorable, the maxim of your action would reveal your true character and the character of the act. The maxim reaches deep into the principle of action, even deeper, in fact, than your own reflection might take you. If you thought you were behaving honorably but were, unknown to yourself, secretly making calculations, the maxim would disclose that fact. Maxims represent, in effect, the account you would blurt out under the influence of a truth serum.

Reason, Kant understands, must suffer a kind of Passion in which it descends from its realm of pure form into a modality capable of work in the world. Without such a self-translation, reason has no point of contact with experience and the senses, and drifts off in airy inconsequence. Language, in the dual forms of objective law and subjective maxims, saves reason from this fate. The implied idea of language behind the maxim seems to be that language speaks originally the truth, that the primary and essential function of language is to represent accurately and honestly, to carry the truth from one mind to another—or, in the specific case of a maxim, from the heart of action itself to the public arena. Kant is aware, even hyper-aware, of the possibility of dishonest uses of language, and spends a good deal of energy worrying about lying and other forms of verbal duplicity (see Kant 1993). But the maxim represents what seems to be a normative use of language in being concerned with intellectual truth and not with individual expression or intention.

The operative concept appears, in other words, to be that of a language of primordial transparency, untouched by historical contingency or by what Saussure would call arbitrariness, a language purged of the errors, defects, and abuses that had so concerned Locke and Hume. Kant seems, too, to be setting aside the critique of language in the 1746 *Essai sur l'origine des connaissances humaines* by the Abbé de Condillac, who raised the issue of linguistic arbitrariness, inquired into the origin and development of languages (plural), and emphasized the volitional character of language use. By attributing to language a power to determine thought, Condillac initiated a line of inquiry that was to be extended by von Humboldt, Herder, Max Müller, Ernst Renan, and many others for whom language was the surest indicator of a national, cultural, or ideological character. It was in the climate of such thinking on language, indeed, that Hegel proposed to complete the work of Kant by incorporating into the theory of ethics the role of the State and the historically determined Spirit of the People. When Hegel declared that, "*What is rational is actual and what is actual is rational*," he sought, in essence, to deflect attention away from an ideal and perfectly transparent Language—the necessary linguistic form of maxims—and toward contingent, variable, and imperfect languages (Hegel 1967: 10). The critique Kant set aside was eventually in a position to set aside Kant himself.

Kant may have failed to develop his theory of language because he felt that the reliance of reason on language was something of an embarrassment that would only get worse the more he said. The evolutionary or historical approach that would eventually dominate linguistic discussion in the nineteenth century and beyond rendered the nonideal and even nonsensical features of natural languages even more apparent (see Harris and Taylor 126–38). But for others who came after Kant, the ethical law was not determined by reason alone, and the relation between language and the law did not necessarily constitute a theoretical or ethical impurity. For some of these thinkers, in fact, the thought that the law was determined or conditioned by language awakened the exciting possibility that the law might actually be "irrational" without ceasing to be the law. And this, while hardly what Kant had in mind when he introduced the maxim into his account of the categorical imperative, has proven to be the more durable and adaptable form of the argument about the law as language.

The Irrational Law: Nietzsche, Levinas, Deconstruction

Ethical imperatives are compelling mental events. Trying to account for their extraordinary force, Kant had described ethical intuitions as having a mechanical or even mathematical quality that announced their impersonal origins, their derivation from reason. Nietzsche, by contrast, trained his relentlessly skeptical eye on questions of origin and value, which he addressed by a highly speculative "genealogical" method that held nothing sacred, certainly not reason. He began, that is, with the feeling of compulsion and nonnegotiability associated with ethical judgments and worked backward, trying to explain where such judgments came from, how they acquired their distinctive impersonality and force, and what interests they continued to serve. What *is* the conscience? Why do we approve *morally* of some things and not others? What are the psychological, political, and anthropological origins of the sense of law that forms our conscience?

His answers to these questions were startlingly similar to the ones Freud would propose little more than a generation later. Nietzsche's account of the content of the conscience as "everything that was during the years of our childhood regularly *demanded* of us without reason by people we honoured or feared," for example, anticipated Freud with an uncanny exactitude (Nietzsche 1996: #52). But radical differences divide the two thinkers. Freud held the human mind to be constant and unalterable in its basic structure, whereas Nietzsche believed that it was in a state of continual alteration, changing in response to external pressures. Nietzsche actually holds mind as such to be something of small consequence in comparison with the animal or organic determinants of human nature, including a ceaseless quest for mastery and self-preservation, and the ongoing effort to avoid pain. In fact, the role of mind, for Nietzsche, consisted largely in concealing its own irrelevance and impotence, the admission of which would represent both an intolerable confession and a damaging principle of ineffectiveness or inefficiency as the organism made its way in the world. And while Freud became convinced that the road to health lay through the analysis of recovered memories, Nietzsche argued precisely the opposite, that health depended upon forgetting.

Such divergent theories of mind reflect differing understandings of language. For Freud, language is less interesting for the concepts represented by it than for the words themselves, which present a matchless analytical and therapeutic opportunity. As I will argue in greater detail below, the Freudian account of the mind and the role of the analyst hinges on the emancipatory effect of true or undistorted speech. Nietzsche's hostility to this and related notions is difficult to overstate, since a very great portion of his philosophical activity takes the form of rejecting them.

He posits, first, a will to falsehood behind linguistic production. The "fundamental human drive," he says, is "the drive toward the formation of metaphors" (1979: 88). By "metaphor," Nietzsche means not only fanciful figures of speech, but also the preliminary business of attaching a nerve stimulus to an image and then imitating the image by means of a sound, the result being a "word." This doubly false unit is then combined in arbitrary and illogical ways with others in order to produce concepts, which can then be arranged into structures that achieve an appearance of schematic rationality by thoroughly damping down the "vivid first impressions." The totality of language is nothing more than a massive heap of dead husks of metaphors animated not by a wish to represent reality but by a passionate desire to return to some primal fantasy, "to refashion the world which presents itself to waking man, so that it will be as colorful, irregular . . . charming and eternally new as the world of dreams" (1979: 89).

Add to this inspired account of language a virtually biological demand by the human organism for self-esteem, a demand that requires the continual production of more metaphors and even outright lies, and you are prepared for Nietzsche's arguments on the origin of moral sensations. In the orgy of short-term self-interest that defines the state of nature, ethical imperatives, Nietzsche says, take root in pain: the sun, soil, and water of ethics is bodily punishment. Even the most primitive societies saw to it that those who cheated or injured others were punished, an eye for an eye. After countless aeons of such punishment, the evolving human mind finally began to germinate a mental faculty by which it could regulate itself and thereby avoid more punishment. Gradually, human beings acquired the capacity to make promises and keep them; and finally, they developed the feeling that laws should be obeyed not because of the consequences of breaking them, but because they are reasonable and right. Thereafter, "conscience" becomes a stern and watchful overseer of action and even of thought. We cannot, of course, admit to ourselves that the basis of conscience is fear, any more than a society can afford to state openly that its laws and customs constitute not guides to right conduct, but threats. And so a constant pressure is exerted all around to repress the truth about the genealogy of morals.

This pressure is applied on and through language, which is both agent and effect of an overdetermined will to falsehood. When evaluations come to appear as facts, when adjectives dissolve into nouns, force has faded to black. When things have reached the state Hume described, in which the very nature of language appears to inform us what is good and evil, then power (Nietzsche would say) has managed to conceal its operations by disappearing into nomenclature, a perfect ethical evaporation. Nietzsche directs us to the history of this process of linguistic deceit and cover-up as the very essence of ethics itself, with etymology becoming an exciting, if often mistaken, means of historical detection. The various signs for "good," for example, all lead back to an identical "*conceptual transformation*," in which terms originally associated with nobility or aristocracy become disconnected from the ruling power, generalized, and set in opposition to terms that once meant simply "common" or "plebian," but which come to stand for "bad" in a broader and more fundamental sense (1969: 4). Power becomes morality in language, especially in those terms that Bernard Williams described as ethically "thick," both "world-guided" and "action-guiding." In fact, the most telling criticism of Williams is that he discovers ethics in precisely the same place as Nietzsche, in complex words—but that, unlike Nietzsche, he discounts the factors of self-interest, a will to deceit, an active desire to forget the truth, and power in the production of those words.

The "slave revolt in morals" also takes linguistic form, when the opposition good/bad is replaced with that of good/evil, with reversed referents, so that the nobility, once decisively on the "good" side of things, become recast as the "evil" ones, their place being taken by the former underclass. "Wherever slave morality comes to predominate," Nietzsche says, "language exhibits a tendency to bring the words 'good' and 'stupid' closer to each other" (1973: 260). In all cases, and at all times, language is where power goes to die, or rather to enter a kind of witness protection program, assuming a false identity that will enable it to live, perhaps forever, a mere innocuous, uncontroversial—and therefore incontrovertible, short of another revolution—fact. Against the drift of language, Nietzsche insists that *"there are no moral facts whatever,"* only interpretations, and misinterpretations at that (1968: 55–66).

Nietzschean language is not just a lie, but a means of inhibiting thought. From the point of view of morals, the chief utility of language is that it discourages critical reflection; as Hume almost said, it encourages us in the mistaken belief that we can obtain the truth "without any reasoning" (or as Nietzsche would say, "stupidly"). The most profound and disturbing truth posited by Nietzsche is that nobody is truly accountable in a moral sense, for we only do what our nature and circumstances dictate. It is only through "the seduction of language (and of the fundamental errors of reason that are petrified in it)" that we come to believe in a distinction, especially favorable to those who are weak and whose impulses are resistible, between action and agent. This distinction "doubles the deed," so that we say, for example, "the lightning flashed," suggesting that the lightning was independent of its flashing, and therefore that it was free to flash or not (1969: 45). In the same way, people are encouraged, even compelled, to think of themselves as free and accountable so that their actions come to appear morally assessable. Morality is thus the consequence of what Whorf—who used precisely the same example, of a flash of light—called "fictional entities" arising within grammar (Whorf 243). And with this thought in place, we can begin to understand how mere degraded slaves, thinking linguistically, could imagine that reality favored their cause, and could therefore mount a "slave revolution" in the name of a "higher imperative"; indeed, we can even begin to work through a persistent problem in Nietzsche's version of history and even prehistory, of how it can be that "the weak" invariably defeat "the strong." With no less a force than grammar working for them, the weak scarcely need God on their side in order to be invincible.

Certain features of the idea of language have long been attractive to ethical philosophers. Both language and ethics have been represented as counterinstinctual, something animals are incapable of, and yet at the same time as "natural" to human beings; both involve representation and judgment; and both are said to involve the exercise of freedom in a framework of custom, regularity, and law. Nietzsche exploited all these affiliations, but he also promoted a view of ethics that entailed a specific and controversial account of language.

This account had not yet been formulated because Saussure had not yet thought of it. And yet, when once Nietzsche has chronicled the "tyranny of arbitrary laws" in moral thinking, when he has detailed the systematic and interlocking character of moral evaluations, when he has described morality as an historical phenomenon that produces at any given moment an apparently ahistorical system, when he has labeled morality as mere "*semeiotics*"— when all this has been done, all that remains for Saussure to do is to gather these elements together and to label the whole business "general linguistics" (Nietzsche 1973: 188; 1968: 55).

Language represents, for Nietzsche, the subtle tool of brute force, the rational face of an irrational law. For Emmanuel Levinas, too, language discloses an ethical law that cannot be reduced to rationality; but Levinas has a higher opinion of both irrationality and the law than Nietzsche. For him, the ethical law is itself ethical: it is not imposed by force, and cannot be described as "arbitrary." The Levinasian law is rigorous, to be sure, but it is also right. Grounding this law becomes, for Levinas, a matter of ethical as well as theoretical urgency.

A Talmudic scholar who came to France from Lithuania in the 1920s, Levinas became highly, if improbably, influential in French avant-garde philosophy from the 1960s to the 1980s. Many found in his thinking weapons with which to attack the pretensions of rationalism and of philosophy itself. For those who felt that philosophy had lost its way in the labyrinths of linguistic details, and had become perversely obsessed with issues of knowledge, Levinas provided a stirring alternative. He pried ethics loose from philosophy, which had tried since the classical era to master it and claim it for its own; and he attempted to restore ethics to what he held to be its former and rightful place above and before philosophy. Ethics was, he insisted, a "first philosophy," an experience that preceded understanding, self-knowledge, ontology, metaphysics—preceded everything, in fact, that the Hellenistic tradition had held to be fundamental to human existence. At the very heart of the ethical experience, Levinas placed the stark encounter not between mind and text, or even between the subject and the moral law stated in abstract terms, but between the subject and the "face of the other." The attempt to undermine philosophy and elevate ethics begins, in short, with the demotion of language and the promotion of the face.

The purity and almost hallucinatory intensity of Levinas's account of ethical obligation set him apart not only from the Greeks, but from virtually all the main traditions of philosophical ethics. He rejects a Kantian rationality as too intellectualized and inhuman to account for the ethical experience. He rejects, too, any neo-Hegelian definition of ethics that refers to customs, traditions, legal codes, or historically evolved communities. He implicitly opposes the analytical orientation in philosophy, for he regards the logical dimension of language not as an index of the law but as a distraction. Almost deliberately archaic, he has no affinity with the self-consciously "modern"—secular, formal, and cognitive—ethics of Habermas, whose emphasis on a consensual "mutual understanding," as detailed below, would have struck Levinas as far too nontraumatic to be considered ethical at all. For Levinas, virtually everything that philosophers have said about ethics is more or less beside the point—needlessly complex at best and complicit with evil at worst. Ethics, he insists, is really very simple: it happens not in an "exchange," not in a negotiation between like subjects, not in a group, not through the rational exercise of free will. It happens in common encounters between A and B in which A experiences an asymmetrical and infinite obligation, a command to which there is no proper response except, "After you, sir."

Although writing in what might be called the genre of philosophy, Levinas does not see himself as a philosopher at all, a point that emerged with great force in an exchange with his most eminent admirer, a youthful Derrida, who, in the course of a complex and extended appreciation, argued that philosophy and linguistic rationality were not, and should not be, so easily abandoned. Sympathetic to Levinas's distrust of the classical equation of language with thought, and to his critique of the pretensions of a "violent" and overmastering rationalism, Derrida still felt that Levinas had exceeded his warrant by simply opposing a Jewish tradition to a Greek one, as if philosophy could be transcended by concentrating on the pure "alterity" of the face. Instead, Derrida wrote, we must "become classical once more," and return to the well of philosophy for another kind of critique that does not depend on ecstatic dreams of thought without language, or of ethics beyond the law (1978b: 151). Indifferent to the career-making compliment paid to him by Derrida's long and influential essay, Levinas wrote a bristling and intransigent reply, insisting that *"Not to philosophize would not be 'to philosophize still'"* (1989b: 186).

But despite Levinas's complaints about the roles assigned to language in classical and modern philosophy, he has an even more profound antipathy to images. More specifically, he opposes the philosophical tradition of associating intellectual mastery with clarity, light, and illumination, all of which are, for him, seductions to be resisted. "Vision," he writes, "is essentially an adequation of exteriority with interiority," an adequation that is altogether illusory, since "the exteriority of discourse cannot be converted into interiority" (1969: 295). In *Downcast Eyes*, Martin Jay places Levinas firmly in the context of a powerful "anti-ocular" disposition that swept across the modern and postmodern French intellectual scene. If, for both classical and Enlightenment philosophy, thoughts were regarded as fully "present" to the mind without mediation, as if they could be "seen," for more recent French thinking, Jay writes, mediation was inescapable; and language, as the primary mode of mediation, assumed new significance as the object of thinking itself.

Levinas's hostility to vision and visuality does place him in the anti-ocular milieu. But he was always a foreigner in France, and shared few of the presuppositions of his contemporaries. His warmly appreciative references to women's "modesty" and "fecundity," not to mention his recommendation of religious ritual as a model of practical action, did not resonate widely in the postmodernist scene. His version of anti-ocularism did not involve a new emphasis on language, nor did he join his contemporaries in celebrating writing in particular or antifoundationalism in general. His objection to images was religious; he insisted that the ban on images was "truly the supreme command of monotheism" (1989d: 141). Still, because he opposed ethics to philosophy, and joined in the denigration of the ocular tradition, he was understood by those with whom he had little else in common, including Derrida, Jean-François Lyotard, Luce Irigaray, and others, to be an intellectual hero, the very conscience of postmodernity (see Irigaray 1986 and 1991; Cohen; Lyotard 1986; Derrida 1978b: 79-153, and 1992).

The differences that remain between Levinas and his admirers converge on the face, which cannot be conceived in an anti-ocular spirit. But the face also marks the point where Levinas differs from himself, the point where the ban on images confronts the denigration of knowledge and rationality and battles it to a standoff. We can observe this mighty struggle from a safe distance in Levinas's effort to describe a paradigmatically "ethical" confrontation in the meeting of Moses and God in Exodus 33, in which God, his back turned, issues a verbal command, neither expecting nor receiving a rejoinder (1989e: 204). Here, Levinas—or rather God—circumvents the problems associated with the imagistic quality of the face by turning away, denying Moses the full-frontal vision of the divine. While "the true essence of man is presented in his face," Levinas comments, it is also the case that "the truth of being is not the *image* of being" (1969: 290, 291).

All the emphasis is on the command, which humbles Moses and awakens him to the "trauma of a fission of the self" (1989b: 186). Levinas is a psycho-analytical as well as a religious thinker, and his fundamental insight, the one that accords most closely with the received wisdom of postmodernity, is that the subject is predisposed to alterity because it is rent by a gaping wound, a radical otherness within. The ethically productive form of this wound occurs whenever we receive a message without distortion or self-interest, or when we speak in a spirit of openness, responsiveness, and nonviolence—when, in other words, our orientation to speech is determined not by our own needs but by the needs of the other. And so the face (including, presumably, the ears), initially advanced as superior to the rational discourse of philosophy, becomes reduced to a mechanism for the production and reception of language.

Can language be somehow purged of rhetoric, false rationality, distraction, narcissism? Can we somehow imagine, and perhaps work toward, a language that would create an ethical imperative without residue, a language of pure naming and command? Levinas seems to believe that we can, but he has an extraordinarily difficult time expunging, even in theory, language's many impurities. Take, for example, his distinction between "saying" and "the said." Levinas much prefers the former, which seems to represent receptive exposure, to the latter, which represents defensive closure, the insulation of the self-mastering subject in all its assertive nonreceptivity. Levinas describes *saying* as "ethical sincerity insofar as it is exposition. As such, this saying is irreducible to the ontological definability of the *said*. Saying is what makes the self-exposure of sincerity possible; it is a way of giving everything, of not keeping anything for oneself" (Levinas and Kearney 28). But as all *sayings* must produce, as a by-product, a *said*, any linguistic practice that seeks to be ethical must commit itself to a continual self-cancellation, an "alternating rhythm of the said and the unsaid, and the unsaid being unsaid in its turn" (1989b: 186). Ethics is easier said than done, but the said itself requires an unsaying, which in turn produces another said, which must then be unsaid, or undone. Beginning with an opposition as clear as that between inside and outside, Levinas edges toward the figure of a Möbius strip.

It is, in fact, fascinating to observe the brilliant clarity of Levinas's linguistic distinctions suffer, one after the other, the same twisting and blending fate. In his major work *Totality and Infinity* (1961), for example, Levinas distinguishes an ethically dubious "expressive function" of language from a more honorable "revealing function" (1969: 73). But as Levinas works on this distinction, it becomes apparent that revealing suggests a visual display, which both violates the taboo on images and reduces things to mere intelligibility and coherence. When this happens, the figure of the other, who, in its absolute singularity, has not been so reduced, begins to look "irrational" by comparison with revealing images, and so a language oriented toward revealing actually works against the authentic other—"a curious result," Levinas notes, in which "language would consist of suppressing the other, in making the other agree with the same!" (1969: 73).

Levinas's distinctions wobble most revealingly when he turns to art, a subject on which he is both decisive and ambivalent. He read Proust as a student in the 1920s in the company of a fellow student, Maurice Blanchot, and this powerful experience disturbed the imposing regularity of his thought for decades afterward. In a 1947 essay on "The Other in Proust," Levinas discovered an ingenious way of honoring both Proust and God, arguing that his own ethics found expression in Proust's amorality. The key was Marcel's subjective indeterminacy, which bestows on the objects of his thought something like the quality of a *saying*—"a scintillating sense of possibility undulled by definition. One would have thought," Levinas commented, "that moral laws rid the world of such glittering extravaganzas more rigorously than natural laws and that magic begins, like a witches' sabbath, where ethics leave off." But no; the very failure of Marcel's love for Albertine ("Tomorrow he will break with the young woman who bores him") perfectly suggests the essence of love as nongrasping and nonappropriative, as commitment to what must remain other (1989c: 162). Through a thematic emphasis on discontinuity in the form of romantic *ennui*, the particular work of art could, Levinas suggests, detach itself from the general category of aesthetics and provide an ethical exemplum—another "curious result."

The enthusiasm for Proust represents one more occasion on which Levinas works himself into a conflict with his own commitments. In *Totality and*

Infinity, he allows for no such exceptions to the ban on aesthetic pleasure, which he elsewhere pronounces a trap for the gaze, even "a descent of the night, an invasion of shadow" (1989d: 131, 132). With good reason, he argues, are Jews compelled to renounce the idolatrous image, for, compared to art, the "work of language"—the work of separation and exteriority—"is totally different" (1969: 74). But at other times, he finds himself turning to qualities of the aesthetic as the best way of disturbing the reign of rationality and imposing that of the face. In a 1966 essay on Blanchot himself, he describes "inspiration" as an infinitely valuable interruption in reason, a "foreign interference in human causality," "a delirium more profound than thought," even an "anarchy" that destabilizes the self and awakens it to a force prior to and more powerful than the ego (1989f: 151). Linked with "obsession," anarchy is pitted, in Levinas's highly abstract and almost figural discourse, against reductive consciousness. But of course, as Levinas recognizes, anarchy by itself possesses no ethical value whatsoever; its good effect is limited to those instances in which it does not appear in pure form but is merely "signaled in consciousness," so that it does not "reign in its own way." In a footnote to this contorted argument, he adds that "the anarchical is possible only when contested by language, which betrays, but conveys, its anarchy, without abolishing it, by an abuse of language" (1989f: 119 n).

Thus the entire ethical effect of language hinges on a betrayal, an abuse. In such compacted, indeed conflicted moments, we see Levinas struggling to bring into alignment the various desires that structure his understanding of the ethical law. Rejecting the misleading clarity of images and of understanding modeled on visual perception, he had turned to language as the worldly site and medium of the ethical obligation. He discovered numerous functions, facets, and features of language that had the effect of imposing or installing the ethical, but found all these immured in a stubbornly nonethical mass of logic, adequation, predication, display, and so forth. For this reason, he could not consider language a pure good, for its ethical dimension was always compromised by the rest. He never succeeded in isolating, even in theory, a purely ethical aspect, component, or feature of language, and as a consequence his account of ethics, which aspired above all else to be simple, remained obscure, conflicted, irreducibly complex.

Does this situation reflect an avoidable failure of rigor? Could Levinas have produced a more self-consistent and encouraging account of language if he had studied the history of languages more deeply, pursued etymology more thoroughly, taken a course in general theoretical linguistics? Obviously not. Levinas does not get the facts of language wrong, he just underestimates the number of such facts. Whatever claims can be made about some of language's aspects, functions, or characteristics, opposite claims can be made to negate them. What I have been discussing as internal conflict or contradiction in Levinas's texts could also be characterized as a measure of Levinas's intellectual integrity, an indicator of his unwillingness to suppress his recognition of language's immensity merely because it would serve his purposes to do so. Registering contradictions, crossing his own tracks, undoing or unsaying his own distinctions, Levinas does not so much succumb to confusion as he bears honorable—one might even say ethical—witness to the real irreducibility of language, and thus to the impossibility of making the kind of case he wants to make.

One way forward, in a theoretical sense, might be simply to give up the task of trying to establish clear and rigorous distinctions between the functions or attributes of language, and simply to accept a principle of linguistic infinity, thereby shedding, almost without effort, a history of error. This is one way of describing the founding gesture of Derridean deconstruction. In the Anglo-American community that discovered him in the early 1970s, Derrida was initially seen as an exuberant herald of the limitlessness of language, the impossibility of stabilizing the mighty force of linguistic dissemination, the jubilant surrender of all principles of containment. For this reason, he was often regarded as a skeptical opponent of the very concept of ethics itself, which he had in fact identified as a repressive force. Thus in attacking Derrida, many felt that they were not simply arguing for one principle of ethics as opposed to another, but for the very idea or possibility of ethics as opposed to none. What only gradually became apparent was that deconstruction began as a meditation on ethics and developed its key concepts and fought its battles in all-but-ethical terms—and this before it ultimately came to grief on the rocks of an ethical crisis.

What his early readers saw in Derrida was a dauntingly complex argument in which ethics functioned as one of the key elements of "logocentrism," a set of distinctions (presence-absence, immediate-belated, interior-exterior, central-marginal, natural-perverted, primary-secondary, life-death, ideal-material) that had been employed in the description of language for so long that they were no longer arguments but premises, the bedrock of philosophical common sense. This bedrock typically became visible, Derrida showed, when the discussion of language turned to writing, which was consistently affiliated with the second of the two paired terms while speech was linked to the first. Since such links were not necessary, Derrida argued, they could only be ethical, reflecting evaluations rather than facts. Thus Saussure's distrust of writing, with its "orthographic monstrosities," reflected not scientific rigor or necessity but a residual humanism that began by isolating some pure or natural essence of language, and then defended it like a medieval knight against threats from the forces of "superstition," "contamination," "tyranny," and "pathology"—all terms Saussure associated with writing. A detailed attention to Saussure and to others in the tradition of "Western metaphysics" would invariably disclose the operation of a dense and half-conscious mingling of prejudices, preferences, privileges, and exclusions that constitute the business end of the "ethic of the living word" (1978a: 139). Thus deconstruction began with a criticism of "l'éthicité de l'éthique" and proceeded to a more properly ethical practice of restoring the outcast writing and related qualities to their proper place, the place they would have if they had not been repressed (1986a: 70).

Early deconstruction thus constituted an ethical criticism of ethics. "The ethic of the living word," Derrida wrote in a passage that lay at the heart of his early work, "would be as respectable as respect itself if it did not live on a delusion and a nonrespect for its own condition of origin, if it did not dream in speech of a presence denied to writing, denied by writing. The ethic of speech is the *delusion* of a presence mastered" (1978a: 139). In such passages, Derrida appeared to criticize all ethics as nonethical, but he made a silent exception for his own argument, which *was* based on an ethical respect for the origin.

Derrida's understanding of the concept of an "infinite" respect was perhaps what drew him in Levinas in the first place. But their infinities were hardly identical, with Levinas describing an infinite responsibility toward the human other and Derrida focusing on respect for the infinite semiosis of the text. For promoting his kind of infinity, Derrida was accounted by many a libertine. But he had said from the very beginning that infinity really described the reader's responsibility toward the text. And gradually, he extended this notion of responsibility to more recognizably ethical circumstances, to the point where, by the late 1980s, his ethical position was not easy to distinguish from that of Levinas despite the profound differences in their basic premises.

This difference was most clearly marked in Derrida's cautious and subtle retrieval of Kant. Given his textual orientation, Derrida was always more responsive than Levinas to the formal dimension of language, and so it was not altogether surprising that Kant's efforts to formalize ethics eventually took root in Derrida's account of an "ethic of discussion." First sketched out in *Of Grammatology*, this ethic involved a two-stage process designed both to ensure the integrity of the text and to open it up to radically new understandings that had the potential of overturning traditional, customary, or commonsensical readings.

The first step in this process is a scrupulous "doubling commentary" that would guard against a wholly unprincipled or wild interpretation by undertaking a work of faithful repetition that established a "probabilistically dominant and conventionally acknowledged" reading (1978a: 144). As Derrida says in an important 1988 text that extended this early meditation, the first duty of the analyst—a "theoretical" duty that is at the same time an "ethical-political duty"—is to establish a dominant account, an account whose dominance is historically established, using whatever resources are available to the scholar (1988: 135). Clearly, Derrida intends to establish in this first layer a formal category of unconditional obligation by describing a task whose execution can be measured in terms of simple competence—a categorical imperative of scholarly discussion.

But this is not all. Having established its fidelity to the text, a deconstructive-ethical reading must then proceed to a second layer or moment, a riskier project of determining a new reading, an *interpretation* based on the lifting of the repression that had been begun in the first. In this second stage the critic enjoys certain liberties denied in the first, but remains unconditionally duty-bound not to "transgress the text toward something other than it, toward a referent (a reality that is metaphysical, historical, psychobiographical, etc.) or toward a signified outside the text"—because, as he says in one of *Grammatology*'s most infamous and cryptic pronouncements, "*il n'y a pas de hors-texte*," which can be translated either as "there is nothing outside of the text" or "there is no outside-of-the-text" (1978a: 158).

It is "not by accident," Derrida concedes in his 1988 text, that he invokes the concept of unconditionality in order to summon up "the character of the categorical imperative in its Kantian form" (1988: 152). But in fact it is precisely at this point that deconstruction parts company with Kant. For the distinction Kant draws between the formal character of the categorical imperative and the contingent nature of other ("hypothetical") imperatives is, in theory, clear and untransgressable. Derrida, on the other hand, regards such distinctions as untenable from the outset: the first stage of "doubling commentary" is, he notes, "*already* an interpretation" (143). Deconstruction thus turns on Kantian thinking, but does so, strangely enough, out of a "Kantian" respect for the resistance of language to clean distinctions, a "respect which, whatever the cost, I neither can nor will compromise." Derrida has, in other words, located within language an ethical imperative that compels his respect, but also compels him to deconstruct the very notion that ethics is defined in terms of respect for imperatives. Thus it is also "not by accident" that, as Derrida writes, he has "always hesitated" to characterize the "injunction that prescribes deconstruction" in Kantian terms, with "hesitation" marking the dilemma (153).

As always in Derrida, the situation is far from simple. But what should be clear is that the task of extrapolating a (neo- or para-Kantian) ethics directly from language sets Derrida at cross-purposes with Kantian rationality, and in that respect, with ethics itself. Still, it is equally clear that Derrida was attempting to preserve the basic idea of an ethical responsibility or imperative even as he sought to refashion the traditional account of it. In this and other ways, deconstruction, thought by many to be a purely subversive and antiethical practice, actually revitalized the subject of ethics for contemporary literary theory.

One way deconstruction restored ethical energy to criticism at large was by provoking outraged attacks against itself. By the 1980s, resistance to deconstructive theory in the Anglo-American academy was beginning to take an unmistakably ethical tone as the claims of the world were pressed with greater vigor against the insularity of the text, and critical debates of that time often took the form of claims and counter-claims for the ethics of worldliness and those of textuality. In these battles, deconstruction was far from defenseless, for it could always claim that its readings, so manifestly unsatisfying and self-canceling, rebuffed readerly desire in an exemplary ethical way by failing to provide any useful, consoling, or rewarding connections between the world and the work.

Paul de Man and his admirers were especially adept at making ethical arguments based on a series of disconnects between author, text, referent, and reader. If the exuberant and proliferating Derrida held that one must say everything the text permits one to say, de Man seemed always to discover forms of negation, sources of prohibition. The gradual recognition by both men of a common and complementary investment not just in a certain view of language or textuality, or in the Jewish contribution to contemporary letters, but in ethics may have consolidated an already intimate relationship and given to it the high seriousness, the sense of great stakes, that informs each of their comments about the other (see de Man 1986: 115–21, and 1983: 102–41; Derrida, 1986b).

Although the controversies surrounding de Man's work were often ethical in character, de Man never made positive ethical arguments, never urged, exhorted, or defined an obligation determined by any notion of the good, the just, or the worthy. In his mature writings, de Man raised the question of ethics in two ways, both of which had the effect of draining the entire issue of value from the subject. First, he simply disparaged the traditional ethical function of literature—presenting worthy exemplars, providing instruction on how to form proper evaluations, refining one's sensibility, revealing the consequences of various acts or decisions—as a series of residual illusions left over from the precritical humanistic era that, sunk in sentimentality, had been incapable of the rigors of real reading. And second, he situated ethics within the field of his central critical concept, "allegory," making ethics a textual function rather than a function of the rational or virtuous subject.

Like other critics who addressed the subject of the ethics of criticism, Derrida had argued for a certain kind of engagement that recognized both the reader's freedom and his responsibilities. In Derrida, the center of ethical reflection is still a human being; Derrida's innovation is to propose principles of ethical obligation pertinent to the act of reading. De Man is almost perfectly deaf to such notions. For him, the entire ethical scenario is worked out as a kind of internal melodrama within the text itself; the reader's share is simply to attend to it, to observe the spectacle. Proper reading, for de Man, is not an act performed on the text, but a submission, an evacuation of self that prepares one to bear witness to the truth of the text.

De Man often depicts this truth in terms of "unreadability," a force of resistance within the text to resolution or finality. The apprehension of a trembling stasis between opposed forces de Man then declares, with deliberate perversity, to be the consequence of an ethical reading. As the reader of Rousseau, Rilke, or Nietzsche discovers that the text does not cohere, and that truth and falsehood are thereby confounded, the distinction between right and wrong is jeopardized as well—hence ethics. In a passage as manifestly important to its author as it is mystifying to many of its readers, de Man says that ethics emerges when the true-false axis intersects with the right-wrong axis:

the term ethical designat[es] the structural interference of two distinct value systems. In this sense, ethics has nothing to do with the will (thwarted or free) of a subject. . . . The ethical category is imperative (i.e., a category rather than a value) to the extent that it is linguistic and not subjective. . . . The passage to an ethical tonality does not result from a transcendental imperative but is the referential (and therefore unreliable) version of a linguistic confusion. Ethics (or, one should say, ethicity) is a discursive mode among others. (1978: 206)

In this luminously obscure passage, with its triumphantly understated conclusion, de Man may have gone somewhat farther than he wanted in stressing the absolute distinction between people and a language that is so alien and masterful that it must, his statements notwithstanding, appear as something like a "transcendental imperative" to which human beings can only bear witness through their passive disquiet, their "confusion." The new linguistic ethicity is still "thematized as a sacrifice, a renunciation," but what used to be a worldly gesture—give all that thou hast and come and follow me, as Christ says—is now wholly cognitive, condensed into the act of reading (1978: 206). Deeply suspicious of the reemergence of self-esteem or complacency even within acts of apparent self-denial, de Man seems to be trying to formulate the principles of an ascesis so radical that it could not even be called a duty, for the subject itself is the object of renunciation: where duty and virtue were, there shall "a discursive mode among others" be. Does ethics still correspond to any value held by a human community? Such a "naïve" question de Man would declare "undecidable."

Everything about de Man was subject to reassessment after the 1987 disclosures of his youthful adventures with fidelity leading to passive confusion. I am speaking, of course, of his "wartime journalism," some 170 articles written during 1941–42 for Belgian collaborationist newspapers. In the course of the wild debate that followed the discovery of these articles, de Man himself was roundly condemned by earnest moralists, and those who defended him found themselves under an attack they could only consider theoretically misinformed, even vulgar, for continuing to insist that the real issue was linguistic, continuing to focus on textual nuances, continuing to *read*.

The effect was often actively de-clarifying, as in the furious exchange between Hillis Miller and the historian Jon Wiener, who had written of de Man as "an academic Waldheim," and of deconstruction as a pernicious school for ethico-political scandal. Once again, it is the less cautious or circumspect Miller who lays bare the mechanism of de Man's position. From his position on the front lines of "the perpetual war on behalf of good reading," Miller responds to Wiener by pointing out not just egregious theoretical naïveté but numerous errors of fact (1989a: 341). Wiener, he charges, had simply not read the relevant texts properly; the facts were "precisely the opposite," "exactly the reverse," and so forth. Both as an historian and as a journalist, Miller says, Weiner has failed in his primary obligation to "get it right" (339).

But what would it mean to get it right? Does a scrupulous practice of reading ensure that the right conclusion will be reached? Miller is on record as believing that it would not. In the chapter on de Man in *The Ethics of Reading* (1986), he stated that, "The failure to read takes place inexorably within the text itself. The reader must reenact this failure in his or her own reading. Getting it right always means being forced to reenact once more the necessity of getting it wrong" (1986: 53). Measuring Wiener's performance against Miller's theory, we might say that in getting things—the date of de Man's death, the meaning of his texts—so utterly wrong, Wiener seems to have established impeccable deconstructionist credentials. Miller, meanwhile, has put his own credentials in question. For by suggesting that getting it right could be accomplished without its shadow, the *necessity* of getting it wrong, Miller seems to have gone over to the other side in the war on behalf of good reading. The perverse conclusion to which all this seems to be leading is that the experience of reading de Man causes anti-deconstructors to bear witness to the truth of deconstruction and committed deconstructors to reaffirm their faith in the undeconstructed truth.

But the more interesting and productive questions concern the relation between de Man's early journalism, which even his defenders consider ethically dubious, and deconstruction as a critical practice that emerged over a quarter-century later. Faithful deconstructive retainers argued, of course, that there was no positive link, or that the later writings inverted the earlier, condemning their errors; others contended that de Man's mature theorizing simply continued the project of the journalism by other means (see Hamacher et al.). Without addressing all the details of these often complex arguments, we can note a number of intriguing lines of continuity between the wartime journalism and the mature literary theory. These include the pronounced and, to many, unseemly interest in the concept of the inhuman, the eager desire to have no independent thoughts, and the disavowal of human agency generally. All these gather into the ethics of language articulated in *Allegories of Reading* and other texts.

Very broadly, the position occupied in his journalism by Nazi Germany as the indisputable destiny of Europe is assumed in de Man's criticism by language, which absorbs humanity as if it were a lesser country like, for example, Belgium, which was misguided to think it had a separate identity in the first place. The cosmopolitan acquiescence in the German occupation of Belgium that must have dismayed many contemporary readers of the journalism became, thirty years and several transformations later, the ascetic devotion to the text, the proud assertion of passivity as a principle. As Geoffrey Hartman explains de Man's early transgressions in the terminology of the older de Man, the young man had been "betrayed" and "trapped by an effect of language, an ideological verbiage that blinded critical reflection" (1989: 21, 22).

In de Man's practice and in Hartman's remarkable characterization of that practice, we can see the danger of thinking of language as an all-but-human or perhaps "inhuman" agent, something capable of trapping, betraying, and blinding the unsuspecting and perhaps even innocent reader. One consequence of this thought is that the notion that ethical responsibility is realized in worthy action is refined virtually out of existence, and replaced by a form of responsibility that involves no more than bearing witness to strictly textual tensions, with the scope of human agency diminished to the vanishing point. In the intellectual climate of de Man, language has fattened itself on the agency stolen from human beings. The ultimate consequence, as the generous comments from Hartman suggest, is that people can, at least in theory, defend themselves from any accusation by pleading linguistic entrapment. The end of the line for the project of extracting an ethical law from a language detached from human purposes is not the deconstruction, but the simple destruction, of ethics itself.

Law and the Language of the Unconscious: Freud, Chomsky, Lacan

The notion that language can trap you, beguile you, and even do your thinking for you while you're not looking may be one conclusion to be drawn from text-based deconstructive criticism, but it is also the key premise of

Whorfian linguistics, which focused on "obligatory phenomena within the apparently free flow of talk," which were "so completely autocratic that speaker and listener are bound unconsciously as though in the grip of a law of nature" (Whorf 221). Whorf directs us not just to the unconscious character of language but to the linguistic character of the unconscious, which can be said to be the founding insight of psychoanalysis, and certainly the one that has proven most durable and adaptable. While Freud developed no general theory of language, he did invent a theory of the mind based on the belief that unconscious mental disturbances produced symptomatic linguistic formations or deformations, and were able to do so because language not only inhabited the unconscious, but, in the form of secondary or unstressed layers of meaning, actually had an "unconscious." By stressing the relation between language and the subject, and by considering linguistic disturbances rather than norms or regularities, Freud in effect proposed a powerful new model of language that diverged sharply from modern linguistic science and the Cartesian premises on which it was based.

Freud's account of the mind posits a complex series of transactions between largely distinct sites or communicative centers within the brain. Repression, for example, works not just on unacceptable instincts that must be kept out of consciousness, but on their "associations," "derivatives," and "ideational presentations," which characteristically take verbal form. It is in distorted uses of language that turbulence, disorder, or misalignment are registered; linguistic complications or oddities often betray the subsurface burbling of psychic disturbances, revealing to the analytical eye both the effort of repression and the repressed energy itself. Since progress toward the cure comes about through the confrontation of the analysand with his or her own verbal formulations and through the social demand to tell one's stories in increasingly coherent and adequate terms, language could be said to contain, in admixture, a therapeutic and even an emancipatory dimension, a will to truth.

Schizophrenics, to take one example, betray their affliction by an overinsistence on bodily organs or "innervations" in their speech. Thus a young girl complained to Freud that her eyes *were not right, they were twisted,* an incoherent comment whose true referent was disclosed only when she later criticized her lover as a man who "looked different every time; he was a shammer, an eye-twister"—a colloquialism meaning "deceiver." "The patient's remarks about her first incomprehensible utterance have," Freud says, "the value of an analysis, for they contain the equivalent of the original words expressed in a generally comprehensible form. . . . I would here lay stress on the point that the relation to the bodily organ (eye) has usurped the place of the whole content of the thought. The schizophrenic speech displays a hypochondriac trait: it has become 'organ-speech'" (Freud 144).

The local point is that, in schizophrenia, "word-relations" dominate over things, but the more general argument is that repressed instincts can enter the "pre-consciousness" by affixing themselves to linguistic formations—to secondary meanings, puns, or even parts of words—where they become susceptible to analysis. Eventually, it is hoped, the suffering patient is brought to the point where he or she can produce more orderly expressions that have the effects of smoothing over the rough spots and releasing repressed energies into the atmosphere, where they can dissipate harmlessly. The ethical project of psychoanalysis, to bring repressed and frustrated instincts to a kind of negotiated settlement with the demands of society, thus works on and through language.

Freud's emphasis on therapeutic practice led him to focus on speech or discourse rather than language as such, the object of linguistic science. And within speech, Freud focused on largely self-contained moments of half-unwitting confession, utterances that must be removed from their contingent context and hauled away, to be reassembled into their true configuration elsewhere. As Emile Benveniste commented, Freud really focused on "style" rather than language (75). Ignoring altogether the possibility of language existing in some sense outside the discourse of a particular subject, Freud may be said to have canceled in advance the premise of Chomskyan psychology, the postulate of a universal language faculty, and, as a consequence, a fixed universal grammar. But this difference, while radical, masks a common investment in the concept of law—the law of the unconscious in the one case and the law of language in the other. By emphasizing the regularity of the operations of the unconscious, Freud actually laid the groundwork for subsequent psychoanalytical thinking on language and ethics in which a principle of law conceived in the most general terms is said to be absorbed as a side-effect of the subject's acquisition of language. Chomsky's linguistics, which Chomsky himself describes as a branch of cognitive psychology, takes this form.

Chomsky contends that a genetically determined capacity for language not only determines the form of our utterances but also solders into our biogenetic system the principles of freedom and creativity. His account of language therefore ramifies in one direction into an account of a fixed and non-manipulable human nature and, in the other, into a normative account of political institutions, which can, he suggests, be judged by the extent to which they foster these principles. It is an argument of breathtaking comprehensiveness that extends from symbolic descriptions of the details of the brain's wiring to jeremiads and polemics on a well-nigh global scale.

The single great fact on which all his work is based is difficult to refute. He points out that the rapidity and assurance with which children learn to produce grammatically correct sentences regardless of how fragmentary or degraded the information provided by their linguistic environment suggests an innate linguistic faculty or capacity. This capacity, he says, takes various forms, but must be identical in all humans; we must, that is, have a "distinct cognitive system" that provides us with a "universal grammar" that can be activated or awakened in such a way as to enable us to learn any human language. Over the years, Chomsky has made a number of attempts to describe this inferred universal grammar.

Famous challenges have been made to all of his attempts, but two basic assertions have survived essentially intact in Chomsky's evolving theory. First, Chomsky says, syntax is autonomous. It can be specified independently of semantics, even if the distinction between these domains is in practice problematic. The formal dimension of language, syntactic rules, like the "module" in the brain in which they are said to be housed, can be understood as a thing apart; and so syntax, despite its very tenuous material existence, serves as Chomsky's version of what Saussure sought in the sign, the "concrete entity" of "language alone." "A language," Chomsky says in *Syntactic Structures*, is "a set (finite or infinite) of sentences, each finite in length, and constructed out of a finite set of elements"; and "a grammar" is "a device that generates all of the grammatical sequences of [the language] and none of the ungrammatical ones" (1957: 13). The finiteness of the "set of elements" and the specific organization of this "device" are what give Chomsky his ontological ground; these are what he infers from available data, what he "observes" and "describes." And second, syntax enables us to produce new sentences in response to new situations. In fact, in Chomsky's ambiguous phrasing, the syntax itself "generates" the sentences, in a production that can be described in a value-neutral way as "creative" since it cannot be programmed or predicted.

Compelling as this argument is, the next phase of Chomsky's work has proven to be difficult for many to follow, or swallow. Having determined the essential properties of the universal linguistic endowment, Chomsky then designates these properties as the defining characteristics of human nature, and translates them into ethical and political imperatives. Since human nature is autonomous and creative, Chomsky reasons, then its natural social and political condition must be one in which those qualities are able to flourish, and any system that discourages this flourishing represents an insult to humanity. We should therefore commit ourselves to working toward a "material and spiritual culture" in which people enjoy the greatest possible degrees of political freedom and moral autonomy, a culture that would "best encourage and accommodate the fundamental human instinct for spontaneous initiative, creative work, solidarity, pursuit of social justice" (1987a: 155). The task of our time, Chomsky concludes, is to imagine and bring into being "a future society that conforms to the exigencies of human nature as best we understand them"—that is, as theoretical linguistics has disclosed them (1979: 80). Because language is our nature, freedom is our destiny and right.

In articulating this chain of arguments, Chomsky draws on, and indeed revives, the very philosophical traditions whose demise Foucault and others celebrated, the rationalist tradition that runs from Descartes through the Enlightenment, and the Romantic tradition that includes Rousseau and especially von Humboldt, who, like Chomsky, combined an emphasis on language as innate human endowment with a libertarian political vision (1966; see also Aarsleff's scornful estimate of Chomsky as historian in 1982: 101–19). Where he differs from his predecessors is in his insistence that ethics and politics have a firm grounding in a body of scientific fact—a body so scientific, in fact, that it has no "body" at all: not only is syntax a mere "system of digital computations" within the brain, a "pattern in the mind," but it is best conceived as theoretically distinct from human bodies. One of Chomsky's earliest supporters among philosophers, Hilary Putnam, congratulated Chomsky with "having dispensed altogether with the assumption 'that the corpus of utterances studied by the linguist was produced by a conscious organism'" (95). The Chomskyan difference, in other words, consists of providing a foundation for ethical and political positions that is so scientifically sound, so universal, that it can stand independent of all the contingencies and particularities associated with human life.

The belief that he has grasped the essentials of human nature undoubtedly contributes to the characteristic moral assurance of Chomsky's attacks on abuses of state authority all over the world. But the vast distance that separates his abstract formulations of syntactic rules and the disorderly world of human endeavor and conflict has led some to suspect that the connection between the two may be construed quite differently, even that it may be nonexistent. Chomsky himself is usually reluctant to make a direct connection, and other linguists generally regard his political activism as incidental to his real work in the "specialized technical field" of linguistics. As the linguist Neil Smith says, "any intellectual relationship between [Chomsky's] linguistics and his political work is extremely tenuous" (180). Chomsky wants, of course, to keep his science technical and value-neutral, and his politics a matter of plain common sense rather than a discourse of the trained elite (1979: 8). Undoubtedly, too, he wants to claim that his work in linguistics neither presupposes nor validates specific values or beliefs. He recognizes, in short, that the integrity of both discourses depends upon the distinction between them.

But if the distinction were absolute, then both would suffer: the linguistics would not yield an account of human nature that had any meaning or force in the world, and the political work, lacking a foundation in fact, would assume (even more than it does) the character of a rant. And in fact, on occasion, Chomsky seems to forget his scruples altogether, as when an essay on "Some General Features of Language" morphs abruptly from a discussion of technical linguistic issues into a philosophical and political discussion of human nature and the just society (1975: 123 ff.). The fascinating combination of exceptionally sere science and extravagantly moralized polemics that constitutes Chomsky's singularity depends, then, on a kind of dotted line drawn between the two fields, with each assigned to a particular sphere that still does not prevent it from energizing, informing, and confirming the other. This delicate balance is accomplished by means of a fissure, a partial tear, in his two central terms, autonomy and creativity, that enables them to function in both discourses while retaining their identity as terms.

Like Hume, then, Chomsky tries to imagine a way to leap over the chasm that divides *is* from *ought*. And like Hume, Chomsky turns for assistance to "the very nature of language," especially to certain words. The question is, however, whether *autonomy* and *creativity* as he defines them are really the same words in both contexts. The referent is clearly quite different in the two contexts, since in the one case they describe the features of an unalterable pattern of signals and switches in the brain to which no particular value need be attached, and in the other case they represent fundamental ethical and political principles that are not perfectly realized anywhere in the world. Are these, then, really the same words in both contexts; has Chomsky successfully identified principles that rule the brain and therefore ought to rule in the world—or has he produced a pair of puns, fortuitous double meanings with no rationale, like bunk (bed) and bunk (hokum)? This is a difficult case to settle, and it would be good if Chomsky would relax his customary refusal to discuss the principles that unify his work and address himself directly to this question, especially since others are proceeding with their own assessments, with the result that he is in danger of being seen as virtually schizophrenic (see Read, "How I Learned to Love (and Hate) Noam Chomsky").

The problem Chomsky and his supporters must confront is how a neutral and automatic faculty can function as a norm for individuals and for public affairs. The fact that untouchables, slaves, homeless orphans, and addicts can constantly produce new sentences—just like their masters, overlords, and social superiors—without any of them undertaking any kind of creative work or pursuing social justice might represent a problem in this respect. The fact that women under the Taliban produced a steady flow of astonishing stuff under their burqas, a production fully equal, statistically speaking, to the verbal innovations of their brothers, husbands, and fathers, does put into question the proposition that creativity and autonomy in one area produces a pressure for the same qualities in another. Without a detailed working-out of the connections between the two distinct and different fields of Chomsky's work, his effort to ground an ethics in the determined facts of language cannot be considered persuasive—especially when the "facts of language" themselves remain unsettled and disputed.

The most sustained and explicit attempt to integrate the thought of the unconscious with a general account of language was undertaken by Jacques Lacan, whose famous declaration that "the unconscious is structured like a language" acquired the status of a postmodern shibboleth. In several important respects, Lacan and Chomsky are so opposed in their approaches and presuppositions that we are not surprised when Chomsky dismisses Lacan as a "conscious charlatan" who spouts nonsense and dares his intimidated listeners to hoot him off the stage (Chomsky 1989: 32). Lacan, after all, demonstrates no interest in the particulars of political struggle, no faith that mankind is endowed with the right to freedom or creative activity, no confidence in the Enlightenment-based notion of truth so crucial to Chomsky. But how are we to explain another comment in which Chomsky accords Lacan a measure of grudging respect, suggesting that he "at least should be read" (quoted in Barsky 195)?

Perhaps Chomsky's guarded approbation on this occasion reflects a half-conceded sense of affinity in their common effort to develop an account of the linguistic subject. If Chomsky had "at least" read that passage in which Lacan asserts that "[man's] nature is woven by effects in which is to be found the structure of language," he might well have found himself nodding in assent (Lacan 1977: 284). But they share an even more profound conviction: that language, as an imperative one cannot escape, binds human beings to ethical principles that it weaves into human nature itself.

Concurring on the main point, Lacan and Chomsky differ on all the details. Chomsky makes language a function of biology, but Lacan extricated psychoanalysis from the grasp of biology by displacing attention from the Act—the infantile trauma, the child's seduction, the parental "No"—to the Word. As Mikkel Borch-Jakobsen points out in his valuable book *Lacan: The Absolute Master,* Lacan at first identified the creative speech act as the core of language and thus of man's nature; but by 1954, Lacan had turned away from what would be the young American's direction, identifying language as the source of a profound nullity within the human subject, the origin and form of the Freudian death instinct (see Borch-Jakobsen 169–96). Human subjects, Lacan argued, are determined by the rules and codes of language in the same sense that the living are subject to mortality as their fundamental condition of being. Lacan continued the Cartesian tradition into which Chomsky would subsequently insert himself, but did so with conceptual tools unavailable to Descartes and, in their emphasis on death and subjection, repellant to Chomsky on several levels (see Chomsky 1966).

Add to these doctrinal differences with Chomsky the striking fact that Chomsky is virtually never mentioned by Lacan or by his numerous commentators, and one can see that Chomsky's contempt is not just inevitable but overdetermined. Perhaps the strangest component of this near-miss by Lacan and Lacanians is the fact that, during the years when the Chomskyan revolution was sweeping the field clean, the primary authority on the science of language in Lacan's texts is still Saussure. Lacan begins his classic position paper "Agency of the Letter" (published in 1957, the same year as Chomsky's *Syntactic Structures*) by declaring, "I shall trust only those assumptions that have already proven their value by virtue of the fact that language through them has attained the status of an object of scientific investigation" (1977: 148). He identifies the source of these assumptions as the *Course in General Linguistics*, "a work of prime importance for the transmission of a teaching worthy of the name," one that has effected nothing less than "a revolution in knowledge"—and makes no reference, even in subsequent publications, to any further revolution, any other science, any other teaching (149). For Lacan, and for Lacanians, it is Saussure, not Chomsky, who provides "compelling scientific 'guarantee'" of the truth of Freud, the truth of language, and therefore the truth of man (Borch-Jakobsen 193).

Lacan came to Saussure in large measure through the work of Claude Lévi-Strauss, who had refashioned anthropology by modeling it on the "laws of language" as propounded by Saussure and subsequently by Roman Jakobson. These laws, Lévi-Strauss felt, were so ironclad and inescapable that linguistics ought to be used as a model for analysis in all the social sciences. Lacan agreed, and specifically included psychoanalysis on the grounds that it, like linguistics, sought to articulate the rules that operated in the unconscious mind. The unconsciousness of linguistic rules was, in fact, one of the primary bases of the claim of linguistics to be a science. As Lévi-Strauss noted in a key essay on "Language and the Analysis of Social Laws," the social sciences had long struggled to establish their scientific credentials in the face of the argument that their results were invariably tainted by the biasing effects of the observer. In response, Lévi-Strauss argued that a social science grounded in structural linguistics would be exempt from this criticism, since knowledge of language, being unconscious, does not modify specific utterances at all. Profoundly affected by this and other works of Lévi-Strauss, Lacan felt by the early 1950s that he had all the materials he needed for a science of language that would yield the laws of the unconscious (see Muller and Richardson 6–19).

While Lacan would later decide that science was "but a fantasy," he sustained for many years an untroubled belief in the capacity of linguistic science to yield the truth (Lacan, Seminar XXV, quoted in Fink 146). And so it is especially disturbing that Lacan's understanding of Saussure is so limited.

For Lacan, Saussure is the apostle of the signifier, the differential mark whose identity was determined only by its relation to other elements in the system. Lacan argued that the signifier was the hidden principle behind the version of Hegel disseminated in the famous Paris seminars of Alexander Kojève in the 1930s and 1940s, which Lacan attended in company with such influential figures as Georges Bataille, Maurice Blanchot, and Sartre. The main lesson of these seminars, summarized by Bataille in terms that directly recall the Saussurean principle of the "chain" in which signifier dissolves into signifier, was that "man always becomes *other*. Man is the animal who continually differs from himself" (363). When Lacan says, in "The Agency of the Letter," that man is "the slave of language," he is trying to concretize Kojève by grounding Kojève's insights into Hegel in the signifier.

For Lacan, the most profoundly suggestive feature of the signifier was its doomed effort to resolve itself into a pure signified, to become the last link in the chain. The absolute division between signifier and signified represented, he argued, a less speculative version of Freud's "first topography," which emphasized the distinction between consciousness and the unconscious. The Freudian unconscious might seize on and deform words or signifiers, but no signifier could ever speak the unconscious fully and directly. Saussure's account of the way the signified keeps slipping away, eluding the vain graspings of the signifier, provided Lacan with an intoxicatingly precise rendering of what Freud described as the slithering associations of the "dreamwork," and also, in a more general sense, of the inability by the conscious mind fully to comprehend or express the unconscious (see 1977: 149, 172; see also Lacan 1992: 295). Chained to its chain, endlessly dissolving into other signifiers like itself, the signifier suggested a powerful explanation of both the Hegel-Kojève principle of otherness and the Freudian principle of frustration, as well as the way in which these two philosophemes fit together.

But in order to make these remarkable connections, Lacan had to stress the signifier at the expense of other Saussurean concepts, including the signified and the sign. Lacan's account of language, and thus of human existence, is thus grounded on an incomplete version of Saussure's thinking. This version accorded nicely, however, with a prevailing antihumanism in Lacan's Parisian milieu. Like many others in that intellectual environment Lacan saw language as more substantial than humanity, imposing its laws on a human subject that, without them, would lack form and force altogether. And like others, Lacan saw those laws imposed on human beings from the outside. Although he sometimes described language as the essential kernel of the human subject, he also insisted that language represented a "cleavage," "break," or "cut" in human existence (1992: 279). This "inhuman" force determines human speech, so that what looks like the free invention of a creative and autonomous individual is actually the discourse of language, an "it" that deploys man as its "material" and "resounds in him, beyond what could be conceived of by a psychology of ideas" (1977: 284). The human subject, according to Lacan, is a structure of lack, a linguistic epiphenomenon, a mirage that exists only "at the level of the enunciation" (1981: 140).

On the strength of Saussure's scientific credentials, which he never questioned, Lacan felt empowered to take a radical step into the field of ethics, calling the discourse of psychoanalysis to a spiritual renewal. The fundamental concept of ethics, as Lacan understood it, was an obligation imposed on the subject by the figure of the other. While the position of the other had, in the previous history of ethical discourse, been assumed by Reason, custom, the State, or the other person, Lacan filled this slot with language, by this means converting psychoanalysis from a therapeutic practice designed to produce integrated social subjects into an ethical discourse with very different goals. He begins his great 1959 seminar on *The Ethics of Psychoanalysis* by stating that "the ethical question of our practice" is related to the fact that every psychology is "nothing more than a mask, and sometimes even an alibi, of the effort to focus on the problem of our own action," so that psychoanalysis as a whole can be understood as "simply another development of ethical reflection" (1992: 19; see also Milner 1991). The remarkable claim of the seminar—that by representing the subject as the slave of language we can understand the task of psychoanalysis and can even get to the bottom of the problem of ethics— represents the most compelling moment of philosophical seriousness in all of Lacan, his most ambitious assault not just on the psychoanalytic establishment but on an entire philosophical tradition as well.

Lacan begins this crucial seminar by pointing out that classical ethics as defined by Aristotle was dedicated to the notion that the appropriate goal of ethical action was the increase of happiness in an orderly or "tidy" society. Kant's immense stature, in Lacan's eyes, derives from his heroic attempt to interfere with this sunny view of the subject's relationship with itself and with social reality. Kant accepts without regret the fact that man is not made for pleasure, that the "good will" on which ethical action depends cannot produce happiness, and that ethics routinely demands a frustration or disappointment of desire. Freud, in Lacan's view, completed Kant's work by establishing in specifically psychoanalytic terms how absolutely nothing in the conflictual nature of the subject is prepared for success in the quest for pleasure. The Freudian pleasure principle, Lacan points out, is "an inertia principle," and the most fundamental desire, incest, meets with the harshest and most unalterable ethical taboo (1992: 27). Lacan felt that he could drive the final nail in pleasure's coffin by revealing the mechanism of this frustration, or castration, in the subject's subjection to language as Saussure described it, a subjection whose mechanism Lacan illustrates by way of *Antigone*.

As Lacan notes, Antigone is driven by a desire that many readers have found disturbing, "criminal," "monstrous," even "idiotic." These judgments, he argues, reflect the perspective of Creon, whom Lacan identifies as the voice of culture, law, the communal good, and practical reason, in order to oppose to him Antigone, with her "natural" commitment to her brother. The culture-nature binary is drawn from Lévi-Strauss, but Lacan's appreciation for anthropology extends only as far as Lévi-Strauss's appropriation of Saussure. And so Lacan proceeds to identify Antigone not with nature as such but with human nature as revealed by the form of the signifier, "the break that the very presence of language inaugurates in the life of man," the "signifying cut" that makes man "what he is in the face of everything that may oppose him" (1992: 279, 282). Insisting on burying her brother even at the cost of her own life, Antigone bears witness to the general proposition that, at the heart of human nature, we find nothing other than the death drive, "the pure and simple desire of death as such" (282). And so Antigone, who offends the law, the sovereign, and the community, becomes in Lacan's analysis a hero of the human condition.

Lacan's account of ethics is structured as series of such paradoxes, one of which is that the disclosure of man's enslavement by language would actually liberate the desire that had been denied by moralists and educators, providing it with a new dignity and urgency. On occasion in this seminar, "desire" refers to one's own path, or pathology, a "particular destiny" of one's own that protests against oppression (1992: 319; see Lee 162 ff.). When moralists advance the claims of the good in general, they strategically elide the question of *whose* good and so provide the same kind of false resolution

as that imposed by the merely apparent unity of the signifier and the signified. The moralizing accommodation of the individual to the larger social
totality produces a general but shallow sense of happiness at the cost of
denying the particular its specific destiny, its singular needs and desires.
Thus the famously paradoxical Lacanian version of the categorical imperative: do not give way as to your desire (see 1992: 319–21).

Although no difference is marked, this use of the term *desire* reflects a
slightly but decisively different concept—informed, strangely enough, by
Saussure—from that of the "particular destiny" of one's own. One would "give
way as to" or "cede" one's desire by persuading oneself that desire had been,
or could be, satisfied, and this would be a betrayal of the law that binds desire
to the infinite signifying chain. The very phrase "your desire" is misleading in
this context, since, for Lacan, desire is not private property; in fact, as a
species-characteristic imposed by language, desire unravels individual identity. "Your" desire leads you on and on and on, always toward the other, just
as—and just because—signifiers acquire their meanings not from the signifieds to which they are arbitrarily attached, but from their place in the system.

The insatiability of desire, the dissimulation of the individual in the field
of otherness, constitutes our best access to the knowledge of death; to "give
way" as to your desire is to attempt to evade the pain and pathos of the human
condition by submitting to a fantasy of wholeness in which desire is satisfied.
When Žižek elaborates on Lacanian ethics, he stresses in particular the role of
desire in this Saussurean sense, as a force that leads on and on from one
chain-link to the next. Ideology, Žižek says, tempts people into identifying
directly not with the split sign but with symbolic fantasies, as if they were not
castrated, as if they were not forever divided from the maternal oneness.
Desire becomes, in this respect, an ethical resistance to ideological closure.
The truth of the human condition, and the lesson on which any analysis worthy
of the name must insist, is that desire can never be gratified, that no signifier
will correspond perfectly to the underlying need that it signifies, for this need
is separated from specific fantasy-objects by a bar. Individual identity is
reducible to the particular place one occupies in the chain of signifiers, the
particular relations one has with other elements in the system, the specific
route tracked by the subject among the vast constellation of signifiers.

Thus, in a magnificent, rolling conclusion to his argument, Lacan asserts
that when Antigone insists on burying Polynices, she affirms as the ultimate

principle of ethical obligation the particular, specific relationship she bears to her brother, a relationship marked by the word *brother* itself, with its mirror-word *sister*, a relationship that is *significant* in every sense, for it is there and only there that Antigone locates her own significance, her own deepest principle of being, her own identity and desire. She does not expect to derive pleasure or satisfaction from her affirmation; indeed, the awful cost of her insistence is apparent from the beginning. But she refuses to deny or betray her own particularity, her own position, in the interests of obedience, ease, and civil order: she refuses to "give way as to her desire."

The stern lesson of desire is presented by Lacan as simultaneously scientific and ethical because it is, or at least purports to be, grounded in the scientific account of language provided by Saussure, in support of the scientific truth of Freud and the proto-scientific truth of Hegel. But, as we need to keep reminding ourselves, Saussure's credentials in the discipline of linguistics have not been taken seriously for many decades. Moreover, with his over-emphasis on the signifier, Lacan's understanding of or fidelity to Saussure is open to serious question (see Borch-Jakobsen 178–79, 274 n. 35). Freud, too, now seems to be more impressive when considered as a supremely gifted philosophical speculator rather than as a biologist of the mind: piece by piece of the Freudian edifice has been chipped off over the years, culminating, to date, in a 1999 essay by the philosopher Colin McGinn called "Freud under Analysis" which argued, in a conspicuously unintimidated tone, that there is, when you consider the matter logically, no warrant for positing anything as lurid or illogical as repression, dreamwork, an internal "censor"—no need, when you come right down to it, for the notion of an unconscious at all.

The quest for the ground of the ethical law, with its long and varied history, was given an extraordinary if unstable license for optimism with Saussure's and then Chomsky's attempts to create a science of language. Interestingly—even fascinatingly—both of these attempts have proven to be capable of providing support for a wide range of ethical arguments. Saussure's text seems highly conservative, even stolid, in its acquiescence to the superior wisdom of the community and tradition, but it has served as scientific authority for projects as remote in spirit from it as the radical democracy of Laclau and Mouffe and the anti-authoritarian anarchism of Lacan. And Chomsky's biological determinism, which appears to be such a reactionary position that almost no self-respecting academic theorist has even felt the need to refute it, leads, for

Chomsky himself, directly to a truly radical project of dissident progressivism on a global scale. Such striking discrepancies between scientific ground and ethical derivative suggest that linguistic science may not be as effective as some might wish in providing a foundation for the law. Some thinkers, in fact, look to language to provide something else altogether—not a principle of foundational rigor, and not a Humean guide to the law, but rather a kind of benign atmospheric influence that exerts an ethical pressure that leads us noncoercively toward the good.

3. Words against War: The Dream of a Virtuous Language

Not everyone welcomes the prospect of a binding law from which no dissent is possible. But so capacious and various is language that those who prefer to think of ethics in terms of gentle corrections and nonjudgmental pressures can still make the linguistic turn in search of support. For thinkers of this persuasion, language represents support itself, an immanent norm that arises not from within Reason or Law, but from within language, conceived as the medium of consciousness and reflection. From this point of view, language could provide the cure for the alienation that afflicts modern life. If only people could attend more closely and sympathetically to the dialogical, interpersonal multivoicedness of language, some, such as Martin Buber and Mikhail Bakhtin, argue, then the cold grip of technology and abstraction might be loosened and we could regain a lost fullness of being. The task that then unfolds before scholars and intellectuals is to make more widely available this sense of the humanizing potential of language.

One of the most influential versions of this species of therapeutic theorizing about language and ethics is to be found in the philosophical project of Hans-Georg Gadamer, of which the brief 1966 essay "Man and Language" represents an especially distilled instance. All of Gadamer's characteristic emphases—"loss of self," the dialogic nature of understanding, the inability of the self to possess itself—are invoked in these few pages in the course of an expansive meditation on the linguistic positioning of man in the world. "In truth," Gadamer writes, "we are always already at home in language, just as we are in the world" (63). Gadamer tries here and elsewhere to explicate Heideggerian metaphysics in a way that would provide more consolation and reassurance than Heidegger does, by translating the traumatic clarity of Being into linguistic terms. As Gadamer put it on more than one occasion, "the Being that can be understood is language."

But Gadamer was not simply impressed by language's presumed transparency to the reflective gaze, its availability to hermeneutic inquiry. As with many of the other thinkers who made the linguistic turn in pursuit of epistemological assurance, another agenda was driving the turn, and this agenda was ethical. Gianni Vattimo writes that "the expanded role assigned to language [in Gadamer's work] is accompanied by—or rather, has its true origin in—the ethical concerns that govern Gadamer's hermeneutics" (132). In language, Gadamer claimed to have identified the very locus of *ethos* itself, the single factor that unified human beings both intra- and intersubjectively. Gadamerian language is historically determined, finite, antiscientific, imbued with social experience; and, to complete the Hegelian inventory, language is said to be the only available form of *logos*. Language speaks us rather than we it, and lucky we are that it does so.

The nature of (Gadamerian) language guides us to where we already are, but might not have known that we were, inducing an ethic of alert humility and discouraging intellectual pride, the desire to dominate, and other forms of distance and alienation. So definite does Gadamer believe the work of language to be that he confidently announces "three things" peculiar to its functioning: first, an "essential self-forgetfulness" evidenced by the unconsciousness of grammar and the fact that language as a whole has a "completely unfathomable unconsciousness of itself"; second, "I-lessness," the orientation of language not to the speaker but to the one spoken to; and third, "universality," by which he means the inclusiveness of dialogue and the fact that speech is "motivated" by its relation to other speech (62ff.). One might almost be tempted to say that the general idea is that language is a kind of amniotic sac—if the model given by Gadamer for this last function were not a courtroom examination. The radically antitechnical character of Gadamer's arguments does, however, foster an illusion of self-forgetful security. The ethos of "Man and Language" suggests nothing so forcefully as the comforts of home in a difficult and distracting world, the security of collective being in a culture of fragmentation. Gadamer has been roundly attacked for a discourse whose ostensible subject is language but whose effect is to provide, as Vattimo charges, "an apology for what already exists"; but perhaps a more telling critique would accuse Gadamer of nostalgia for a state of belonging and intimacy that never existed at all (Vattimo 143).

One way to reply to Gadamer's arguments about language itself would be simply to invert his three points, and to ask whether the reality of language were thereby falsified. Language—a counter-Gadamerian imp of the perverse could argue—is the very medium of consciousness: it functions to make our innermost thoughts explicit, and does so by means—including a great mass of rules, conventions, and other codifiable structural features— that define consciousness itself. Having no mind, language cannot "forget itself," and in fact provides a structure for memory in those who do have minds. Second, since all utterances come from somebody, language is essentially "I-centric," focused in a speaking or intending subject. And third, language enables people to define and assert themselves in the midst of others whose utterances make some kind of claim on them, to resist and even to dominate others by advancing statements of their own. Language is the very mark of one's identity: one has a self in the first instance because one controls one's own language. If none of these counter-arguments is demonstrably wrong, then none of Gadamer's claims can be right; at least, none has the force Gadamer wants to claim for it.

Gadamer's work suggests that one appeal of language to those trying to work through the problems of ethics is that, if some immanent norm could be discovered in language, then the law would be humanized and conformity to it could be represented as a task no more arduous or counterintuitive than a recognition of our own nature. Ethical life is often difficult, and the concepts of struggle, rigor, discipline, and resistance are prominent in the traditional discourse of morality. But the struggle can be made to seem winnable, and even largely won, by an argument that suggests that language takes the entire burden and problem of ethics onto, or into, itself.

Thinkers in the therapeutic vein are, it seems, as sanguine about the ethical force of language as they are fascinated by the number three, which imparts a mystic wholeness to arguments whose lacunae are papered over by the generalizing and consoling rhetoric of humanism. This is the proper context in which to approach Charles Taylor's *Human Agency and Language*, which renews Gadamer's contention that a uniquely self-reflexive human way of being is disclosed by virtue of what Taylor calls "three things that get done in language." The passive voice registers, perhaps, a philosophical reluctance to ascribe agency to language; but, this reluctance voiced, the ascription is powerful and decisive, for the three things include:

1. *Making articulations.* Taylor also uses terms such as "formulating things," "bringing something to explicit awareness," and "drawing boundaries," all of which suggest that language enables people to apprehend some object, act, or quality in contrast to others.
2. *Founding public space.* Language places matters before *us*, enabling a "common vantage point from which we survey the world together."
3. *Permitting the formulation of standards.* Expressing "essential human concerns," standards reflect a uniquely human capacity to posit "second-order desires," desires to have some desires as opposed to others, a key factor in the ethical project of living according to chosen principles. (1985: 263, see 259ff.)

By these means, Taylor argues, language fosters an ethical and therefore a distinctively human being. Possessing language, we are virtually halfway home; the humanistic ethical project of seeing the world in all its marvelous particularity, formulating worthy projects together, and living by principle is all but accomplished and requires only our active assent to its direction.

One presumption common to Gadamer, Taylor, and the thinkers discussed below is not just that a particular use of language can be made morally effective, but that the nature of language itself stands against brute force, duplicity, or coercion. The most confident and ambitious application of such a presumption is the humanistic discourse on war, or "just war" theory. In a widely circulated argument, Elaine Scarry contends that the first victim of war's violence is language, which is reduced on the one hand to propaganda and duplicity and on the other to cries of pain and anguish. War begins, she says, when one side in a conflict attacks the "interior national self-description" of the other, and it is waged over the right to the control of language (129). War itself destabilizes language by undermining or "deconstructing" reference: the chaos of conflict produces a general object-confusion; language is subject to censorship, encryption, and euphemism; imperatives abound, and the deliberate accumulation of injured and traumatized bodies on both sides contributes to war's general "verbal unanchoredness" (115).

Language is the first among war's victims—but, in a hopeful turn common to the humanistic discourse on war, Scarry and others argue that language can also be marshaled against war itself, and against the anarchical order of power that characterizes the relations of nation-states. The "laws of war" and the philosophical discourse that supports them attempt to insert into the presumptively antilinguistic chaos of warfare a deliberate linguistic practice that is or ought to be pacific in its nature. The Geneva Conventions, James Dawes writes, "use language to interfere with force, to create gaps and pauses that break up the momentum and self-amplification of violence" (1999: 237–38). Dawes provides a list of three war-inhibiting aspects of language that is very close to Taylor's, and argues that the statements and declarations required of belligerents by the Conventions are intended to establish participation in a series of linguistic transactions that work as brakes on destruction by forcing people to pause in their awful labors in order to take in a message, a definition, an order, or to prepare a response or a report.

Dawes's many specific examples of language's moral effectiveness are cheering, but hovering over his list of the "objective" antibelligerent properties of language is a far more general, and less easily defended premise, that language *itself and as a whole* is *essentially* pacific. Dawes is understandably more reluctant to make this argument, which is, however, essential to his case, and to linguistically oriented just war theory in general. For if the moral force of language is limited to certain uses in specific contexts, then that force cannot be grasped as a property of language alone, and the antiwar party would lose its most powerful resource. Thus, while Dawes mostly restricts himself to admirably specific comments on particular incidents, he occasionally invokes a more general and unrestricted sense of the agency of language. In war, he writes, "we are strangers in a strange land, bereft of language"; the Geneva Conventions work to restore language to us, their force deriving "from their magnification of language and multiplication of opportunities for discourse" (1999: 242, 238; see also Dawes 2002). But language itself does not militate against war, nor does war in general deprive us of language as such. The Geneva Conventions and other international protocols that attempt to regulate the conduct of war are carefully drafted propositions with implied political backing; they are, in other words, specific contextually situated instances of language, and if they prove to be effective, language itself cannot take the credit.

Nor, to take up another of Scarry's propositions, can language itself be said to enjoy an essential or natural connection to reference or material reality. We should remind ourselves that the same David Hume who argued that language provided a sure guide to ethics also suggested, in "Of Some Verbal Disputes," that language compromised clarity and distracted attention from what should be the real object of reflection, "things." What if this Hume was right, and language served, *contra* Taylor, Scarry, Dawes, and many others, to confuse a public space that was instituted by other means, to complicate clear and simple standards by proliferating meaningless distinctions and to deceive us with lies and pseudo-distinctions, and to permit rationalizations that left evil undetected? What if all the good things that got done in language were undone by other, bad things? Could we still retain any notion that things—especially big things like the cessation of hostilities on an international level—"get done" in language at all? Where is language, and why is a quasi-agency attributed to it, even in the passive voice?

One way of addressing, or seeming to address, such questions is to generate a discourse in which language, or "languages," are depicted as something one attains with directed effort. In *The Ethics of Authenticity*, Taylor writes that "we"—and the use of the unrestricted "we" suggests the "Family of Man" tenor of the argument that follows—"become full human agents capable of understanding ourselves, and hence of defining an identity, through our acquisition of rich human languages of expression" (1991: 33). What would have to be true in order for these sentiments to mean anything at all? Language would have to be multiple; it would have to be partitioned into segments, some of which would constitute a common birthright and others of which would be available only to those fortunate and virtuous enough to "acquire" them. Otherwise, everybody would be a "full human agent" and Taylor would be saying nothing at all. But if he is saying something, and languages are something one does or does not acquire, then there are those—probably a majority—who are not full human agents, but something else. Taylor wisely does not articulate his argument in this way, for if he did, its potential but essential viciousness would be revealed, as would the dubiety of his account of language or "languages" as something one could, or could not, acquire.

The primary value of language in all kinds of ethical argumentation is, as I have noted, that it is possessed by every member of the species, and so stands in the position, at least, of a universal ethical imperative. This enables language to function, in many kinds of optimistic argument, as a site or even as an agent of the moral law. Language has the further, decisive advantage, for the thinkers we are considering in this section, of being more "human," more responsive to social and historical circumstances, and more intimate with individual identity, than, for example, Kant's faculty of reason. The problem, however, is that, Taylor notwithstanding, language itself is acquired without effort—so little effort, in fact, that Chomsky can argue that it is not acquired at all, but possessed—and put to an infinite variety of uses, many of which cannot be represented as worthy or just.

Thinkers who wish to take advantage of the universality of language despite their awareness of its omnidirectional and therefore amoral infinitude sometimes, like Taylor, divide language into parts, with some parts having zero, or negative, ethical value and others qualifying as "rich." Others, such as the social theorist Cornelius Castoriadis, divide language into a regressive "private" part, a remnant of infancy, and a more worthy, socially constructed "public" language, which he calls "language in the full sense of the term" (312). Or they posit distinctions between morally inflected "languages," as when Thomas Szasz urges his fellow analysts to lead their narcissistic or self-absorbed patients away from their current "language of excuses" to a more mature and worthy "language of responsibility" (202, 203). In a Szaszian understanding, language as such has no "nature"; rather, each individual language (of excuses, of responsibility; presumably there are others) has its own particular character, and we declare ourselves by our choice of which language to use. Language emerges as a solution to the traditional therapist's problem of how to define, and indeed to effect, the cure. The real problems, of how to tell one language from another, or how to know if a given language is being used in a sincere, as opposed to a self-serving, ironic, deceptive, or strategic manner, remain, however, unsettled and even unstated.

The more one thinks about it, or reads those who think about it, the more unsatisfactory the word *language* is to describe the ways that people take responsibility or make excuses. The word is chosen, one suspects, for a variety of reasons, all having to do with ease and the desire to be optimistic: because language is experienced as natural, the cure does not require us to learn a new skill; because it is a simple matter to substitute one word for another, we can simply decide one fine day to do right, and so cure ourselves; because we all enjoy the use of language and no word is prohibited to anyone, nobody is incurable. For Taylor, Castoriadis, Szasz, and many like-minded others, the only thing language lacks in order to stand as a site of ethical value is value; but this can be supplied by declaring some portion of language as the fruit of honest labor, a moral accomplishment, and the rest as mere unruly nature.

This approach can be made even friendlier by emphasizing the less formal aspects of language use. The British philosopher Michael Oakeshott, for example, describes morality as "a vernacular language" that we must learn "how to speak . . . intelligently" (78–79). According to Oakeshott, morality must be conceived in terms of human institutions, practices, and conventions, and language represents a knowable and manageable version of these. In a comparably vernacular spirit, Rorty says we should learn from language what kind of fools we are to think that moral laws are absolute or divine in origin. Morality, he says, is just a given community's set of habits, a culture-specific and contingent human artifact—like a language, which makes perfect sense to those who speak it, but not to others. "The demands of a morality are the demands of a language," Rorty says, and if we learn to see both of these as contingent products of time and chance, then we won't take ourselves too seriously, and so will be well suited to life in a liberal democracy (1989: 60). The antiphilosophical appeal of the vernacular approach is clear. What is also clear is that nothing in this "culturalist" or "vernacular" account contradicts anything said by Nietzsche, for whom ethics is a polite term for the end-product of centuries of face-to-face violence.

For vernacular ethicists, violence is associated not with the name of Nietzsche, but rather with Kant, whose categorical imperative, these thinkers contend, dignified what was in fact a species of moral terrorism. In order to serve as a genuine guide to morality, they say, reason must be brought down to earth, its contingency restored, its limitations acknowledged. Reason must accommodate itself to the real needs and character of existence—it must learn, in short, to content itself with being incarnated in language. This, at least, is the fundamental premise behind the most ambitious effort in our time to promote an ethics based on language, Jürgen Habermas's "discourse ethics" (see 1992a: 147–210; 1992b: 57–87; 1993: passim; 1990: 43–115).

Unlike most of the philosophers considered in this section, Habermas does not reject Kant out of hand. He believes, in fact, in such Kantian artifacts as the rational human subject, the capacity of people to consider arguments on the strength of their impersonal "validity" alone, and the legitimacy of universal ethical principles. His contribution to the tradition being discussed here consists of a modification of Kant in the direction of modern liberal society, using conceptual resources supplied by other Enlightenment thinkers, including Rousseau and Hegel, as well as by contemporary philosophy and social theory. These are used to leaven the Kantian faculty of reason, which Habermas argues is too "monological" to be consistent with modern society, too abstract and immaterial to be persuasive to many today as a genuine force, too tightly associated with the category of the self-aware subject. What is needed, he contends, is an account of ethics that takes practices in the "lifeworld" as seriously as it does consciousness, an account he came to call "discourse ethics."

In the early formulations of discourse ethics, its Enlightenment pedigree was clearly marked in the extravagant claims Habermas made for the good things language does. If, for Gadamer, the "unconsciousness" of language resisted the universalizing pressures of reason, for Habermas, the situation was reversed: language, he argued, brought unconscious or irrational interests and needs to light so that they could be subjected to rational testing. Language itself, he said, was oriented toward an ideal of rationally motivated, undistorted, transparent communication. Since the use of language as such represents an implied commitment to mutual understanding, trust, and accord, an ethical principle in the form of an "ideal speech situation" is built into the very structure of human existence. Functioning "counterfactually" even in our most degenerate, tyrannical, duplicitous, inauthentic, or scurrilous interactions with each other, this ideal circumstance is free from all coercion and oriented toward consensus. In it, all parties have equal access to the conversation, and none has undue influence over the others; thus, only the "unforced force of the better argument," a phrase that occurs often in Habermas, can have persuasive power.

Of course, Habermas did not deny that deceptive rhetoric, threats, lures, half-truths, outright lies, or other "strategic" uses of language were possible, even commonplace, but he represented these as corruptions or perversions of the premises, tacit understandings, and rules implicit in the ideal speech situation, and therefore violations of the essential communicative nature of language. We can, he said, see all around us "subsystems" of great complexity that foreground "purposive-rational understanding" in which actions are coordinated through "steering mechanisms such as money and power," and these do in fact threaten the functioning of society (1984: 342). But all strategic or duplicitous uses of language are hobbled by a "performative contradiction" that, Habermas suggests, will eventually tell against them. For, as he insists in a revealingly essentialist gesture, language "with an orientation to reaching understanding" is "the original mode" of language use, upon which others are merely "parasitic" (1984: 288).

The ideal speech situation serves as a directly normative force when it functions as a judgment on any given utterance or exchange. And it becomes nothing less than "the single principle of morality" when it is aligned with accounts of individual or cultural maturation (Habermas 1983: 119). Habermas is attracted to highly specific accounts of the moral development to be effected by linguistic means. In a move controversial to other Marxists, for whom the openness of the historical process was an article of faith, Habermas argued that cognitive and moral developments accompanied progress in linguistic ability. Drawing on work by Jean Piaget, Jane Loevinger, and especially Lawrence Kohlberg, Habermas developed an abstract scheme, illustrated by charts, of such growth patterns. He tinkered with Kohlberg's six stages of moral development, and even added a seventh, in which mankind is tied together "as members in a fictive world society" (1979: 80).

Many readers of Habermas have found all of these stages, and the very notion of stages, nothing but fictive. With most adults loitering in what Kohlberg would call the "conventional" or even "pre-conventional" stages, the acme of ethical consciousness represented by the final stage seems too counterfactual, too distant from actuality, to function as an effective norm in the real world. Why, Habermas's critics ask, would any real person ever feel obliged to measure his or her utterances against such an impossible ideal of transparency and rationality? And what actual conversation could accurately be described as a mutual argumentative interchange oriented toward understanding, in which "every person who accepts the universal and necessary communicative presuppositions of argumentative speech and who knows what it means to justify a norm of action implicitly presupposes as valid the principle of universalization" (1990: 86)? And in what real human interaction is it agreed, even implicitly, that no speaker may contradict himself or use the same expression with different meanings, and that all speakers must assert only what they really believe, without internal or external constraint? So hypnotically invoked by Habermas's massively assured prose, the whole architecture seems, from a skeptical point of view, fantastic. As a specialist in skepticism, Stanley Fish charges that, "however many times Habermas *describes* the ideal speech situation, it remains little more than the expression of a fervent desire, and we are still without an answer to the question of how that desire is to be achieved" (452).

In 1968, when he wrote *Knowledge and Human Interests*, Habermas already seemed to anticipate such complaints. Responding proleptically, he proposed an account of language in which the general direction of the desired moral development was already evident in this universal human endowment. Language, he said, contributed to the mastery of "internal nature" by operating "like a transformer. When psychic processes such as sensations, needs and feelings enter into the structures of linguistic intersubjectivity, they are transformed from inner states and episodes into intentional contents" (1971: 170–71). By means of this process, civilization evolves from totalistic, mythic, nonreflective thinking to a linguistic transformation of normative fundamental agreements, and thereby to the unleashing of the rationality always potential in communicative action. As we pass through the stages of moral development, we simply advance along the way of language. What raises us out of nature? What impels us along the evolutionary path? For Habermas, the answer is clear: the driving force is "the only thing whose nature we can know: *language*" (1971: 314).

As a dimension of human life that is necessary and universal, language locks in a series of propositions whose ideal and counterfactual character Habermas clearly understands. By representing moral development as a consequence of linguistic transformation, however, Habermas severely compromises the freedom on which Kantian, and indeed all modern ethics depends. An act that cannot be represented as having been freely chosen possesses no ethical value whatsoever. In fact, the oxymoronic notion of a compulsory ethical project appears to derive not from the best of modernity's options, but from its worst, the political or cultural regimes in which obedience to doxa is required as a principle of solidarity. On intriguing occasion, Habermas tries to imagine an escape from the suffocating virtue of having a path of moral transformation dictated by language, but he is unable to conceive of this alternative space except as a hellish vacancy of purpose. If we did not have the normative pressures exerted by language, he says, we would lack an "inner center"; we had better not even think of leaving the home of language, for doing so would take us straight back to the "the monadic isolation of strategic action, or schizophrenia and suicide" (1990: 199, 102).

But if no actual speech act is perfectly communicative, if all utterances are impure, if honesty is not simply "policy" (i.e., strategic) but the very *best* policy, and if, therefore, language as a whole (if it could ever *be* a whole) is neutral with respect to the values Habermas seeks to promote, then what ethical value can be attached to it? At this point, I can do no better, and no worse, than to repeat, and to underscore the force of, the "what if" questions put to Habermas by one of his most sympathetic and intelligent readers, Martin Jay:

> But the question must be asked, What if other dimensions of language are privileged over those Habermas has chosen to stress? What if language is conceived as having more than one telos, other than the goal of achieving undistorted speech? What if the metaphoric, polysemic, playful capacity of language is highlighted, rather than its discursive function? What if the mimetic dimension of language, which Benjamin and Adorno praised for reducing the gap between man and nature is privileged over the reflective, which sets man apart from nature? What if the context-dependent, connotatively varied meanings of a restricted code are seen as preferable to the context-independent univocality of the intellectuals' elaborated code? What if the capacity to lie or utter counter-factual statements is seen as more central to language than the capacity to tell or seek the truth? What if linguistic consensus can be achieved by methods more akin to sophistic rhetoric than true rational discourse?
>
> What if language's deep structure, which Habermas has so far neglected to study, can be understood to work against or even undermine the pragmatic utterances that strive for perfect communicability? . . . In short, *what if language is not seen as the antidote to nature and man's embeddedness in it, but rather as at least in part an expression of man's irrational "naturalness" itself?*

"If so," Jay concludes, "then Habermas' already weak and tentative reconstruction of the Western Marxist concept of totality"—and the same would go *a fortiori* for the ethical project to which Habermas has devoted so much of his attention—"would have to be accounted as weaker still" (1984: 508–9).

Always a responsive reader of his critics, Habermas has more recently downplayed the term *language*, stressing instead the near-synonym *discourse*. For the purposes of his discourse theory of law and democracy, *discourse* indicates a linguistic formation determined by social, theoretical, political, or institutional characteristics (see McCarthy, ch. 4). Necessarily, *discourse* is more worldly and concrete than *language*, and multiple rather than single: the Kantian discourse of philosophical morality, for example, proceeds along a different track from the Hegelian discourse of political self-expression within a given community. The advantage of "a discourse theory of law and democracy"—the subtitle of Habermas's massive 1992 book *Between Facts and Norms*—is that it encourages us to think that these two philosophical discourses might communicate without any loss of integrity, since they are both, after all, enfolded into the larger category of—discourse. "Law," in the optimal form Habermas undertakes to imagine, is the process of mediating, through democratic means, the conflicting claims of different discourses. The worldly *force* of discourse thus compels from each side a compromise, a renunciation of the belief that it is sufficient unto itself. And because discourse carries more worldly weight than consciousness, but is not as crystallized as, for example, the state, or as "overly concrete notions of 'the people,'" it can stand as an exemplary medium for democratic negotiation—solid but not petrified, responsive to history and change without being flaccid or indifferent (1998: 185). The mere fact of discourse, or discourses, leads directly to "public communication" in a democratic polity.

Discourse constitutes, then, a marvelous solution to the political-philosophical problem of how to accommodate both Kant and Hegel, norms and facts, reason and experience, conscience and communal self-understanding. Referring to a "higher-level intersubjectivity" than that of the "philosophy of consciousness," and to a somewhat lower or more mobile level of intersubjectivity than a state-centered understanding of politics, the very name of discourse theory accomplishes a certain worldly-theoretical work. But the objections of Fish, and the questions of Jay and of numerous others, remain, hanging in the air. Does *discourse*, like *language*, name a social reality or merely a "fervent desire" to reconcile all oppositions in a dialectician's heaven? What if language, the deep ground of discourse, were other than Habermas describes it; what if language had no "essential nature" or "primary function" whatsoever; what if *language* turned out to name nothing, or *no thing* at all? What, then, would become of discourse and its theory? And what if the commitment to democracy were a function of cultural, historical, and institutional factors rather than of the logic of language?

It is a telling feature of Habermas's work that it provokes, even among its most sympathetic readers, such a great number of questions, questions left unformulated by Habermas himself because, many suspect, the answers would be inconvenient. The fact that they can be asked without eliciting an immediate rejoinder suggests the fragility of an account of modernity that rests on the uncertain base of a tendentious statement of the true nature or "original mode" of language, a construction that appears—once again, even to Habermas's admirers—as a list of preferences promoted to the status of an immanent norm rather than the kind of objective and disinterested account of reality that Habermas says he wants to promote.

The project of scanning language in search of some effective force that might be cultivated in the service of a political project continues to be an attractive one, especially in the American context. In a powerfully influential version of the recurrent attempt to merge postmodernism and feminism, Judith Butler tries to locate in language some principle that would enable people, preeminently women, to escape victimization at the hands of those who would denigrate or label them. Without some such principle, she worries, people would be vulnerable to "hate speech" and other forms of verbal assault. Fixed by the words of others, they would, moreover, be incapable of the kinds of improvisation that Butler had, in her well-known book *Gender Trouble* (1990), described as the essence of identity itself.

Gender identity, she had argued in that book, is established by performance: we select from among the menu of gestures circulating about in the culture, and use these to act out an identity by which we become known to ourselves and others. Unencumbered by a core of need or necessity, identity is mobile and negotiable, subject to change. This account of identity as a "stylized repetition" of certain acts met with incredulity in some quarters from those who could not imagine themselves as having or even wanting such powers of self-fashioning. And it was greeted with outright hostility by others who charged that, having asserted that identity was "constructed," Butler had no consolation to offer those who found their identities constructed by others in ways they would never have chosen for themselves. Sensitive to these criticisms,

Butler then began to cast about for some principle of resistance to the hostile constructions of her argument by others. She found this principle not, of course, in an inner, unconstructed core of pure self-identity, the possibility of which she had already dismissed. Nor did she locate resistant agency in the realm of social action, which is subject to all manner of external influences. Instead, she found it in language.

Like Habermas and many others, Butler seeks to fortify an argument rich in particular positions and commitments by referring to the logic of language. For Habermas, language is oriented toward understanding while for Butler it is a particular mode of action, but they agree on the deeper premise, that the nature of language can be deployed in a normative argument. They even agree that the nature of language has been identified by a particular linguistic theorist, J. L. Austin, whose *How to Do Things with Words* distinguishes between "constative" and "performative" uses of language on the basis that one makes truth-claims and the other brings into being the state it names— the difference between "these two people are married" and "I now pronounce you man and wife." The radical difference between Habermas and Butler that will eventuate in a vision of an orderly and unified liberal community for one and a libertarian vision of eccentric self-fashioning for the other is marked only when we zoom in one more level. For Habermas, we should draw from Austin the lesson that the constative is the "original" mode of language on which others are parasitic, while for Butler, we learn from Austin that the power of language is centered in the performative (see Habermas 1984: 342; Butler 1997: 13–20, 43–52, 141–59). The intentions or true meaning of the enigmatic Austin may remain elusive, but what these two readings establish beyond a doubt is "how to do things with words."

In *Gender Trouble*, Butler had stressed the power of repeated actions to establish identity, but in *Excitable Speech* (1997), the actions in question are primarily speech acts, a category also established by Austin. Identity, she concedes in this later text, is often fixed by others, who use names and their associations to denigrate, stereotype, dominate, wound, or subordinate. The implied background to this assertion may be the widely disseminated arguments of Maurice Blanchot in *Writing of the Disaster* to the effect that the powers of language were somehow implicated in the Holocaust, that the very systems of ordering and meaning that the Holocaust forever shattered were complicit in its violence. In the wake of Blanchot, many came to believe that the very act of naming constituted a human-rights crisis. This view of the power of language was taken over by such leftist interventions as the "critical race theory" and antipornography movements, both of which argued that speech itself could constitute a direct form of injury. Butler, however, saw a danger in this collapsing of speech into conduct, pointing out that it could easily serve to justify state intervention into the domain of speech, and thus an unintended curtailment of freedoms.

Freedom of speech is guaranteed in the U.S. Bill of Rights, but at a more fundamental level, it is, Butler argues, an intrinsic part of language. For evidence, she points to Austin's catalogue of the various "mistakes," "failures," and "infelicities" that attend performatives. The most general explanation of such misfires is that since every element in language, from letters and phonemes up to discursive or social conventions, exists prior to a given usage, language itself escapes even the most determined efforts to master it, to concentrate its force on a certain object at a precise moment. Every aspect and element of language circulates in a potentially infinite number of contexts, and so each act of designation both fixes and volatilizes identity. Even the most unambiguous and decisive speech acts—pronouncing people man and wife, letting the games begin, calling the meeting to order—contain within themselves a principle of self-difference, a reference to a prior, socially established ritual and a temporal extension, that escapes the present moment and exceeds any individual intention. Thus the theoretical argument is that hateful utterances cannot succeed in their aim of fixing a victimized identity because, in the long run, utterances themselves testify to a general condition of unfixity.

Moreover, to be subject to naming—as one is when, for example, one is the intended victim of hateful or derogatory speech—is in subtle ways to be placed in a position of agency. Our vulnerability to linguistic injury is, Butler argues, not altogether dissociable from our capacity to assume the position of speaker, to use language in an instrumental sense. If we are constituted by language as objects, we are also constituted in language as agents. And this means that we are always in a position of being able to spin terms in a given direction. So not only does language, in its difference-from-itself, require a "new" meaning on each occasion, but being in the position of speaker enables us to determine that meaning for ourselves. By describing oneself defiantly as *queer, bitch, chickenhead, terrorist, slut, geek, wop, nerd, nigger, righteous, old-school, fat, princess, egghead, gangster,* or *bad*, one can, Butler argues, redefine these terms, robbing them of their sting and even appropriating some of their power.

We should not, it follows, seek redress of grievances by banning the use of certain terms, because the regulation of speech risks "destroying something fundamental" about language (Butler 1997: 27). What Butler describes as an "ethical dilemma brewing at the inception of speech" pits language's capacity for violence and wounding—its "traumatic residue"—against its fundamental condition of freedom and indeterminacy (28, 38). The theoretical argument, and the ground of the qualified worldly optimism that characterizes the entire project, depends therefore on an identification of the fundamental nature of language, which she locates in what Austin calls the "mistakes" or "infelicities" that beset linguistic performances. If performatives were basically effective, if direct and necessary consequences flowed from certain kinds of speech acts, if trauma were not merely a residue but an essential and uncontestable feature of language use, the entire argument would collapse in every way. It is only when freedom is securely identified as fundamental and trauma as epiphenomenal or residual that one can have, as Butler's subtitle promises, a "politics of the performative."

But as Butler herself understands, things aren't so easy. We confront an ethical *dilemma*, rather than a clear ethical choice, because there is no self-evident principle of decision. The fundament does not declare itself unequivocally, in either a theoretical or a practical sense. We are never simply in a position to honor the fundament and cast aside the residue because it is unclear which is which; and the reason for this unclarity is simply that language—a term she does not even try to disentangle from the larger category of communication or meaning-bearing phenomena—has no fundament, no single quality or feature that grounds, much less contradicts, the others. Trauma, or the capacity to wound, has as good a claim as freedom to fundamentality—and so, too, does "communicative rationality," the Habermasian principle that would seem to restrict people's ability to redefine terms to their liking. In short, Butler's highly sophisticated and subtle theoretical argument is structured around a wish rather than a fact, and her argument is open to precisely the same set of questions that Martin Jay addresses to Habermas: what if other dimensions of language are privileged over freedom; what if language has more than one telos; what if the capacity to resignify or recode terms constitutes its own kind of trauma . . . ?

• • •

All the thinkers discussed in this section share the belief that the nature of language provides grounding for a particular account of ethics; language, they believe, is *a good thing*, and gives people resources both theoretical and practical in their efforts to live worthy lives. Because it emerges within human existence, language, they argue, must be friendly to humans, respectful of their inclinations, interests, capacities, and desires. But they cannot escape the problem we have already seen so often before in this account of the fortunes of the concept of language over the past century. Language is not a limited whole, a determined entity. It has no single character, no essence, no dominant or fundamental quality. In its infinitude, it lends support to countless hypotheses and projects, but also undercuts them. The brutal fact is that all ethically desirable features of language can be negated by opposite features that can, with equal warrant—that is, no warrant at all—be advanced as the essence of language. Language can, in other words, also be represented as an antiethical agent, a negative indicator of the law, and it is to these arguments that we must now turn.

4. Language against the Law: Postmodernism, Feminism, and the Fundamentals of Language

So far, I have been exploring two possible paths leading out of Hume's assertion that the nature of language provides a guide to ethical judgment. Those thinkers considered in section 2 held, in general, that language functions as a force of law that, regardless of whether it is rational or irrational, binds human beings in ways they are not free to determine. For these thinkers, language is not a guide to virtuous conduct but a site of obligation, a law to which we are bound by virtue of our constitution as linguistic beings. Section 3 discussed a different orientation, in which language itself embodies and fosters not law but virtue, not obligation as such but an inclination toward the good. Regardless of their differences, both paths presume a positive alliance, a direct relationship, between language and ethics. In this section, I want to consider contemporary versions of another possibility, raised but deemphasized by Hume, that a capricious and irresponsible language destabilizes the very concept of an ethical law.

Among the most influential and controversial of the thinkers who make such an argument is Jean-François Lyotard. Not all of Lyotard's sprawling and eccentric *oeuvre* can be characterized so compactly, but several of his more important texts have mined the resources of language in search of a force capable of subverting an oppressive law he identifies with order, rationality, or intelligibility. What makes this project so tricky is that both the law and its subversion are linguistic. In the 1971 *Discours, figure*, Lyotard identified a virtually Nietzschean dialectic within language between a mask of formal equipoise and intelligibility and, beneath that, an eruptive force of anticonceptual figurality. Allied with other binary oppositions such as difference and identity, the visual and the audible, the line and the letter, and the primary process and the secondary process, this dark internal struggle of figure and discourse defines the dynamic character specific to language.

In certain of Lyotard's works—in particular the 1974 *Libidinal Economy*, in which he achieved a maximum of revolutionary exuberance from which he subsequently backed off—he pressed these arguments even further, to the point of declaring war between a "discourse" he identified with language as such and a force of figurality that opposes language from some nonlinguistic outside. In a section of *Discours, figure* called "The Dream-Work Does Not Think," Lyotard disputed, for example, Lacan's argument that "the unconscious is structured like a language" on the grounds that Lacan lacked the imagination to see that the unconscious was in essence nonlinguistic. According to Lyotard, the unconscious is affiliated with a figurality that does not just perturb language, but "possesses" or "haunts" it, disrupting its intelligibility through "games played by the figure on the words which form its legend" (1989: 28; see Jay 1993: 567–70).

But, perhaps intuiting that any opposition to language as such could only end badly for figurality, Lyotard was generally careful to position the resistance to intelligibility on the inside of language. He also, however, argued that language was invariably worked on from the outside as well as the inside, both by what he calls a violent and hallucinatory "primal phantasm" that composes the raw material of the signifier, and by that part of the world that is irreducible to language. Language is thus disturbed on all sides in a turbulence so general that one hardly knows whether language is threatened or defined by it. Language comes to seem both vulnerable and unassailable—both like a dictatorship on the brink of collapse, and like a liberal state constantly refreshed and relegitimated by challenges to its own order.

One of the most fascinating aspects of Lyotard's work was that, from the very beginning, it was haunted, if not possessed, by the work of an other. Within the thought of this most programmatically disorderly and experimental thinker reposes the austere figure of Levinas, the "conscience of postmodernity." It was in Levinas's promotion of the "Hebraic" values of exteriority and incommensurability over the "Hellenic" virtues of knowledge and adequation that Lyotard discovered not just the real principle behind the "libidinal intensities" he wanted to celebrate, but also the key to the far more profound subject of justice. In two texts conceived in the late 1970s, *Just Gaming* and *The Differend*, Lyotard outlined an ethic of justice that derived from Sophism, Hume, Kant, and, most decisively, from Levinas.

The law that governs judgment, Lyotard contended in these texts, is a law of original segregation in which what he variously called "language games," "phrase regimes," or "genres of discourse" were essentially distinct and equal, with none capable of claiming legitimate jurisdiction over any others. From Levinas, Lyotard extracted a warrant for his argument that "the language game of prescription [should be] kept in its purity," uncontaminated by the "ontological discourse" cultivated by the knowledge-obsessed Greeks (1985: 64). Kant becomes, in the context of this argument, a proto-Levinasian thinker, and the categorical imperative is held to reaffirm the formal purity of prescription since the directives of reason have, Lyotard said, no empirical content, "no relation to knowledge" (86).

The contention that an "abyss" separates prescriptions from descriptions means even more than it seems to. For on this basis, Lyotard concluded not only that no *ought* follows from an *is*, but also that there are no standards that can define just action, proper decisions, right conduct. When coupled with a postmodern rejection of the "metalanguage" in which questions of justice could be phrased in the abstract, such arguments entailed, for Lyotard, the conclusion that we must now judge intuitively, "without criteria" or any normative standards, on a "case by case" basis. As we ponder ethical questions, we are adrift in contingency with no guidance from above. We cannot float above the scene, recumbent on clouds of general principles, but must slog it out down among the phenomena. Bereft of concepts and deprived of access to a transcendent law, we are left alone with language and must find our way in the welter of genres, regimes, and games.

The Lyotard of *Just Gaming* is a purist. Prescriptions such as the Golden Rule or the Ten Commandments compel obedience, he says, not because they explain the world so perfectly, but because they explain nothing, not even themselves. Since prescriptions cannot be confused with descriptions, there can be no evidence for an imperative. Our obedience must therefore be un-questioning, and we should not attempt to challenge an imperative by point-ing toward some set of facts that might invalidate it. Lyotard offered as an exotic model for postmodern ethical obligation the Cashinahua Indians, the central fact of whose existence is that, for them, to hear a story is to be obli-gated to retell it, and to remind listeners that what they are about to hear is a repetition. Cashinahua narrators bring Levinasian "passivity" to a fine per-fection, and possess the additional virtue of applying this virtue of obedience in the exercise of language.

Up to a point, Lyotard simply endorsed, in a characteristically idiosyn-cratic way, the Levinasian revision of Kantian ethics in which the law be-comes figured as a function not of reason but of language. But he ultimately took this argument in a radically anti-Levinasian direction by claiming that "the task is one of multiplying and refining language games" in a process that would eventually generate "a literature, in the best sense of the term, as an enterprise of experimentation . . . a general literature if one can put it this way" (1985: 49). Lyotard called this hoped-for literature "pagan" in recogni-tion of the fact that "pagans are artists" (61). Under the pagan dispensation, language games become aesthetic exercises: all of language is just that, lan-guage, with each genre or micro-discourse operating according to rules as arbitrary and as distinct as those of chess, tennis, courtship, physics, con-tracts, detective stories, legal codes, love letters, or promises. The "task" assigned us by the nature of language is to keep all these games separate by treating all discourses as though they were species of literary experimenta-tion dedicated to exploring their own internal mechanisms.

Lyotard did not hesitate to label as "oppression," "terror," or even "torture" the consequences of any "imposition" of one game or discourse on another; an unregulated proliferation of minorities seemed to be the only circumstance Lyotard approved. But as his numerous critics were quick to point out, the cure may be worse than the poison. Terry Eagleton, for example, noted that small is not always beautiful: "What small narratives does Lyotard have in mind? The current, gratifyingly minor tributary of British fascism?" (1990: 399). Nor is large always evil. When we try to guide our decisions by reasons or principles others might endorse, we are not necessarily engaging in oppression. Nor, to round off this list of complaints, does one strike a blow for justice by promoting judgment without criteria, which might in practice take the form of arbitrary proclamations without even an attempt to achieve a common ground or consensus. As his interviewer in *Just Gaming*, Jean-Loup Thébaud, pointed out, a politics based solely on a cultivation of minority perspectives "would renew the very difficulties you were recalling yourself but a while ago" in that none would be able to claim superiority to any other, thus inhibiting the realization of justice; to which Lyotard replied, "Yes. You are flagging a difficulty, and one does risk falling back into a kind of indifferentism that is the bad side of the pagan line I am trying to trace" (1985: 96). Despite their emphasis on "pragmatics," Lyotard's texts offer no practical advice on how to get around this or other bad sides, and so cannot be said to provide trustworthy counsel, even in a theoretical sense, about political or ethical issues.

One way of accounting for the bad sides of Lyotard's thinking is to point out their origin in the decision to refer theoretical arguments in ethics and other fields to a partial and tendentious account of the nature of language. His arguments expose themselves to easy contradiction in large part because all such accounts of language are easily matched and negated by other arguments with equal claims. His claim, for example, that in the optimal linguistic state, language games or genres of discourse exist in a condition of perfect difference and equality has no decisive response to make to opposing assertions that language games always strive for dominance, that description and prescription impose on each other, that language games have no natural boundaries, and that a condition of impurity and heterogeneity is "natural" to language. But Lyotard's opponents fare no better than he when they try to refute him by making different claims about the nature of language. In a Habermasian moment, Eagleton suggests, *contra* Lyotard, that language includes within itself normative, genre-transcending standards, without which we could not even begin to judge events; but even if language did contain such standards, the argument would only be pertinent if those standards constituted the true nature, the indisputable essence of language. And there is precisely the same amount of evidence for this claim as Lyotard marshals for his—none at all. Language does not force us to judge either with or without criteria, purely or impurely. Nothing in the nature of language obligates people to judge any particular way because there is no nature of language.

Lyotard seemed to become aware of some of these problems in the course of writing *Just Gaming*, for *The Differend*, with its extended meditations on Kant and Levinas, and its opening declaration that, "There is no 'language' in general, except as the object of an Idea," is both a subtler and a philosophically tougher book (1988: xii). More rigorously antihumanistic than its predecessor, *The Differend* surrenders not only the humanist subject, but several of Lyotard's own notions. These include the term "language game," which had, he belatedly realized, implied the theoretically retrograde notion of a human player (see Readings 197ff.). Also abandoned is the priority of the prescriptive in favor of a general principle of incommensurability between discourses. And, most significantly, *The Differend* gives up the quest for "purity" launched in *Just Gaming* by acknowledging the inescapability of "linkage" between phrases.

But the difficulties, acknowledged by even the friendliest of critics, remain, taking the general form of a return of the illicit gratifications of humanism. To stress, as Lyotard does, the "performativity" of language is not to abolish human agency but simply to displace it onto a new site, which is thereby made into a conscious agent—in short, humanized. "No one doubts," Lyotard writes in this vein, "that language is capable of admitting these new phrase families or new genres of discourse." No one doubts, in other words, that language is *capable*, even that it is *more* capable—more commanding, more autonomous, more effective in realizing its intentions—than the human beings who pretend to use it: "human beings who thought they could use language as an instrument of communication," he says, "learn . . . that they are summoned by language" (1988: 13).

Just as thorny a problem for Lyotard as the unseemly return of the human in the form of conscious agency was the contradiction between the multiplicity of justices he sought to promote and the singularity of the general commandment he said was imposed by language, to "Be plural." This contradiction may in fact represent a differend in Lyotard's own thinking, an incommensurability between means and end. For Lyotard is looking to language to provide a general principle that will unsettle the very notion of general principles, and success in such an enterprise may well be indistinguishable from failure.

Lyotard forms common cause with those versions of feminist thinking whose self-conception is minoritarian and oppositional. Both criticize various aspects of humanism and leftover residues of Enlightenment rationality, but for our purposes, the most significant common denominator is a joint investment in the general proposition that language can harm and oppress—often through the very features that thinkers such as Taylor and Habermas describe as emancipatory. Both begin, in other words, with the premises that the psychological or ideological subject is determined by the linguistic subject; that language has an ethical character; that language is complicit in the established order; and that the most effective resistance to this order is the mobilization of the more subversive properties of language.

For many feminist thinkers, the established order is, first of all, a symbolic order. The patriarchy exercises its power by controlling access to this order, and can do so because everyone must speak, and so must buy into whatever order is encoded in language. In the previous chapter, we noted the arguments of such English-speaking socio-linguists as Nancy M. Henley and Dale Spender, whose exposés of a sex-and-gender system of inequities within the English language culminate in the fine rage and high spirits of the renegade theologian Mary Daly. More rebellious and oppositional, but also less utopian, than they, Daly urges that women actively take up the sword against certain deep-laid features of language, beginning with the word "I," which is, to her, both an ethic and an ideology, a linguistic phallus that must be "broken" or "cut" in order to remedy the "woman-breaking effects of language" (327).

In *Webster's First New Intergalactic Wickedary of the English Language*, Daly and Jane Caputi list hundreds of "phallic usages" and offer as a practical corrective an equally large number of redefinitions that "[free] words from the cages and prisons of patriarchal patterns. Under the rule of snools," they write, describing the dim bulbs of the phallocracy, "words are beaten down, banalized, reduced to serving the sentences of father time. They are made into ladies-in-waiting, wasted and worn in the service of thought-stopping grammar" (3). The phallocracy has long been guilty of abusing women by "thrusting into their minds and mouths man-made seminal ideas, infecting their victims with such communicable diseases as logorrhea and verbigeration, culminating in logocide, verbicide, gynocide, biocide" (34). And the worst effects occur, Daly says, in "ethical" sentences that operate according to a principle of "agent-deletion" by stating a truth with no reference to the person whose interests that truth supports, as in "It is thought to be the case that . . ." or "This is surely intolerable" (Daly 324 ff.). By "castrating" official language, plumbing the forgotten depths of words, and spinning networks of new or buried associations, "websters" can wake ancestral memories of hidden elemental meanings, revitalizing language and liberating themselves.

Daly's seriocomic effort to geld ethical language and invent another by writing a new dictionary suggests a lively unwillingness simply to suffer the effects of language, an eagerness to seize the initiative. French feminists such as Julia Kristeva, Hélène Cixous, Monique Wittig, Catherine Clément, and Luce Irigaray have made similar arguments in a far more academically sophisticated register. When the language in question is French, it seems, the inquiry becomes less explicitly political, less focused on lexical issues and specific injustices, and more universal in its applicability.

The French spirit is less separatist than the American, more theoretical and cosmopolitan. It is also less firmly anchored in the practice of a "subversive" or "radical" literary criticism and more "literary" in its own right, more concerned with the powers of the "aesthetic" or "imaginary" to disrupt systematicity in general. While some American feminists have, in the spirit of Virginia Woolf's *A Room of One's Own*, cultivated the idea of a literature or criticism or history "of one's own," French women writers, several of whom eschew the term "feminist" altogether, have adapted the insights of such powerful father-figures as Lacan, Derrida, and Roland Barthes, in an effort to identify the ways in which the "otherness," "specificity," or "difference" of women has disappeared from the scene of language altogether. For many French feminists, the ethical questions surrounding language are concerned not with oppression as such but rather with exclusion, often through a linguistic version of what psychoanalysis would call repression. For them, the issue is not the way in which language victimizes women, but the ways in which, under a patriarchal dispensation, language fails to represent them. Freudian psychoanalytic theory, in which women "appear" under the sign of deficiency, lack, absence, envy, becomes in this sense exemplary for other discourses, including philosophy, linguistics, and science. As Irigaray puts it, "discursive logic" itself, with its built-in preferences for abstraction, identity, sameness, and ungendered neutrality, "has always put the feminine in a position of inferiority, of exploitation, of exclusion with respect to language" so that women have been effectively castrated not of the penis but "of words" (1985a: 161; see also 1985b: 142).

Included among the list of defendants in such charges is post-Kantian ethics, with its cultivation of what one philosopher calls the "view from nowhere," the "universal subject," and its strict indifference to bodiliness, historical circumstance, contingency, and especially to gender. " 'Frenchwomen,' stop trying," Irigaray urges, "Do what comes to mind, do what you like: without 'reasons,' without 'valid motives,' without 'justifications.' You don't have to raise your impulses to the lofty status of categorical imperatives" (1985a: 203). Within the discourse of the universal ethical subject, woman can only appear, Irigaray argues, as an unrepresentable and disruptive excess incapable of being gathered into "any proper meaning, proper name, or concept, not even that of woman" (1985a: 156). Thus the "ethics of sexual difference" or "herethics" outlined in French discourse takes the form in part of a celebration of woman's specificity through the practice of an "*écriture feminine*," a "*parler-femme*" that reconstitutes language according to an "other logic" in a way more expressive of woman (see Kristeva 1989b: 184–85; see also Irigaray 1993; and Whitford).

How would this "other logic" work? How would one actually go about speaking or writing, as Irigaray's translators put it, "(as) woman" (1985a: 135)? While arguing that such speech can be spoken, but not spoken about, Irigaray has nevertheless been specific about her program of ethical insubordination in passages such as the following, which I quote at length because it is echoed in many other celebrations of the feminine linguistic difference.

> Turn everything upside down, inside out, back to front. *Rack it with radical convulsions*, carry back, reimport, those crises that [woman's] "body" suffers in her impotence to say what disturbs her. Insist also and deliberately upon those *blanks* in discourse which recall the places of her exclusion and which, by their *silent plasticity*, ensure the cohesion, the articulation, the coherent expansion of established forms. Reinscribe them hither and thither *as divergencies*, otherwise and elsewhere than they are expected, in *ellipses* and *eclipses* that deconstruct the logical grid of the reader-writer, drive him out of his mind, trouble his vision to the point of incurable diplopia at least. *Overthrow syntax* by suspending its eternally teleological order. . . . Make it impossible for a while to predict whence, whither, when, how, why . . . something goes by or goes on. . . . (1985b: 142)

Torching all "good forms" and "proper terms," such a style is the natural expressive medium of a being—woman—who, as Irigaray put it, "*has sex organs more or less everywhere*," who is "indefinitely other in herself" (1985a: 28).

Such passages have been very widely cited, and have made Irigaray a celebrity in academic feminism. But they have been cited, and swaddled, in dominant-discourse prose; there has been no outbreak of rackings and convulsions by women in response to its call, which now seems to mark a singularly strange moment in a movement that specialized in the exotic, rather than a plausible version of a general ethical principle. Why have women, not to mention publishers, been unwilling to overthrow syntax in pursuit of indefinite otherness and infinite sexual excitement? Several reasons might be offered. First, the call is itself made in rational, syntactically conventional terms. Second, it provides no way to distinguish meaningful and valuable convulsions and ellipses from nonsense and mere silence. Third, it would, if accomplished, only serve to marginalize women further. In the area in Yemen in which the family of Osama bin Laden originated, the veiled, sheltered women are reported to be so secluded that they speak their own dialect, but empowerment is neither the intention nor, presumably, the effect of this act of *parler-femme*. Fourth, the recommended deformations would only confirm, to a patriarchal sensibility, the presumed female predisposition to hysteria; indeed, the attempts by some feminists to revalue or recuperate hysteria itself might only sink woman even more deeply into her characteristic malady. Fifth, a woman who spoke or wrote like this might appear to some to be trying, belatedly and pathetically, to append herself to a tradition of innovation dominated by such figures as Rimbaud, Swinburne, Hopkins, Joyce, and Conrad, and by the theorists Deleuze, Lacan, Lyotard, and Derrida. And sixth, many people may feel that syntax— the source, for Chomsky, of human rights beginning with free speech and political autonomy—might not be the villain in women's oppression.

Despite all this, some might have found the risks worth taking if they felt that a vital ethical principle was at stake. The real reason why Irigaray's summons to revolution echoed in an empty square was that it corresponded to no recognizable ethical principle; and the reason for this might have been that it proceeded from a view of language that could not hold up to scrutiny. Language is an urgent issue for Irigaray and others because it responds to two conventional beliefs. First, language seems to be ubiquitous, at once entwined with the most intimate recesses of personal identity and deeply inwoven with the processes of the larger world; and second, it seems to be a limited whole, a concrete object. The combination of these common conceptions produces the illusion that we can work on language and fashion it to our liking—and can thereby renovate ourselves and improve the world. But if language were a limited thing with a determined character, then it would not be the sort of thing that diffused itself throughout inner and outer space; it would not be the universal medium of expression, communication, and meaning in general. If language were the sort of thing that could be changed at will, it would not be worth changing; and any segment or dimension of it that can be altered at will does not deserve the general name of *language*.

The difficulties associated with ethics seem to defy resolution. We feel, but have difficulty proving, that there must be some grounding for our sense that mere desire or self-interest ought to be overruled by "principle"; we want to believe, in advance of compelling reasons, in some superior power that illuminates the right path, informs our judgment, guides our steps aright, inclines us toward the good; we want to feel that we are or ought to be in command of our destinies; we want to feel that we occupy a definite place in the order of things that defines our responsibilities and obligations. Or, on the other hand, we want to feel that we can identify the malign agency responsible for our failures to realize ourselves as optimally as we might wish. In search of certitude and a warrant for hope, many thinkers have sought to enlist the aid of language in solving problems in ethics. As it became increasingly confident of its status as a science, the discipline of linguistics abetted the quest for the site of the ethical law, unconsciously and unwillingly in the case of Saussure, and programmatically in the case of Chomsky. So insistently, in fact, have ethical thinkers turned to language and linguistic thinkers to ethics that it almost appears impossible to provide a modern account of either without somehow introducing the other.

Thus it should be clear that while both those theories of language that have introduced ethical ideas and those theories of ethics that have referred themselves to linguistic ideas have been criticized here, no positive alternative is proposed or even imagined. The critique has concerned the level of self-awareness displayed by theorists who have, in general, failed to recognize and pursue the implications of their own thinking, and have contented themselves with gestures toward a solution rather than a truly rigorous working-out. But even on this point, we must avoid self-congratulation, for the failures of rigor or self-knowledge detailed above may well constitute not lapses but conditions of intellectual work of this kind.

This kind is the "modern" kind. Modernity, it is often said, is defined by the "legitimation crisis" that accompanies the loss of traditional grounds and guardrails. This loss both created the need for a discipline of ethics and ensured that such a discipline would be perpetually in crisis. In search of grounds in a crisis atmosphere, a number of disciplines have made the linguistic turn, hopeful that a science of language would be able to provide what they were not able to provide for themselves. But no science of language has been able to do what sciences are supposed to do, to identify and describe an object, whether phenomenal or ideal, that does not reflect prior normative judgments, attitudes, or orientations toward life in general. Thus the circularity of so many arguments for the relationship of language and ethics, which proceed not from linguistic fact to ethical value but from value to value through the procedural intermediary of language, not from observed particulars to theoretical generalization but from generalization to generalization with a phantom object in between. And so I am not arguing that if language did not exist, it would have to be invented, but rather that language—considered as a limited entity with a determined essence that can be revealed by observation and inference—does not exist and has been invented.

5. Coda: On Culture

Recent years have seen what seems to be a hostile takeover of language by culture. In literary studies, a discipline in which changes in general theoretical paradigms are often first registered, the crucial moment came when a group of critics centered in California began to mount an organized resistance to the language-centered discourses of deconstruction and postmodernism that then prevailed. In time, the "New Historicism" began to describe itself as a practice of "Cultural Poetics" that sought to place literary texts firmly in the context of a culture that enfolded and determined them. Since the late 1980s, a cultural, sociological, and even an anthropological orientation has sunk deep roots into the practices of literary history and criticism, which have rapidly learned to invoke categories of race, class, gender, and ethnicity in place of signifiers and signifieds.

As an academic concept, "culture" is remarkably robust, and seems to require no support from language at all. But many accepted formulations of the concept of culture, even those that take a sociological point of view, employ such para-linguistic concepts as *representation*, *articulation*, and *coherence*. Virtually all of them presume the distinction on which Lévi-Strauss and Benveniste insisted, between nature as the domain of "simple" and "self-contained" facts and culture as the domain of those things that "are connected to something else" and thereby generate meaning (Benveniste 38–39). The identification of culture and meaning was premised on the argument that language represented the human difference, the feature of human existence that distinguished it from the rest of creation. And the most congenial account of language, with respect to this identification, was provided by Saussure, who defined the object of his work as the life of signs in society, and whose signal contribution was the description of language as an immense mesh of signs pointing to other signs.

Take as an example of the way in which linguistic concepts or premises entered the field of culture the work of the anthropologist Clifford Geertz, under whose benign aegis "cultural studies" arose in North America over a generation ago. Geertz was famously influenced by the New Critics, and tried to apply their practice of close reading to the practices that he encountered in the field, which he described as a "rich ensemble of texts." "Doing ethnography," he said, "is like trying to read (in the sense of 'construct a reading of') a manuscript" (4–5). But beneath the general model of formalist literary criticism lay a more profound if less explicit debt to Saussure that determined his basic understanding of culture itself. "The concept of culture I espouse," Geertz said, "is essentially a semiotic one" (9). The reliance of the most prominent anthropologists on semiotics ensured that Saussure would be taken, by anthropologists and others, as the central linguist, and that structuralism and semiotics would be understood as the most vital principles of linguistic science, long after the discipline of linguistics itself had moved on.

One consequence of this determination of the concept of culture by a certain view of language has been that the study of culture has been opened to theoretical influences by a number of thinkers who have figured in this book, including Althusser, Gramsci, Habermas, and Hall. Another consequence is that literary theorists and thinkers have been encouraged, by themselves and others, to feel that they had privileged access to culture. In the Anglo-American academy, many of the leading figures in the currently fashionable discourse on culture are literary or linguistic in their orientation, including Raymond

Williams (*Culture and Society*), Fredric Jameson (*The Cultural Turn*), Edward Said (*Culture and Imperialism*), Terry Eagleton (*The Idea of Culture*), Christopher Herbert (*Culture and Anomie*), Steven Connor (*Theory and Cultural Value*), John Guillory (*Cultural Capital*), and Geoffrey Hartman (*The Fateful Question of Culture*). And so the last, often unacknowledged consequence is that, in the Anglo-American academy, the concept of culture, insofar as that concept is theorized at all, remains to a large extent an artifact of the theoretical, and specifically the linguistic, branch of literary study.

One of the stories in Italo Calvino's *Cosmicomics* describes the passing of the dinosaurs, an event experienced by the very last dinosaur on earth, already living in a changed world populated by diminished specimens, "New Ones" for whom "dinosaur" is the subject of myth and fable. "I had learned many things," the dinosaur says at the end,

> and above all the way in which Dinosaurs conquer. . . . the more the Dinosaurs disappear, the more they extend their dominion, and over forests far more vast than those that cover the continents: in the labyrinth of the survivors' thoughts. From the semidarkness of fears and doubts of now ignorant generations, the Dinosaurs continued to extend their necks, to raise their taloned hoofs, and when the last shadow of their image had been erased, their name went on, superimposed on all meanings, perpetuating their presence in relations among living beings. Now, when the name too had been erased, they would become one thing with the mute and anonymous molds of thought, through which thoughts take on form and substance: by the New Ones, and by those who would come after the New Ones, and those who would come even after them. (112)

In an era of culture, and whatever comes after, language is Dinosaur.

LANGUAGE AND HUMANITY

Language comes so naturally to us that it is easy to
forget what a strange and miraculous gift it is.
—STEVEN PINKER, *Words and Rules*

It is acutely distressing for those who have staked a great deal on
the nature of language to see that experts in the field cannot
agree on the most basic principles. I am thinking here specifically
of the 1999 debate, conducted in the pages of the *Times Literary
Supplement*, between Pieter A. M. Seuren and Roy Harris. In *Western Linguistics*, Seuren had distinguished between Western and
non-Western linguistics on the basis that the latter is "strongly
dominated by religion," while the Western tradition "has been
characterized from the very beginning by a sharp rejection of religious thought and is therefore basically secular and nonreligious.
Neither Homer . . . nor the Christian Bible," Seuren wrote, "played
a significant part in the coming about of linguistics in the western
world" (1998: xii). Reviewing this book, Harris disagreed. The Classical concept of *logos*, he pointed out, was a "religious" concept;
Plato, Aristotle, and others who wrote on language were "religious"

teachers; and as for the Bible, Harris said, it is nothing less than "the most important text in the entire history of western linguistics from late antiquity down to the nineteenth century" (Harris 1999b; see also Harris 1999a, and Seuren 1999a and 1999b). The few but memorable moments in which the Bible renders linguistic concepts into narrative were, Harris contended, "far more influential in moulding European thought than anything a Greek grammarian or philosopher ever wrote," and served as the basis for common sense well into the modern era. A Western linguistics conceived as secular is simply in denial, and Seuren's book in particular is "a sad example of how a fixation with the outmoded topos of 'science' versus 'religion' can still . . . distort the history of ideas" (1999b).

But a fixation with victory and defeat in academic controversy could easily distract attention from the crucial fact that both men actually agree on an unstated major premise, that modern linguistics is not, as Seuren puts it, "a real science" (1998: xi). As we saw in the first chapter, Harris argues that language simply cannot support a properly scientific inquiry because the principle of the division of labor on which the disciplines are based requires an object that can, in principle, be separated from the rest of human life, and this cannot be done in the case of language. Fully integrated into every aspect of existence, language cannot be conceptualized holistically, as a discrete entity whose nature corresponds to the questions framed by a particular privileged methodology. As Saussure says, there is no "unity" to language; and as Chomsky suggests, there is nothing in the world corresponding to the word *language*. The sense even among linguists that they are dealing with something that exceeds all disciplinary parameters may account for what Harris criticizes as unreflected "religious" residues in linguistic thought; it may even contribute to what Seuren describes as a sectarian professional ethos given to dogma and dominated by "parochial group arrogance and the brazen-faced presentation of nonsense as the latest wisdom" (1998: 527). Harris feels that we will never achieve a science of language, while Seuren feels that we might achieve it some day if people would just get serious and reject faith-based approaches, but they agree that we are currently nowhere near that goal and that "religion" is part of the reason why.

The question is important in the context of this inquiry because one of the main reasons that modernity has turned to language as the solution of its various problems is undoubtedly because of the extraordinary prestige as a master concept that language has long enjoyed in the Western tradition. Because of this prestige, many have felt that knowledge of language constituted insight into the deepest and most universal truths about the human condition. And since this prestige derived largely from the prominence of language in the Bible, we need to understand Biblical claims about language if we want to understand modern thinking on the subject.

Two of these claims are centered, with maximal epigrammatic efficiency, in the opening verses of the Gospel of John: "In the beginning was the Word, and the Word was with God and the Word was God. He was in the beginning with God; all things were made through him, and without him was not anything made that was made" (John 1:2–3). Clearly intended as a majestically lucid and powerful assertion, this brief passage in fact raises a number of questions, and even introduces confusion into "the beginning" as it strains to say the unsayable and perhaps even to think the unthinkable. Where, precisely, is the Word—in God, or "with" God? What could it mean to say that the Word is God? Have we been calling God by the wrong name? Are there two Gods, or one God with two phases or dimensions? Is there a part of God that is Word and another part that is not? And how—to move on to the second sentence—can the Word be said to "make" things, much less make everything that is made? What does it mean to say that all things are made "through" or "with" the Word?

The Word as "Son" of God is John's solution to the problem of how to account for the agency of God as a worldly force that human beings can understand. But this identification of the Word as the intelligible, ongoing, and manifest agency of God is itself problematic, for it involves two distinct assertions, that the Word is God and therefore beyond man's ken—pure, inscrutable essence; and also that it is not God but merely with God, something that God uses to make things with, like an instrument or a tool. But this is not all. In the very beginning—of the text, not the universe—we encounter another way of conceiving of language altogether, as the defining mark of the human. When Adam names the beasts, he asserts both authority over them and difference from them, and defines the human species as the possessors of language, thus giving Biblical warrant to a humanistic tradition that has been, for the most part, secular, philosophical, and scientific.[1] "According to the Bible," then, language appears to form one part of a triad: God-Man-Word. I would argue, however, that a more profound understanding of the

Bible, and of language, emerges when we consider this triad itself to signify the concept of language. The Bible does not, after all, use the term *language* in the passages I have been considering, and this frees us to entertain another, and more spacious thought, that the Biblical concept of language is not confined to the Word, but is rather a composite in which elements of transcendence, humanity, and instrumentality form variable components.

This way of thinking about language did not expire with the decline of faith in a secular and rationalistic culture. In fact, while Harris asserts a Biblical influence "down to the nineteenth century," a strong if speculative case can be made that the three-part composite concept that can be cobbled together from Biblical passages really only comes together as a powerful and unified entity in what I have been calling the modern thought of language. It is precisely when the larger belief structure of religion has been set aside as safely irrelevant to the project of science that its component parts, liberated from their context, can impose themselves neutrally, invisibly, as categories of thought rather than articles of faith.

We can actually see all three energies struggling to emerge from a religious matrix in a single sentence from Archbishop Trench's 1851 *The Study of Words*: "Man starts with language as God's perfect gift, which he only impairs and forfeits by sloth and sin."[2] As the gift of God, language is divine in origin, properly belonging to God in the first instance. The modern or nonreligious form of this proposition drops the factor of divinity but retains transcendence and superhuman power. Even in Saussure's spare scientific account of language alone, language has a power denied to mere language-users, as it "chooses," "interprets," and "decomposes" its elements. In the post-Heideggerian, poststructuralist, postmodernist ethos of the past half-century, a superhuman language has taken on an inhuman and somewhat sinister life of its own, becoming, in some accounts, a shadowy, potentially malignant form of agency with the power to cloud men's minds, to think their thoughts for them, even to make them and everything else that is made besides. The highly elaborated set of tropes in which the supreme agency of language was given voice in the disciplines of philosophy, psychoanalysis, and literary theory has actually migrated, in recent years, to other disciplines. The anthropologist Derek Bickerton argues, in a series of assertions that seem to issue directly from Paris in the 1960s rather than Hawaii (Bickerton's home base) in the 1980s, that language is not merely the product of evolution but is rather "the direct root and cause of all those mental characteristics that distinguish us from other creatures," an independent agent that "puts its own spin on the way we execute biological imperatives" (1995: 156, 157). Not even John credits language with greater power than Bickerton, who asserts, with a flourish, that language "created our species, and created too the world that our species sees" (1992: 255).[3]

If we stress another moment in Trench's sentence, however, another aspect of the modern concept of language comes into focus. As "perfect gift," language gives Trench a way of measuring the effects of sin on the human condition. Given to us in perfect condition, language is now degenerate, having been overtaken by rust and decay in the forms of confusion, obfuscation, and imprecision.[4] Some modern theorists, such as Steven Pinker in the epigraph to this chapter, retain the notion that language is a "gift," but this has become a conventional and empty figure of speech. Far more significant is the assumption behind this figure, that language is, like a gift, a material or all-but-material thing—a "concrete object," as Saussure puts it, or at least the referent of a concrete noun. It is this aspect of language that is expressed in the notion of "the Word." Linguistics becomes modern when it determines that language itself is a medium, an instrument, a system—in short, an object of external and objective knowledge that cannot be confused with the knower, a thing with no more intimate relation to language-users than a hammer has to a carpenter or a 3-iron to a golfer. Beyond the massive and quite specific dependency of particular thinkers on Saussure's theory of signs, modern intellectual history in general, with its numerous linguistic turns, is profoundly indebted to his insistence that the nature of language can be known, its features described, its limits set.[5]

So insistent was Saussure that language was a concrete object rather than a kind of organism that a kind of vacuum was created in the other two poles of the modern thought of language, God and Man. In modern and especially postmodern philosophy and critical theory, as we have seen, the idea of language as a superhuman agency gained ascendancy. But inside the discipline of linguistics, the Chomsky revolution turned scholarly attention to Man. In Chomsky's work, Trench's first claim, that "Man starts with language," has evolved into a series of anti-Saussurean propositions—that language is centered in the individual, not society; that language is essentially expression, not communication; that the linguist should focus on language rather than on a language; that language is governed by necessary, not arbitrary laws; and that freedom and creativity are the essence of language, not regularity and convention. But the most fundamental claim, the one that heralds the revolution most unmistakably, is that language is not a social but a biological fact, the key not to society but to human nature. Under this description, the goal of linguistics is not to become one of the human sciences but to found a general and authoritative science of the human.

In his efforts to establish such a science, Chomsky tries to eliminate all conceptual overtones. He does so by focusing on the language faculty instead of language itself, a concept that has no place in Chomsky's work—except, as we have seen, in the titles, which announce a subject of great philosophical prestige. Language is not, in fact, the subject of Chomsky's linguistics, but the word *language* is the hinge that links his highly focused inquiries into the language faculty with his ethics and politics, which require a principle of universality. Indeed, Chomsky does not begin to use the word *language* in his titles until he begins to discover this larger ethico-political project, well after he had succeeded in revolutionizing linguistics.

The centrality of this more spacious conception of Man to Chomsky's approach to linguistics becomes immediately apparent when we consider the version of his position offered by one of his most brilliant interpreters and advocates, Ray Jackendoff. While Jackendoff announces as his goal the Chomskyan task of "better understand[ing] human nature," his results in this endeavor are strangely nul, for what he uncovers is a mere capacity to generate mental representations within the system of constraints and possibilities structured by the brain (1996: 21). Jackendoff's "language" is so reduced that it excludes such basic linguistic functions as reference and meaning, to include which, he says, would amount to "an invocation of magic" (28). In fact, in his effort to get at the linguistic thing itself, he is even forced to distinguish between language and mind, which he characterizes as two "distinct forms of mental information" (185). He draws no normative conclusions about human behavior or human life whatsoever, and consequently his account of Man is as shriveled as his account of language. Like Chomsky, he retains the concepts of language and humanity in the titles of his books (*Patterns in the Mind: Language and Human Nature*), but the work itself constitutes a monument to formalism, and Chomsky, the passionate moralist, could hardly be gratified by such support.

What seems to have been lost on Jackendoff is Chomsky's quite specific and, by comparison, rich understanding of the human. This failure is, of course, understandable given Chomsky's insistence on the scientific character of his work, not to mention his occasional reluctance to unify his two projects into a single comprehensive argument. This insistence, and this reluctance, have made it possible for even as sophisticated a thinker as Jackendoff to proceed on the assumption that Chomsky believes that human nature as revealed by the language capacity is simply an ability to manipulate the system of possibilities that apply to syntax.

For Chomsky, however, the concept of the human is established not by linguistics alone, but also by the philosophical tradition, prominently including Descartes. He situates his work in a tradition of Cartesian rationalism, in which a theory of human flourishing is based on an account of innate capacities, the most fundamental of which, he argues, is the language faculty. In this tradition, he argues, the autonomy of syntax entails the ethical and political autonomy of the human subject. Incapable of rule-governed creativity, beasts cannot be considered subjects in this larger sense; as Chomsky points out, Descartes argued that the beast was "merely an ingenious machine, commanded by natural law. Man's freedom and his consciousness of this freedom," on the other hand, "distinguish him from the beast-machine" (Chomsky 1987a: 145). Humans share with primates certain elements of a conceptual system that involves object identification and the capacity to attribute intent to other organisms, but the capacity to conceive of a "discrete infinity"—the most obvious example being the infinite number of natural numbers—is, Chomsky says, an exclusively human trait. When, at some point in the distant past, the conceptual system hooked up with the computational capacity, the result was an ability to formulate an infinite number of new sentences over an unbounded range. And this new capacity, Chomsky says, produces "a totally new organism" living in "a total new world" (1982: 21, 22). And so, while language is an evolved capacity, it constitutes "the essential difference between man and animal" (1966: 3). This difference is profound: like Descartes and Rousseau, Chomsky believes that humans are "metaphysically distinct from non-humans" (1979: 92).

It is strange to hear Chomsky speak of metaphysics, but even stranger to hear him then suggest, in another text, that human nature is still, at this late date, encumbered by a primitive and not fully human mental apparatus. We are, he suggests, still faced with evolutionary work to do, for only if we cultivate those faculties to which language bears witness can we anticipate a future condition in which "animal nature is transcended and human nature can truly flourish" (1975: 134 *RL*). It appears from this striking quote that Chomsky has not fully thought through the implications of evolution with respect to "animal nature," and has therefore left a major part of his own theory in the dark. In fact, he has always been relatively incurious about evolution and unenthusiastic about scholarly efforts to develop the details of the process by which the language capacity was produced in the modern human brain; he has even cautioned that, as the product of slow and imperfect modifications, the brain may not be equipped to fathom the world "in its deepest scientific aspects . . . a warning that we might well bear in mind in a period when pseudoscientific pretense serves so well the needs of dominant coercive ideologies" (1975: 124).[6] This cryptic utterance comes very close to suggesting that the entire subject of language and evolution gives aid and comfort to the ruling powers, who would naturally seize on any suggestion that the human instinct for freedom originated in the beast-machine as a sign that freedom deserved no more respect than other animal appetites. Indeed, Chomsky gives the impression that if he had been present for the 1866 meeting of the Linguistic Society of Paris, he would have voted with the majority in banning papers on language and evolution.

It was with the intention of fortifying Chomsky on the subject of evolution that Steven Pinker wrote *The Language Instinct*, an entertaining book that begins with the assertion that Chomsky is misguided in his resistance to the subject. (Pinker says Chomsky is "too flip"—perhaps the only time Chomsky has been so accused.) According to Pinker, a genetically determined language faculty must have evolved along with the rest of our capacities, from simple to complex forms, to the point where grammatical structures are now a human instinct, like sonar in bats or web-spinning in spiders (Pinker 1995: 357). Pinker wants to clarify and support Chomsky's identification of language with human cognition and human nature by adding a kind of evidence that Chomsky omits, for no reason Pinker can understand. His case is so commonsensical, so amiably presented; it all seems so harmless and charming; the prehistory of language seems like a set of fun facts anyone would be interested to know. So why does Chomsky seem so indifferent, even hostile, to this line of inquiry? One of them knows something the other doesn't—but which one?

Pinker begins with the unexceptionable claim that Chomsky's theory entails the argument that the language faculty evolved very slowly within the human brain, in obedience to the law of natural selection. Even in its most primitive forms, Pinker says, speech must have provided a highly efficient way of sharing complex kinds of information. "It makes a difference," he notes, "whether you understand me as saying that if you give me some of your fruit I will share meat that I will get, or you should give me some fruit because I shared meat that I got." A more complex structure such as recursion "allows sentences like *He knows that she thinks that he is flirting with Mary* and other means of conveying gossip, an apparently universal human vice" (1995: 368). Whether the issue is fruit and meat, or Mary and her beau, language provides an evolutionary advantage, one that begins small, in the "first traces of language," but grows, through the processes of natural selection, ever larger (352).

What about these "first traces of language"? When—and what—were they? Indifferent to particulars, Pinker suggests that they might have begun to appear as early as *Australopithecus afarensis*, the famous "Lucy" fossil, from about 3.2 million years ago; or perhaps even earlier, from the time of the human-chimp split, about 5–7 million years ago (1995: 352–53). And here we may be able to see why Chomsky so vigorously resists the evolutionary argument, and why the affable Pinker, who seems to think he is merely helping Chomsky out by putting his magnificent but incomplete theory on a firm evolutionary footing, providing a component that Chomsky really ought to have provided himself, may actually be Chomsky's worst nightmare. Chomsky has not demonstrated a sustained interest in chimp nature or chimp rights. Primates are suffering unjustly all over the world, but the only ones he gets exercised about are those with a language module in their brains.[7] For him, the thought that language *had* first traces that might be retained by today's primates would constitute a decidedly unwelcome distraction. Even worse than distracting, from Chomsky's perspective, would be Pinker's functionalism, which stresses the evolutionary advantage represented by the ability to share information, rather than the capacity for individual "creativity" that grounds Chomsky's anarchist-libertarian political stance, or the instinct for "freedom" that anchors his philosophical arguments.

If Pinker does not register these concerns, the reason may be that he has no evident philosophical or political agenda; although he insists that speech is restricted to the human species, there is, for him, no cost in tracing language back to prehuman origins, nothing worrisome in relinquishing the notion of human uniqueness, nothing at stake in conceding that language "for all we know . . . could have had a gradual fade-in" (1995: 347, 346). As long as "the modern adult language instinct" is granted to be "unique in the modern animal kingdom," that's all he cares about (366, 342). His cavalier tone obscures, however, the fact that the real effect of his intervention is to detach language from Chomsky's normative presuppositions by loosening the human grip.

We may well wonder whether the account of language that results from the emphasis on evolution is still "Chomskyan"; but a more interesting question is whether it is still an account of language. To answer this question, we must pursue the evolutionary argument further, beyond the level of detail concerning those first traces of language than Pinker himself provides.

A good deal of recently accumulated—and, to many, controversial—evidence suggests that even in the absence of a computational capacity, primates are capable of grasping rudimentary grammatical distinctions. Among the most aggressive apostles of primate intelligence, Sue Savage-Rumbaugh and Roger Lewin have studied thousands of the "utterances" produced by a talented bonobo chimp named Kanzi, and have discovered a number of intriguing regularities. By tapping on a "lexigram," a keyboard with dozens of symbols, Kanzi, they say, not only associates things with arbitrary symbols, but also regularly puts the action before the object. He follows more complex patterns as well: when two actions are involved in the utterance, Kanzi typically places those involving greater distance between the two parties first, suggesting that he grasps not just semantic isolates but syntactic structures. These invented structures, Savage-Rumbaugh and Lewin assert, indicate a "cognitive substrate" to language, not a fully developed grammar but a preliminary structuration best regarded as "proto-grammar" that must have existed in the common ancestor to humans and chimps (Savage-Rumbaugh and Lewin 1994: 165).[8] From their point of view, Chomsky is right when he says that the language capacity is innate, but wrong when he insists that the structure of language is prewired only in the human brain (163). For Chomsky, as we have seen, *innate* means unique to humans; for Savage-Rumbaugh and Lewin, who hold human beings to be "African apes, of an unusual kind," innateness signifies the biological continuity of the human species with its primate ancestors (280).

The claim for primate command of proto-linguistic skills is supported by recent work on the origins of language not in brain chemistry, but in gesture. In *Eve Spoke: Human Language and Human Evolution*, Philip Lieberman traces the origin of language to neural mechanisms initially adapted to regulate precise manual movements. Language, he argues, emerged initially not as a genetic endowment but as a kind of cultural skill like tool-making. Language may have originated as visible bodily action, in which a sense of grammatical distinctions was inscribed in movement rather than words. But once established, a system of gestures would, through a process of self-modification, have played a significant role in the further development of the human brain.[9] At a very generous estimate, humans have only been able to speak for a few hundred thousand years, a very short time, as Lieberman points out, for something as complex as grammar to be hardwired into our brains. Grammar, or its component parts, must have been loaded into the system much earlier, during the long run-up to anatomically modern humanity when we were gesturing with increasing expressiveness and urgency. It makes perfect sense, from this point of view, that some of the most impressive proto-linguistic accomplishments yet recorded should come in the area of hand signals. One chimp, the legendary Washoe, reportedly learned over two hundred signs in American Sign Language; and while this claim has been disputed, it is generally conceded that some chimps have mastered the use of signs to a certain extent. And this small encroachment on the exclusive human possession of language, including grammar, makes the evolutionary argument even more compelling, and compelling in a slightly different way, than Pinker seems to want to realize (see Fouts and Mills).

According to Pinker, "the first steps toward human language are a mystery" (1995: 351). He is willing to leave it at that, but surely the evolutionary argument itself obliges us to inquire into that mystery, to construct some account of the origins of language, the straining and groping of primitive organisms for the regularity and repeatability that secure the possibility of meaning. One who has made the attempt, Robin Dunbar, argues that one of the very earliest forms of proto-language is primate grooming. When primates pick the burrs, bugs, and scabs from each other's fur, he says, they are not simply providing a cleaning service. Nor is the utility of grooming confined to the production, in the groomees, of endogenous opiates, enhancing as these are to one's quality of life. What grooming really does, according to Dunbar, is establish an elementary social bond that mitigates the threat of predation and facilitates the development of a sense of common cause in order to ensure the survival of the group. In other words, grooming is a primitive form of communication that meets a number of individual and group needs.

Through grooming, apes assess each other's moods, create shared strategies, impart intentions, reconcile with each other, and forge alliances. Combined with such hoots and grunts as apes can make, grooming does everything needed in these respects until the group reaches a certain size—about 120 or so, when there simply aren't enough hours in the day to do a really thorough job, a job you could be proud of. At this threshold, which was reached with the advent of *Homo sapiens*, or modern man, a powerful alternative form of group bonding was triggered: "vocal grooming," which emerged "slowly over a long period of time" (Dunbar 115). Gradually, expressive noises replaced the older form of grooming as a form of communication. This means that the "first" purpose of what we now call language must have been the communication of information about the little doings, feelings, and reflections of the members of the group, information that had been transmitted one at a time in the early days, when the group was smaller.

In other words, Dunbar says, the fateful first steps toward language were taken not only by Mary and her suitor, but by those who talked about them. The most primitive instances of speech in the reddening dawn of language consisted of little stories about each other, the "tittle-tattle of life," which remains, Dunbar points out, the subject of the vast majority of human conversations today (4). Gossip, in short, is both the most rudimentary form of language and the most advanced form of grooming: pick a little, talk a little. On the basis of complex calculations of group size, Dunbar concludes that language proper in the form of expressive noise with a rudimentary grammatical structure arrived with the first of our species, no earlier than 500,000 years ago, as "a cheap and ultra-efficient form of grooming. . . . In a nutshell, language evolved to allow us to gossip" (79).

To understand why primate groups became so large, we need to imagine a vast process that began about five million years ago, and this will require us to posit one of those species-narratives whose charming whimsicality, like an animated cartoon where corporeal transformation is the rule, makes evolutionary psychology one of the few academic disciplines capable of reaching a wider audience. We begin at the point when one strain of the great Old World apes, their small and fragmentary groups happily grooming and gibbering away in the rain forest, abandoned their protected life in the trees and established a new, knuckle-walking way of life, first on the edge of the forest, then in the woodland, and then in the open country. About 1.8 million years ago, *Homo ergaster* (closely related to *Homo erectus*) appeared, fully upright if not precisely graceful. Standing in the sun, this creature shed much of its body hair, keeping only the protective covering on the head and shoulders. Less hair meant greater efficiency in cooling, which enabled the species to become more mobile (Dunbar 107–8). At just this time, the primate brain grew. After hundreds of thousands of years of little or no growth, the brain suddenly became 50 percent larger; over the next 1.3 million years or so, it nearly doubled its size once again. Then, with the first appearance of *Homo sapiens* half a million years ago, the rate of growth underwent a further rapid increase until roughly 250,000 years ago, when brains attained modern levels of 1,350–1,400 cc. Bigger brains, Dunbar argues, enabled bigger groups, and bigger groups required their members to possess the language their brains could sustain.[10]

But how did our brains grow? According to the "expensive tissue hypothesis," in order for one organ to grow, another has to shrink, and there aren't that many candidates (see Aiello and Wheeler). The obvious candidate is the gut, which is much larger in leaf-and-fruit-eating primates than it is in humans, for the reason that "a big vat" is required to ferment and process the raw leaves (Dunbar 126). In order for the gut to shrink, there must have been a change to a food source much more efficient in delivering energy. And that was meat, which does not require a big vat to process, and is far richer in nutrients than fruit or leaves. The initial increase in brain size was connected, Dunbar argues, to a dietary shift from fruits and vegetables to meat. In pursuit of meat, our ancestors would have spent less time in the trees and more on the ground, becoming ever more dependent on the two-legged life and on each other. The shift to a diet composed primarily of meat, or, as Leslie C. Aiello ambiguously puts it, "animal-based products," entailed a more mobile and cooperative style of living, and larger and more firmly bonded groups required more complex forms of interaction and communication than had been required in the shelter of the trees. And so, Aiello says, dietary change, and the accompanying morphological and cognitive developments it gave rise to, preceded and propelled the development of language. Language comes out of the mouth because meat goes into it.

Meat-eating entails other changes as well. Since, as Aiello notes, animal food would not be directly accessible to weanlings, there would be a longer period of helplessness or infancy, and prolonged mother-infant food sharing. Complex communication would become not an option but a necessity, a matter of survival. Aided by such factors as continuous sexual receptivity, certain kinds of relationships would become habitual, then ingrained. Females would have a tremendous incentive to "encourage provisioning from other members of the group and particularly from males." For their part, males would find that "improved levels of attentiveness" would be rewarded. Eventually, females would discover that the principle of secrecy manifest in concealed ovulation could be extended to social practices. Indeed, "there would be a strong incentive for females to use deceptive tactics to encourage provisioning from the male (in possible return for sexual access) while at the same time there would be an equally strong incentive for the males to use deceptive behavior to gain sexual access to the female without engaging in the levels of provisioning that might be to her best benefit." It's but a short step, apparently, from eating carrion to faked orgasm and false promises of continued respect and affection in the morning. Low as these are, they represent social intelligence of a high order, and social intelligence, Aiello says, "is a fundamental prerequisite for the origin of fully developed modern human language" (29).

Like Dunbar, Aiello contends that the first traces of human language did not appear before 500,000 years ago, at least five million years after the chimp-human split. She dismisses any claim that primates can understand more than the most rudimentary linguistic concepts. And yet, in a gesture that affiliates her with Dunbar's linking of grooming and gossip, she asserts that the social intelligence of primates involves planning and anticipation of a kind that is "one and the same as those operations that provide the cognitive foundations for human language learning and understanding" (29).

One major plot element in this evolutionary dream-narrative remains missing. Chimps cannot speak, according to many (but not all) researchers, because their brains are smaller than ours; but even if their brains grew, their large and clumsy faces could not produce language. The chimp vocal apparatus does not have our delicate musculature, our superfine coordination between jaw, lips, tongue, in respect to teeth, palate, and pharynx. Moreover, the chimp larynx is too high in the throat to enable sufficient variation in vowel sounds. Such faces are needed to chew leaves, roots, and tubers; but most animal-based products can be bitten off and chewed by smaller mouths and teeth—the kind seen in *Homo ergaster*, the first meat-eater.

Once we change diets, we can do with less face than before, and a small lower face becomes an evolutionary advantage. Savage-Rumbaugh and Lewin point out that the heavy ape jaw actually inhibits fully upright locomotion by tilting the entire animal forward, producing a shambling gait unsuited for long distances. A lighter and more delicate (meat-eating) face enables the head to be positioned directly above the body so that the animal can speed along and thereby become more nomadic. The vertical positioning also entails the spectacular "free benefit" of bending the vocal tract at a ninety-degree angle, so that the tongue does not lie flat in the mouth as it does in apes, but takes a turn down into the throat, with excellent consequences for our ability to produce finely graded and rapid sequences of consonants and vowels (Savage-Rumbaugh and Lewin 234, see also 226-29). Unlucky prey: their flesh is literally food for thought, helping to make the body and the mind that can hunt it. But lucky predator, whose diet not only nourishes the body but also enlarges the mind and helps create the vocal tract that enables it to communicate with other minds so it can hunt more efficiently, and do other things as well.

With our cunning lips, our supple and flicking tongues, our low larynxes, we can begin to produce complex phonemic sequences; we can cluck about our neighbors and hoot at their eccentricities. We can deceive and cheat each other. We can reflect on past dining experiences and anticipate future meals, the difficulties, pleasures, and meaning thereof. And with these and related reflections, the episodic character of archaic life is broken; life becomes a single, continuous thing. We are in a position to acquire natures, rights, destinies, ideologies, ethics—identity in general. We are on our way to becoming the creatures that Chomsky imagines us to be.

Among the most committed opponents of the human uniqueness argument, Savage-Rumbaugh and Lewin contend that apes have all the parts of the brain that govern language use, and that Kanzi in particular has mastered the understanding of abstract signs. The differences in mental capacity between humans and apes, they insist, are quantitative rather than qualitative. In terms of basic social intelligence—structured, complex, open-ended, extended in time and space, and dependent on sensory data—the smartest primates lack for nothing, and only the wrong kind of face keeps them from expressing their thoughts vocally. If their prize bonobo had the requisite neuro-muscular control to produce consonants and vowels, Savage-Rumbaugh and Lewin say, "[we] have little doubt that Kanzi would be able to speak" (249, see also Savage-Rumbaugh, Shanker, and Taylor).

Why can't Kanzi speak? Dunbar and Aiello say that, clever though he is, he's still too dumb. He and his kind never underwent the dietary transition to meat, and so the species needs the big jaw and the large gut to process vegetable matter, and their brains therefore cannot increase in size. But— Savage-Rumbaugh and Lewin would respond—even without meat and the face to eat it, primates have low levels of everything it takes: fully developed language skills may be peculiar to human beings, but Pinker's first traces are evident in primate capacities. And as even Pinker recognizes, no anatomical evidence has been adduced to support Chomsky's suggestion that the human brain contains a special "language acquisition device" or a "linguistic module" with instructions for universal grammar. And so we must conclude that language, broadly defined—including not only meaningful sounds structured in grammatical patterns, but also those gestures that manifest social intelligence of the kind that underpins "meaning" as such—cannot be considered absolutely definitive of humanity, or to constitute a bright line between humans and other primates.

The evolutionary argument introduced by Pinker does not, therefore, complete Chomsky's identification of language and the human; rather, it decomposes both categories by smudging the borderlines between humans and other animals. The sheer contingency of the evolutionary process suggests a certain flukiness about the human difference. Thinking about the vast improbability of the concatenation of circumstances that shrink the primate gut, enlarge the brain, develop the vocal tract, and thereby enable the germination of language, one finds oneself contemplating not a "total difference" between species, but rather a series of lucky turns in the evolutionary adventure. And so language, once considered the Rubicon between man and beast, may actually, in the light of evolution, be considered to be the bridge. The ancient triad of God, Man, and Word is now giving way to a fourth term, Nature, which seems not to join the others but to contain them, its mechanisms of organic self-modification fully capable of eliminating all metaphysical distinctions.

In the work of Jackendoff, the study of syntax inspired by Chomsky results in a formalism devoid of moral resonance and even of mind. Also inspired by Chomsky and seeking only to support his arguments, Pinker, too, produces a lobotomized version of Chomsky's position, undercutting the basic concept of a distinct human nature from which specific ethical and political commitments can be derived. Pinker is, of course, absolutely correct to think that language demands an evolutionary explanation. But evolutionary functionalism need not be the value-neutral account of simple adaptation and advantage that he suggests. In his widely read book *The Moral Animal*, Robert Wright argues that evolution has been driven by factors that, at first glance, strongly appear to cut across the natural grain, and to moderate if not cancel out the impulses to self-assertion and self-protection that we might associate with a "state of nature." Language in particular, Wright says, most likely evolved through a set of self-reinforcing "positive feedback mechanisms" of the sort that that create evolutionary advantages for intelligence in all species. Such mechanisms involve the selective transmission of nongenetic "cultural" information from animal to animal, and can actually accelerate evolution.

The most pertinent example of such a mechanism is "reciprocal altruism," the capacity, once scarce and fragile but now instinctual across the human species, to forge mutually beneficial relationships. The conceptual power and memory required to forge these relationships take intelligence, and those that have what it takes will thrive at the expense of those who do not. In both the long and the short runs, such moral or nearly moral emotions as affection and empathy work on behalf of the species' deeper interests. Even in the very earliest stages, Wright argues, language would facilitate and concretize such emotions, and so promote the evolution of a "morality gene" that provides human beings with a highly advantageous faculty of sympathetic fellow-feeling. On this basis, evolution as a whole can be said to be not a blind striving, but a purposive, even spiritually suggestive, progression, one with "religious" overtones. "It is certainly true," Wright concludes, "that Darwinism can make a person saintly" (1994: 376). An evolved language faculty can, in other words, still be considered a moral force in the world, but this force does not derive from the brain's capacity to generate sentences, but from the more primitive or elemental capacity to communicate and to express mutual interest, a capacity that primates undoubtedly possess.

With such speculations, in which language, evolution, and the values and practices that define a moral and meaningful human world in a continual process of self-creation are grasped together in a unified account, language is restored to its ancient status as a mystery, both the central mystery and the mysterious center of human being. One of the most mysterious aspects of language is its apparently infinite availability to observation and description, when, in fact, *language* is a word for that for which there are no words, a chaos, as Chomsky says, not worth thinking about. Not worth thinking about but excellent to think with, the unqualified term *language* commends itself to us primarily as a proxy for a host of concerns, questions, and anxieties—our position in the order of things, our rights and obligations, our relation to law, our beginnings and ends, the relation between faith and knowledge, the scope of our agency, the extent of our responsibilities, the origin of evil, the sexual divide (the Word as "he," the "phallic" signifier), the laws of our being—that otherwise frustrate the desire for a formulation that would satisfy rationalist sensibilities. What we talk about when we talk about language are things that cannot be spoken of in a literal or direct manner. By thinking of language, we try to identify a vital streak that runs through the universe, a streak that includes and defines the human. Language is, or has been said to be, nature, human nature, and nonnature; it is divine spark, species endowment, point of primate commonality, and alienated instrument; it is deep instinct and cultivated rationality. The distinctive power, resonance, and suggestiveness of the concept derives from its unique capacity to serve as evidence for all these, as well as from its power to suggest, at a deeper level, that they are all somehow connected in a continuum.

Thus the term *language* stands as a luminous and highly concentrated token of the multiple mysteries of human life. While, as Bickerton notes, "language is, of all our neural capacities, the deepest below the threshold of our awareness," the smothering ubiquity of observable linguistic facts encourages us to think we can understand what language is all about, and suggests that we can approach the foggy immensities and deeper enigmas that have always preoccupied thoughtful humans as if they were a tool, a system, a gift, a thing we could know (1992: 5). It used to be possible to discuss such abstractions in the terms appropriate to their mythic or metaphysical character; but in our time, evidence is always demanded, and questions like these seem impossible even to articulate. An ancient mystery that is, in some of its dimensions, available to scientific interrogation, the subject of language gives us a way to talk about things that matter, but resist quantification, resolution, or even definition. Indeed, as I have tried to demonstrate in this book, the displacement of the undiscussable onto the empty signifier *language* constitutes the central intellectual project of the past century.

In a previous chapter, I noted that linguists from von Humboldt to Chomsky are likely to preface or to conclude their discussions by acknowledging that even specialists are "just beginning" to understand the object, or that their discipline is still "immature." I am arguing here that the adolescent or weanling period in our understanding of language is likely to be protracted indefinitely since the object under analysis fades under examination like the Cheshire Cat, leaving only a gently mocking smile—a smile that, come to think of it, bears more than a passing resemblance to the swooping arc of Saussure's speaking circuit. The error of thinking that we can know the true nature of language is stubborn, so stubborn in fact that it ought not to be considered an error at all, but rather a trace of an archaic desire to know the unknowable. Who knows but what this desire itself may provide a truer measure of "humanity" than any falsely clarified or reduced notion of language that we are likely to formulate?

NOTES

1. This ancient claim is not, of course, exclusively Biblical. Isocrates says that "because there is born in us the power to persuade each other and to show ourselves whatever we wish, we have . . . escaped living as brutes" (quoted in G. Kennedy 8–9); Quintillian, that "God, that all-powerful Creator of nature and architect of the world, has impressed man with no character so proper to distinguish him from other animals, as by the faculty of speech" (quoted in Pei 24); Condillac, that language gives men memory, consciousness, and free will, distinguishing them from brutes (1974); Descartes, that "all men, the most stupid and the most foolish, those even who are deprived of the organs of speech, make use of signs, whereas the brutes never do anything of the kind; which may be taken for the true distinction between man and brute" (cited in Torrey 287); Hegel, that "the forms of thought are, in the first instance, displayed and stored in human *language*. Nowadays we cannot be too often reminded that it is *thinking* which distinguishes man from the beasts" (Hegel 1989: 1: 31); Walter Benjamin, that *"Man alone has a language that is complete both in its universality and in its intensiveness"* (66); Suzanne Langer, that "between the clearest animal call of love or warning or anger, and a man's least, trivial *word*, there lies a whole day of Creation" (94); and Ian Tattersol, that humans are distinguished from all other species by their ability to use symbol systems, specifically language (1998). Since the beginnings of time, it seems, human beings have told themselves that bestiality was banished, and a human essence defined, by language, our first and greatest endowment.

2. Richard Chenevix Trench 1892: 27, 22–23. In many respects, Trench is a traditional, even a reactionary thinker, for whom language is chiefly of interest for the traces it contains of humanity's divine origins. But this concern actually puts him in contact with contemporary thought. Writing eight years before *The Origin of Species* and twenty before *The Descent of Man*, Trench combines quasi-theological arguments with the evolutionary emphasis that has reinvigorated the study of language in recent years. Not only did he describe language as "fossil poetry," "fossil morality," "fossil ethics," and "fossil history"; he also raised the general question of the evolution of language (see 1–45 passim). Steven Pinker, some of whose claims are discussed below, wrote an academic best-seller that argued that language has

evolved to the point where it is now as "instinctual" as animal behavior. But it was Trench who argued nearly a century and a half earlier that language has evolved; that mankind possesses a language "capacity," and that "man makes his own language, but he makes it as the bee makes its cells, as the bird its nest; he cannot do otherwise" (14, 15). For the arguments supporting Pinker's position, see Pinker 1995: 18–21, and 342–69.

3. At one point, Bickerton makes this argument by saying that language "is the hen, while human cognition is the egg" (1995: 160). As the context makes clear, Bickerton is trying to say that the hen preceded the chicken. But elsewhere, he is more faithful to the traditional chicken-egg conundrum, outlining a "gradualist scenario" in which the primate brain had begun to develop the potential for language until, through some possibly quite contingent event, the "final connection" was made, and a "stumbling, halting protolanguage" was converted into "the superb and infinitely flexible instrument that all of us control today" (1995: 82, 83, 85). For a discussion of how this archaic process is illuminated by the conversion of pidgin into creole languages, see Bickerton 1981.

4. The role of language in modern scenarios of the fall of man has yet to be fully assessed, but it would be a rich field of study. A generation ago, Ngugi wa Thiong'o warned about the imperial power of the English language to alienate Africans from their original, native culture. Ngugi foreswore the further use of English as a way of preserving an authentic African sensibility, and hoped others would do the same. The same sense of determined optimism in the face of formidable obstacles informs an essay that Ngugi might well have read in his youth, George Orwell's "Politics and the English Language." Orwell argues that the English language circa 1946 had fallen into a bad state. Dead metaphors, jargon, the habit of thinking in phrases rather than words: all reflected and promoted an intellectual passivity that favored the propagation of orthodoxy and the increasing consolidation of power in the hands of bureaucrats. Still, Orwell suggests, this sorry state of affairs could be reversed if only we could manage to restore English to its original condition, which he represents by a passage from the King James translation of Ecclesiastes. But that text, while written in a splendid English plain style, was produced in a political atmosphere of Puritan agitation and royal oppression that could hardly be called enlightened on either side; nor does the ethos of Ecclesiastes, with its world-weary refrain "all is vanity," and its leisurely fantasies of slaves and concubines, suggest an invigorating climate of popular democracy. Ngugi might well concur with the hypothesis that even the purest English is a degenerate instrument, but one wonders whether any language could deliver the deeper authenticity Ngugi and Orwell have in mind.

5. This orientation also dominates a variety of other disciplines where language is an object of study. For biologists, language is a functional system evolved for communication; for philosophers, it is a "social art"; and for computer scientists working on artificial intelligence, language is a "skill" (Young 175, Churchland 388, Newell 441). All of these rationalist discourses agree that language is external to human being, invented rather than instinctive or natural.

6. For other antinatural selection utterances, see Chomsky 1972: 97–98, and 1987b:

167. For an early, brief, but penetrating discussion of the impact of evolution on the study of language from Darwin to Chomsky, see Roy Harris 1980: 168–87.

7. The intimate but often obscure relations between Chomsky's work in linguistics and his political analyses and polemics present a standing challenge to those who would understand his thinking. One way of approaching the subject might be to begin by noting the strict formalism of his work in linguistics, the insistence on the formal autonomy of syntax, the unwillingness to consider semantics as worthy of a scientist's attention, the dedication to uncovering the invariant mental structures that constitute the language faculty. One might then note the peculiar ironic coldness with which Chomsky chronicles American terrorism, the conspicuous absence of anything like moral passion in his recitation of fact after bloody fact, the refusal to identify in any explicit way with any interest group or ideological perspective, the insistence that he stands in simple and direct relation to the obvious truth. A common feature in both discourses is a flight from the uncertainties or ambiguities of judgment and, *a fortiori*, from a context-specific responsiveness to the fluid complexities of the interpersonal world. For Chomsky, it seems, U. S. imperialism constitutes the "deep structure" of the global political order, a structure that becomes especially visible when catastrophe strikes.

8. Savage-Rumbaugh and Lewin do not consider a question asked by Roy Harris: do the accomplishments of primates in manipulating signs really indicate an *intending consciousness* of the sort that we would consider essential to language, or do they represent some more rudimentary associative skill? See Harris 1990: 18–79.

9. See Frank R. Wilson 1999. For a fine-grained inquiry into the intimate and interanimating relations between gesture and language, see David McNeill 1992. In *Gesture and the Nature of Language,* David F. Armstrong, William C. Stokoe, and Sherman E. Wilcox study the primary sign languages of deaf communities, as well as other, more established sign languages such as American Sign Language, which, they contend, qualifies as "a natural human language" (5). Throughout, they treat visible signing as a basis for subsequent linguistic evolution, even asserting "deep links" between symbolic and nonsymbolic gestures (46). While neither of these books concerns evolution, both make, as it were, evolution-compatible arguments by stressing the quasi-syntactic character of the aspect of communication that primates seem to be most successful at deploying. McNeill explicitly opposes Chomsky's notion of a discrete linguistic "module" in the human brain.

10. In general, the argument from brain size is made by anthropologists and primatologists; linguists typically contend that it is wiring or organization rather than gross volume that enables language. See Pinker 1995: 363–64; and Bickerton 1995: 41–49. For a more detailed, if still highly speculative, account of how the primate brain evolved into a human (fully linguistic) brain, see Derek Bickerton and William H. Calvin, *Lingua ex Machina: Reconciling Darwin and Chomsky with the Human Brain.*

Works Cited

Aarsleff, Hans. 1967. *The Study of Language in England, 1780–1860.* Princeton, N.J.: Princeton University Press.

—. 1982. *From Locke to Saussure: Essays on the Study of Language and Intellectual History.* Minneapolis: University of Minnesota Press.

Aiello, Leslie C. 1998. "The Foundations of Human Language." Nina G. Jablonski and Leslie C. Aiello, eds., *The Origin and Diversification of Language.* Wattis Symposium Series in Anthropology. Memoirs of the California Academy of Sciences, no. 24. San Francisco. 21–34.

—, and Peter Wheeler. 1996. "The Expensive Tissue Hypothesis." *Current Anthropology* 36. 199–211.

Althusser, Louis. 1965. *For Marx.* Translated by Ben Brewster. New York: Vintage Books.

—. 1984. *Essays on Ideology.* London: Verso.

Armstrong, David F., William C. Stokoe, and Sherman E. Wilcox. 1995. *Gesture and the Nature of Language.* Cambridge: Cambridge University Press.

Austin, J. L. 1962. *How to Do Things with Words.* Cambridge, Mass.: Harvard University Press.

Ayer, A. J. 1952. *Language, Truth, and Logic.* New York: Dover Publications.

Balibar, Etienne. 1988. "The Vacillation of Ideology." Cary Nelson and Lawrence Grossberg, eds., *Marxism and the Interpretation of Culture.* Urbana: University of Illinois Press. 159–210.

Barsky, Robert F. 1997. *Noam Chomsky: A Life of Dissent.* Cambridge, Mass.: MIT Press.

Barth, Hans. 1976. *Truth and Ideology.* Translated by Frederic Lilge. Berkeley: University of California Press.

Barthes, Roland. 1967. *Writing Degree Zero. Writing Degree Zero and Elements of Semiology.* Translated by Annette Lavers and Colin Smith. Boston: Beacon Press.

—. [1972] 1990. "How to Begin?" *New Critical Essays.* Translated by Richard Howard. Berkeley: University of California Press. 79–90.

Bataille, Georges. 1988. "Hegel, l'homme et l'histoire." *Oeuvres complètes* XII. Paris: Gallimard. Quoted in Borch-Jakobsen 91.

Baynes, Kenneth, James Bohman, and Thomas McCarthy, eds. 1991. *After Philosophy: End or Transformation?* Cambridge, Mass.: MIT Press.

Bell, Daniel. 1960. *The End of Ideology.* Glencoe, Ill.: Free Press.

Benhabib, Seyla. 1992. *Situating the Self: Gender, Community and Postmodernism in Contemporary Ethics.* New York: Routledge.

Benjamin, Walter. 1996. "On Language as Such and on the Language of Man." *Selected Writings, Volume 1, 1913–1926*. Edited by Marcus Bullock and Michael W. Jennings. Cambridge, Mass.: Harvard University Press, Belknap Press. 62–74.

Benveniste, Emile. 1971. *Problems in General Linguistics*. Translated by Mary J. Meek. Coral Gables, Fla.: University of Miami Press.

Bernasconi, Robert. 1986. "Levinas and Derrida: The Question of the Closure of Metaphysics." Cohen. 181–204.

—, and Simon Critchley, eds. 1992. *Re-Reading Levinas*. Bloomington: Indiana University Press.

Bickerton, Derek. 1981. *Roots of Language*. Ann Arbor, Mich.: Karoma Publishers.

—. 1992. *Language and Species*. Chicago: University of Chicago Press.

—. 1995. *Language and Human Behavior (The Jessie and John Danz Lectures)*. Seattle: University of Washington Press.

—, and William H. Calvin. 2000. *Lingua ex Machina: Reconciling Darwin and Chomsky with the Human Brain*. Cambridge, Mass.: MIT Press.

Blanchot, Maurice. [1980] 1995. *The Writing of the Disaster*. Translated by Ann Smock. Lincoln: University of Nebraska Press.

Borch-Jakobsen, Mikkel. 1991. *Lacan: The Absolute Master*. Translated by Douglas Brick. Stanford, Calif.: Stanford University Press.

Boulez, Pierre. 1968. *Notes of an Apprenticeship*. Translated by Herbert Weinstock. New York: Knopf.

Butler, Christopher. 1994. *Early Modernism: Literature, Music, and Painting in Europe, 1900–1916*. Oxford: Clarendon Press.

Butler, Judith. 1990. *Gender Trouble: Feminism and the Subversion of Identity*. New York: Routledge.

—. 1997. *Excitable Speech: A Politics of the Performative*. New York: Routledge.

Calvino, Italo. 1968. *Cosmicomics*. Translated by William Weaver. New York: Harcourt Brace Jovanovich.

Cameron, Deborah. 1985a. *Feminism and Linguistic Theory*. New York: St. Martin's Press.

—. 1985b. "What Has Gender Got to Do with Sex?" *Language & Communication* 5. 19–27.

Carnap, Rudolf. 1967. "On the Character of Philosophical Problems." Rorty 1967. 54–62.

Castoriadis, Cornelius. 1998. *The Imaginary Constitution of Society*. Translated by Kathleen Blamey. Cambridge, Mass.: MIT Press.

Chomsky, Noam. 1957. *Syntactic Structures*. The Hague: Mouton & Co.

—. 1966. *Cartesian Linguistics: A Chapter in the History of Rationalist Thought*. Lanham, Md.: University Press of America.

—. 1972. *Language and Mind*. New York: Harcourt Brace Jovanovich.

—. 1975. *Reflections on Language*. New York: Random House.

—. 1979. *Language and Responsibility*. Based on conversations with Mitsou Ronat. Translated by John Viertel. New York: Pantheon Books.

—. 1980. *Rules and Representations*. New York: Columbia University Press.

—. 1982. *Noam Chomsky on the Generative Enterprise: A Discussion with Riny Hurbregts and Henk van Riemsdiik*. Dordrecht: Foris.

—. 1986. *Knowledge of Language: Its Nature, Origin, and Use.* New York: Praeger.

—. 1987a. "Language and Freedom." *The Chomsky Reader.* Edited by James Peck. New York: Pantheon Books. 139–55.

—. 1987b. *Language and Problems of Knowledge: The Managua Lectures.* Cambridge, Mass.: MIT Press.

—. 1989. "An Interview." *Radical Philosophy* 53 (Autumn). 30–39.

—. 1990. "Language and Problems of Knowledge." Martinich. 509–27.

Churchland, Patricia. 1986. *Neurophilosophy.* Cambridge: Cambridge University Press.

Cohen, Richard, ed. 1986. *Face to Face with Levinas.* Albany: State University of New York Press.

Condillac, Abbé de. 1974. *Essay on the Origin of Human Understanding.* Translated by Thomas Nugent. New York: A.M.S. Press.

Connor, Steven. 1992. *Theory and Cultural Value.* Oxford: Blackwell.

Cooke, Deryck. 1959. *The Language of Music.* London: Oxford University Press.

Corngold, Stanley. 1989. "On Paul de Man's Collaborationist Writings." Hamacher et al. 80–84.

Coward, Rosalind, and John Ellis. 1977. *Language and Materialism.* London: Routledge & Kegan Paul.

Culler, Jonathan. 1986. *Ferdinand de Saussure.* Revised edition. Ithaca, N.Y.: Cornell University Press.

Daly, Mary. 1978. *Gyn/Ecology: The Metaethics of Radical Feminism.* Boston: Beacon Press.

—, and Jane Caputi. 1987. *Websters' First New Intergalactic Wickedary of the English Language.* Boston: Beacon Press.

Davidson, Donald. 1986. "A Nice Derangement of Epitaphs." *Truth and Interpretation: Perspectives on the Philosophy of Donald Davidson.* Edited by Ernest LePore. Oxford: Blackwell. 433–46.

Davis, Robert Con, and Ronald Schliefer. 1991. *Criticism and Culture: The Role of Critique in Modern Literary Theory.* Harlow: Longman.

Dawes, James. 1999. "Language, Violence, and Human Rights Law." *Yale Journal of Law & the Humanities* 11 (Summer) 2. 215–50.

—. 2002. *The Language of War.* Cambridge, Mass.: Harvard University Press.

de Man, Paul. 1978. *Allegories of Reading: Figural Language in Rousseau, Nietzsche, Rilke, and Proust.* New Haven, Conn.: Yale University Press.

—. 1983. *Blindness and Insight: Essays in the Rhetoric of Contemporary Criticism.* 2nd edition. Theory and History of Literature, vol. 7. Minneapolis: University of Minnesota Press.

—. 1984. *The Rhetoric of Romanticism.* New York: Columbia University Press.

—. 1986. *The Resistance to Theory.* Foreword by Wlad Godzich. Theory and History of Literature, vol. 33. Minneapolis: University of Minnesota Press.

Derrida, Jacques. 1973. *Speech and Phenomena and Other Essays on Husserl's Theory of Signs.* Translated by David B. Allison. Evanston, Ill.: Northwestern University Press.

—. 1978a. *Of Grammatology.* Translated by Gayatri Chakravorty Spivak. Baltimore: The Johns Hopkins University Press.

—. 1978b. *Writing and Difference*. Translated by Alan Bass. Chicago: University of Chicago Press.

—. 1984. "Deconstruction and the Other." Dialogue with Richard Kearney. Kearney, ed., *Dialogues with Contemporary Continental Thinkers: The Phenomenological Heritage*. Manchester: Manchester University Press. 107–25.

—. 1986a. *Altérités*. Paris: Editions Osiris.

—. 1986b. *Memoires for Paul de Man*. Translated by Cecile Linday, Jonathan Culler, Eduardo Cadava, and Peggy Kamuf. New York: Columbia University Press.

—. 1988. "Afterword: Toward an Ethic of Discussion." *Limited Inc*. Edited by Gerald Graff, and translated by Samuel Weber and Jeffrey Mehlman. Evanston, Ill.: Northwestern University Press. 111–60.

—. 1992. "At This Very Moment in This Work Here I Am." Bernasconi and Critchley. 11–48.

—. 1994. *Spectres of Marx: The State of the Debt, the Work of Mourning, and the New International*. Translated by Peggy Kamuf. New York: Routledge.

Dolar, Mladen. 1996. "The Object Voice." Renata Salecl and Slavoj Žižek, eds., *Gaze and Voice as Love Objects*. Durham, N.C.: Duke University Press. 7–31.

Dunbar, Robin. 1996. *Grooming, Gossip, and the Evolution of Language*. Cambridge, Mass.: Harvard University Press.

Eagleton, Terry. 1990. *The Ideology of the Aesthetic*. Oxford: Basil Blackwell.

—. 1991. *Ideology: An Introduction*. London: Verso.

—. 2000. *The Idea of Culture*. Oxford: Blackwell.

Eco, Umberto. 1995. *The Search for the Perfect Language*. Translated by James Fentress. Oxford: Blackwell.

Elliott, Gregory, ed. 1994. *Althusser: A Critical Reader*. Oxford: Blackwell.

Engels, Friedrich. 1978. "Letter to Mehring." Robert C. Taylor, ed., *The Marx-Engels Reader*. New York: Norton. 765–67.

Everdell, William R. 1997. *The First Moderns: Profiles in the Origins of Twentieth-Century Thought*. Chicago: University of Chicago Press.

Fink, Bruce. 1995. *The Lacanian Subject: Between Language and Jouissance*. Princeton, N.J.: Princeton University Press.

Fish, Stanley. 1989. *Doing What Comes Naturally: Change, Rhetoric, and the Practice of Theory in Literary and Legal Studies*. Oxford: Clarendon Press.

Foucault, Michel. 1970. *The Order of Things: An Archeology of the Human Sciences*. New York: Vintage Books.

—. 1972. *The Archeology of Knowledge and the Discourse on Language*. Translated by A. M. Sheridan Smith. New York: Pantheon.

—. 1977. *Language, Counter-Memory, Practice: Selected Essays and Interviews*. Edited by Donald F. Bouchard, and translated by Donald F. Bouchard and Sherry Simon. Ithaca, N.Y.: Cornell University Press.

—. [1966] 1990. "Maurice Blanchot: The Thought from Outside." Michel Foucault and Maurice Blanchot, Foucault/Blanchot. New York: Zone Books. 7–60.

Fouts, Roger, and Stephen Tukel Mills. 1997. *Next of Kin: What Chimpanzees Have Taught Me about Who We Are*. New York: William Morrow.

Freud, Sigmund. [1915] 1963. "The Unconscious." *General Psychological Theory.* Edited by Philip Rieff. New York: Macmillan. 116–50.

Gadamer, Hans-Georg. 1976. "Man and Language." *Philosophical Hermeneutics.* Translated by David E. Linge. Berkeley: University of California Press. 59–68.

Geertz, Clifford. 1978. *The Interpretation of Cultures.* New York: Basic Books.

Goodman, Nelson. 1976. *The Languages of Art.* Indianapolis: Hackett.

Graham, Joseph. 1992. *Onomatopoetics: Theory of Language and Literature.* Cambridge: Cambridge University Press.

Gramsci, Antonio. 1971. *Selections from the Prison Notebooks of Antonio Gramsci.* Edited and translated by Quintin Hoare and Geoffrey Nowell Smith. New York: International Publishers.

Guillory, John. 1993. *Cultural Capital: The Problem of Literary Canon Formation.* Chicago: University of Chicago Press.

Habermas, Jürgen. 1971. *Knowledge and Human Interests.* Translated by Jeremy J. Shapiro. Boston: Beacon Press.

—. 1979. *Communication and the Evolution of Society.* Translated by Thomas McCarthy. Boston: Beacon Press.

—. 1983. "Arnold Gehlen: Imitation Substantiality." *Philosophical Profiles.* Translated by Frederick G. Lawrence. Cambridge, Mass.: Harvard University Press. 111–28.

—. 1984. *Theory of Communicative Action,* vol. 1. Translated by Thomas McCarthy. Boston: Beacon Press.

—. 1987. *The Philosophical Discourse of Modernity.* Translated by Frederick G. Lawrence. Cambridge, Mass.: MIT Press.

—. 1990. *Moral Consciousness and Communicative Action.* Translated by Christian Lenhardt and Shierry Weber Nicholsen. Cambridge, Mass.: MIT Press.

—. 1992a. *Autonomy and Solidarity.* Edited by Peter Dews. London: Verso.

—. 1992b. *Postmetaphysical Thinking: Philosophical Essays.* Translated by William Mark Hohengarten. Cambridge, Mass.: MIT Press.

—. 1993. *Justification and Application: Remarks on Discourse Ethics.* Translated by Ciaran Cronin. Cambridge, Mass.: MIT Press.

—. 1998. *Between Facts and Norms: Contributions to a Discourse Theory of Law and Democracy.* Translated by William Rehg. Cambridge, Mass.: MIT Press.

Hall, Stuart. 1981. "In Defence of Theory." Raphael Samuel, ed., *People's History and Socialist Theory.* London: Routledge & Kegan Paul. 378–85.

—. 1982. "The Rediscovery of 'Ideology': Return of the Repressed in Media Studies." Michael Gurevitch, Tony Bennett, James Curran, and Janet Woollacott, eds., *Culture, Society, and the Media.* London: Methuen. 56–90.

—. 1986a. "On Postmodernism and Articulation: An Interview with Stuart Hall." With Lawrence Grossbert. *Journal of Communication Inquiry* 10: 2. 45–60.

—. 1986b. "The Problem of Ideology—Marxism without Guarantees." *Journal of Communication Inquiry* 10: 2. 28–43.

Hamacher, Werner, Neil Hertz, and Thomas Keenan, eds. 1989. *Responses to Paul de Man's Wartime Journalism.* Lincoln: University of Nebraska Press.

Hare, R. M. 1952. *The Language of Morals.* Oxford: Oxford University Press.

—. 1963. *Freedom and Reason.* Oxford: Clarendon Press.

Harris, Randy Allen. 1993. *The Linguistics Wars.* New York: Oxford University Press.

Harris, Roy. 1980. *The Language-Makers.* Ithaca, N.Y.: Cornell University Press.

—. 1981. *The Language Myth.* London: Duckworth.

—. 1987a. *The Language Machine.* London: Duckworth.

—. 1987b. *Reading Saussure: A Critical Commentary on the* Cours de linguistique géné-rale. London: Duckworth.

—. 1988. *Language, Saussure and Wittgenstein: How to Play Games with Words.* London: Routledge.

—. 1990. *The Foundations of Linguistic Theory: Selected Writings of Roy Harris.* Edited by Nigel Love. London: Routledge.

—. 1996. *Signs, Language and Communication: Integrational and Segregational Approaches.* London: Routledge.

—. 1998 (October 23). Review of Seuren, *Western Linguistics. Times Literary Supplement.* 37.

—. 1999a (July 9). Letter to the Editor. *Times Literary Supplement.* 17.

—. 1999b (August 27). Letter to the Editor. *Times Literary Supplement.* 19.

—. 2000. "Saussure for all Seasons." *Semiotica* 131: 3–4. 273–87.

—, and Talbot J. Taylor, eds. 1997. *Landmarks in Linguistic Thought I: The Western Tradition from Socrates to Saussure.* London: Routledge.

Hartman, Geoffrey. 1989. "Looking Back on Paul de Man." Waters and Godzich. 3–24.

—. 1997. *The Fateful Question of Culture.* New York: Columbia University Press.

Hawkes, David. 1996. *Ideology.* London: Routledge.

Hegel, G. W. F. 1967. *Hegel's Philosophy of Right.* Translated by T. M. Knox. London: Oxford University Press.

—. 1989. *Hegel's Science of Logic.* Translated by A. V. Miller. Atlantic Highlands, N.J.: Humanities Press International.

Heidegger, Martin. 1962. *Being and Time.* Translated by John Macquarrie and Edward Robinson. New York: Harper & Row.

—. 1971. *On the Way to Language.* Translated by Peter D. Hertz. Cambridge: Harper & Row.

—. 1975. *Poetry, Language, Thought.* Translated by Albert Hofstadter. New York: Harper Colophon Books.

Henley, Nancy M. 1987. "This New Species That Seeks a New Language: On Sexism in Language and Language Change." Joyce Penfield, ed., *Women and Language in Transition.* Albany: State University of New York Press. 3–27.

Herbert, Christopher. 1991. *Culture and Anomie: Ethnographic Imagination in the Nineteenth Century.* Chicago: University of Chicago Press.

Hodge, Robert, and Gunther Kress. 1993. *Language as Ideology.* 2nd edition. London: Routledge.

Hudson, W. D. 1969. *The Is-Ought Question.* London: Macmillan.

Hume, David. 1975. *Enquiries concerning Human Understanding and concerning the Principles of Morals.* 3rd edition. Edited by L. A. Selby-Bigge. Oxford: Clarendon Press.

—. 2000. *A Treatise of Human Nature.* Edited by David Fate Norton and Mary J. Norton. Oxford: Oxford University Press.

Irigaray, Luce. 1985a. *This Sex Which Is Not One.* Translated by Catherine Porter with Carolyn Burke. Ithaca, N.Y.: Cornell University Press.

—. 1985b. *Speculum of the Other Woman.* Translated by Gillian C. Gill. Ithaca, N.Y.: Cornell University Press.

—. 1986. "The Fecundity of the Caress." Translated by Carolyn Burke. Cohen. 231–56.

—. 1991. "Questions to Emmanuel Levinas." Margaret Whitford, ed., *The Irigaray Reader.* Oxford: Basic Blackwell. 178–89.

—. 1993. *An Ethics of Sexual Difference.* Translated by Carolyn Burke and Gillian C. Gill. Ithaca, N.Y.: Cornell University Press.

Jackendoff, Ray. 1994. *Patterns in the Mind: Language and Human Nature.* New York: Basic Books.

—. 1996. *Languages of the Mind: Essays on Mental Representation.* Cambridge, Mass.: MIT Press.

Jameson, Fredric. 1998. *The Cultural Turn: Selected Writings on the Postmodern, 1983–1998.* London: Verso.

Jay, Martin. 1984. *Marxism and Totality: The Adventures of a Concept from Lukács to Habermas.* Berkeley: University of California Press.

—. 1993. *Downcast Eyes: The Denigration of Vision in Twentieth-Century French Thought.* Berkeley: University of California Press.

Johnson, Barbara. 1995. "Writing." Frank Lentricchia and Thomas Docherty, eds., *Critical Terms for Literary Study,* 2nd edition. Chicago: University of Chicago Press. 39–49.

Johnson, Sally, and Ulrike Hanna Meinhof, eds. 1997. *Language and Masculinity.* Oxford: Blackwell.

Kamenka, Eugene, ed. 1983. *The Portable Karl Marx.* Harmondsworth, England: Penguin Books.

Kant, Immanuel. 1977. "Metaphysical Foundations of Morals." Carl J. Friedrich, ed., *The Philosophy of Kant.* New York: Modern Library. 140–208.

—. 1993. "On a Supposed Right to Lie because of Philanthropic Concerns." *Grounding for the Metaphysics of Morals.* Translated by James W. Ellington. Indianapolis: Hackett. 63–67.

Kaplan, Ann E., and Michael Sprinker. 1993. *The Althusserian Legacy.* London: Verso.

Katz, Jerrold, ed. 1985. *The Philosophy of Linguistics.* Oxford: Oxford University Press.

Kearney, Richard, and Mark Dooley, eds. 1999. *Questioning Ethics: Contemporary Debates in Philosophy.* London: Routledge.

Kennedy, Emmett. 1978. *A Philosopher in the Age of Revolution.* Philadephia: American Philosophical Society.

Kennedy, G., ed. and trans. 1963. *The Art of Persuasion in Greece.* Princeton, N.J.: Princeton University Press.

Kristeva, Julia. 1989a. *Language the Unknown: An Initiation into Linguistics.* Translated by Anne M. Menke. New York: Columbia University Press.

—. 1989b. "Stabat Mater." *The Kristeva Reader.* Edited by Toril Moi. New York: Columbia University Press. 161–85.

Lacan, Jacques. 1977. *Ecrits: A Selection.* Translated by Alan Sheridan. New York: W. W. Norton & Co.

—. 1981. *The Four Fundamental Concepts of Psycho-Analysis.* Edited by Jacques-Alain Miller, and translated by Alan Sheridan. New York: W. W. Norton & Co.

—. 1992. *The Ethics of Psychoanalysis 1959–60.* Book VII of *The Seminar of Jacques Lacan.* Edited by Jacques-Alain Miller, and translated by Dennis Potter. New York: W. W. Norton & Co.

Laclau, Ernesto. 1977. *Politics and Ideology in Marxist Theory: Capitalism—Fascism—Populism.* London: NLB; Atlantic Highlands, N.J.: Humanities Press.

—. 1996a. "The Death and Resurrection of the Theory of Ideology." *Journal of Political Ideologies* 1: 3. 201–220.

—. 1996b. *Emancipations.* London: Verso.

—. 2000. *Contingency, Hegemony, Universality: Contemporary Dialogues on the Left* (authored by Judith Butler, Ernesto Laclau, and Slavoj Žižek). London: Verso.

—, and Chantal Mouffe. 1985. *Hegemony and Socialist Strategy: Towards a Radical Democratic Politics.* London: Verso.

Langer, Suzanne. 1960. *Philosophy in a New Key: A Study in the Symbolism of Reason, Rite, and Art.* Cambridge, Mass.: Harvard University Press.

Lecercle, Jean-Jacques. 1985. *Philosophy through the Looking-Glass: Language, Nonsense, Desire.* London: Hutchinson.

Lee, Jonathan Scott. 1990. *Jacques Lacan.* Amherst: University of Massachusetts Press.

Lefort, Guy. 1986. *The Political Forms of Modern Society: Bureaucracy, Democracy, Totalitarianism.* Edited by John B. Thompson. Cambridge, Mass.: MIT Press.

Lenin, V. I. 1973. *Collected Works,* vol. 5. Translated by Joe Fineberg and George Hanna, and edited by Victor Jerome. Moscow: Progress Publishers.

Levinas, Emmanuel. 1969 [1961]. *Totality and Infinity: An Essay on Exteriority.* Translated by Alphonso Lingis. Pittsburgh: Duquesne University Press.

—. 1989a. *The Levinas Reader.* Edited by Séan Hand. Oxford: Basil Blackwell.

—. 1989b. "God and Philosophy." *The Levinas Reader.* 166–89.

—. 1989c [1947]. "The Other in Proust." *The Levinas Reader.* 160–65.

—. 1989d. "Reality and Its Shadow." *The Levinas Reader.* 129–43.

—. 1989e. "Revelation in the Jewish Tradition." *The Levinas Reader.* 190–210.

—. 1989f [1966]. "The Servant and Her Master." *The Levinas Reader.* 150–59.

—, and Richard Kearney. 1986. "Dialogue with Emmanuel Levinas." Cohen. 13–34.

Lévi-Strauss, Claude. 1963. *Structural Anthropology.* Translated by C. Jacobson and B. Schoepf. New York: Basic Books.

—. 1966. *The Savage Mind.* Chicago: University of Chicago Press.

Lieberman, Philip. 1998. *Eve Spoke: Human Language and Human Evolution.* New York: W. W. Norton & Co.

Locke, John. 1975. *Essay Concerning Human Understanding.* Edited by Peter H. Nidditch. Oxford: Clarendon Press.

Lyotard, Jean-Francois. 1971. *Discours, figure.* Paris: Klincksieck.

—. 1985. *Just Gaming.* Theory and History of Literature, vol. 20. Translated by Wlad Godzich. Minneapolis: University of Minnesota Press.

—. 1986. "Levinas' Logic." Cohen. 117–58.

—. 1988. *The Differend: Phrases in Dispute.* Theory and History of Literature, volume 46. Translated by Georges Van Den Abbeele. Minneapolis: University of Minnesota Press.

—. 1989. *The Lyotard Reader.* Edited by Andrew Benjamin. Oxford and Cambridge, Mass.: Blackwell.

Macey, David. "Thinking with Borrowed Concepts: Althusser and Lacan." Elliott. 142–58.

MacIntyre, Alasdair. 1966. *A Short History of Ethics.* New York: Macmillan.

—. 1981. *After Virtue.* Notre Dame: University of Notre Dame Press.

—. 1988. *Whose Justice? Which Rationality?* Notre Dame: University of Notre Dame Press.

Martinich, A. P. 1990. *The Philosophy of Language.* 2nd edition. New York, Oxford: Oxford University Press.

Marx, Karl. 1983a. "From *Capital,* Volume 1." Kamenka. 369–504.

—, and Friedrich Engels. 1983b. "From *The German Ideology,* Volume One." Kamenka. 162–96.

—. 1983c. "Preface" to *A Contribution to the Critique of Political Economy.* Kamenka. 158–61.

McCarthy, Thomas. 1978. *The Critical Theory of Jürgen Habermas.* Cambridge: Cambridge University Press.

McGee, Daniel T. 1997. "Post-Marxism: The Opiate of the Intellectuals." *Modern Language Quarterly* 58 (June) 2. 201–25.

McGinn, Colin. 1999 (November 4). "Freud under Analysis." *The New York Review of Books* 46: 17. 20–24.

McNeill, David. 1992. *Hand and Mind: What Gestures Reveal about Thought.* Chicago: University of Chicago Press.

Meyer, Leonard. 1967. *Music, the Arts and Ideas; Patterns and Predictions in Twentieth-Century Culture.* Chicago: University of Chicago Press.

Miller, J. Hillis. 1983. "Mr. Carmichael and Lily Briscoe: The Rhythm of Creativity in *To the Lighthouse.*" Robert Kiely and John Hildebidle, eds., *Modernism Reconsidered.* Harvard English Studies 11. Cambridge, Mass.: Harvard University Press. 167–89.

—. 1986. *The Ethics of Reading: Kant, de Man, Eliot, Trollope, James, and Benjamin.* New York: Columbia University Press.

—. 1989a. "An Open Letter to Professor Jon Wiener." Hamacher et al. 334–42.

—. 1989b. " 'Reading' Part of a Paragraph in *Allegories of Reading.*" Waters and Godzich. 155–70.

—. 1989c. "Is There an Ethics of Reading?" James Phelan, ed., *Reading Narrative: Form, Ethics, Ideology.* Columbus: Ohio State University Press. 79–101.

Milner, Jean-Claude. 1990a. *Introduction à une science du langage.* Paris: Seuil.

—. 1990b. *For the Love of Language.* Translated by Ann Banfield. Houndsmills, U.K.: Macmillan.

—. 1991. "Lacan and the Ideal of Science." Alexandre Leupin, ed., *Lacan and the Human Sciences.* Lincoln: University of Nebraska Press. 27–42.

Mitchell, W. J. T. 1986. *Iconology: Image, Text, Ideology.* Chicago: University of Chicago Press.

Mulhern, Francis. 1994. "Message in a Bottle: Althusser in Literary Studies." Elliott. 159–76.

Müller, Max. 1882. *Lectures on the Science of Language*. 2 vols. London: Longmans, Green.

Muller, John P., and William J. Richardson. 1982. *Lacan and Language: A Reader's Guide to Ecrits*. New York: International Universities Press.

Naess, A., et al. 1956. *Democracy, Ideology and Objectivity: Studies in the Semantics and Cognitive Analysis of Ideological Controversy*. Oslo: Norwegian Research Council for Science and the Humanities, University Press.

Newell, Eric. 1990. *Unified Theories of Cognition*. Cambridge, Mass: Harvard University Press.

Ngugi wa Thiong'o. 1986. *Decolonising the Mind: The Politics of Language in African Literature*. London: James Currey.

Nietzsche, Friedrich. 1968. *Twilight of the Idols*. In *Twilight of the Idols; and, The Anti-Christ*. Translated by R. J. Hollingdale. Harmondsworth, England: Penguin.

—. 1969. *On the Genealogy of Morals*. *On the Genealogy of Morals and Ecce Homo*. Translated by Walter Kaufman. New York: Random House.

—. 1973. *Beyond Good and Evil: Prelude to a Philosophy of the Future*. Translated by R. J. Hollingdale. Harmondsworth, England: Penguin.

—. 1979. "On Truth and Lies in a Nonmoral Sense." *Philosophy and Truth: Selections from Nietzsche's Notebooks of the early 1870's*. Translated and edited by Daniel Breazeale. Atlantic Highlands, N.J.: Humanities Press. 79–97.

—. 1996. *The Wanderer and His Shadow*. In *Human, All Too Human*. Translated by R. J. Hollingdale. Cambridge: Cambridge University Press.

Norris, Christopher. 1988. *Paul de Man: Deconstruction and the Criticism of Aesthetic Ideology*. New York: Routledge.

Oakeshott, Michael. 1975. *Of Human Conduct*. Oxford: Oxford University Press.

Orwell, George. 1984. "Politics and the English Language." *The Orwell Reader: Fictions, Essays, and Reportage*. With an introduction by Richard H. Rovere. San Diego: Harcourt Brace & Company. 355–66.

Pavel, Thomas G. 1992. *The Feud of Language*. English version by Linda Jordan and Thomas G. Pavel. Oxford: Basil Blackwell.

Pecheux, Michel. 1982. *Language, Semantics, and Ideology: Stating the Obvious*. Translated by Harbans Nagpal. London: Macmillan.

Pei, Mario. 1984. *The Story of Language*. New York: Penguin.

Pietz, William. 1987. "The Problem of the Fetish, I." *Res* 13 (Spring). 23–45.

—. 1993. "Fetishism and Materialism: The Limits of Theory in Marx." Emily Apter and William Pietz, eds., *Fetishism as Cultural Discourse*. Ithaca, N.Y.: Cornell University Press. 119–51.

Pinker, Steven. 1995. *The Language Instinct*. New York: HarperPerennial.

—. 1999. *Words and Rules: The Ingredients of Language*. New York: Basic Books.

Powers, Harold S. 1980. "Language Models and Musical Analysis." *Ethnomusicology* 24. 1–60.

Putnam, Hilary. 1964. "Minds and Machines." A. R. Anderson, ed., *Minds and Machines*. Englewood Cliffs, N.J. 72–97.

Quine, W. V. O. 1967. "The Semantic Ascent." Rorty 1967. 168–72.

Read, Rupert. 2000–2001. "How I Learned to Love (and Hate) Noam Chomsky." *Philosophical Writings* 15–16 (Autumn–Spring). 23–47.

Readings, Bill. 1991. *Introducing Lyotard: Art and Politics.* London.

Ricoeur, Paul. 1986. *Lectures on Ideology and Utopia.* Edited by George Taylor. New York: Columbia University Press.

Rorty, Richard, ed. 1967. *The Linguistic Turn: Recent Essays in Philosophical Method.* Chicago: University of Chicago Press.

—. 1989. *Contingency, Irony, and Solidarity.* Cambridge: Cambridge University Press.

—. 1991. "Pragmatism and Philosophy." Baynes et al. 26–66.

Rossi-Landi, Ferrucio. 1990 [1982]. *Marxism and Ideology.* Translated by Roger Griffin. Oxford: Clarendon Press.

Russell, Bertrand. 1940. *An Inquiry into Meaning and Truth.* London: G. Allen and Unwin, Ltd.

Said, Edward. 1993. *Culture and Imperialism.* New York: Alfred A. Knopf.

—. 1994. *Representations of the Intellectual.* New York: Vintage Books.

Sampson, Geoffrey. 1979. *Liberty and Language.* Oxford: Oxford University Press.

—. 1980a. *Making Sense.* Oxford: Oxford University Press.

—. 1980b. *Schools of Linguistics.* Stanford, Calif.: Stanford University Press.

Sapir, Edward. 1949. "Psychiatric and Cultural Pitfalls in the Business of Getting a Living." *Selected Writings of Edward Sapir in Language, Culture, and Personality.* Edited by David G. Mandelbaum. Berkeley: University of California Press. 578–89.

—. 1956. "The Status of Linguistics as a Science." *Culture, Language and Personality.* Edited by David G. Mandelbaum. Berkeley: University of California Press. 65–77.

Sattel, Jack. 1983. "Men, Inexpressiveness and Power." Thorne et al. 119–24.

de Saussure, Ferdinand. 1949. *Cours de Linguistique Générale.* Edited by Charles Bally and Albert Sechehaye, in collaboration with Albert Reidlinger. 3rd edition. Paris: Payot.

—. 1997. *The Course in General Linguistics.* Edited by Charles Bally and Albert Sechehaye, in collaboration with Albert Riedlinger, and translated by Roy Harris. Chicago: Open Court.

Savage-Rumbaugh, Sue, and Roger Lewin. 1994. *Kanzi: The Ape at the Brink of the Human Mind.* New York: John Wiley & Sons.

—, S. Shankar and T. J. Taylor. 1998. *Apes, Language and the Human Mind.* Oxford: Oxford University Press.

Scarry, Elaine. 1985. *The Body in Pain: The Making and Unmaking of the World.* New York: Oxford University Press.

Segal, Harold B. 1998. *Body Ascendant: Modernism and the Physical Imperative.* Baltimore: The Johns Hopkins University Press.

Semiotexte I, no. 2 (1974) and II, no. 1 (1975).

Seuren, Pieter A. M. 1998. *Western Linguistics: An Historical Introduction.* Oxford: Blackwell.

—. 1999a (June 11). Letter to the Editor. *Times Literary Supplement.* 17.

—. 1999b (July 23). Letter to the Editor. *Times Literary Supplement.* 17.

Smith, Neil. 1999. *Chomsky: Ideas and Ideals.* Cambridge: Cambridge University Press.

—, and Dierdre Wilson. 1990. *Modern Linguistics: The Results of Chomsky's Revolution.* Harmondsworth: Penguin.

Spender, Dale. 1980. *Man Made Language.* London: Routledge & Kegan Paul.

Sprinker, Michael, ed. 1999. *Ghostly Demarcations: A Symposium on Jacques Derrida's "Specters of Marx."* London: Verso.

Starobinski, Jean. 1971. *Les mots sous les mots: Les anagrammes de Ferdinand de Saussure.* Paris: Gallimard (English translation, *Words upon Words.* New Haven, Conn.: Yale University Press, 1979).

Szasz, Thomas. 1988. *The Ethics of Psychoanalysis: The Theory and Method of Autonomous Psychotherapy.* Syracuse, N.Y.: Syracuse University Press.

Tattersol, Ian. 1998. *Becoming Human: Evolution and Human Uniqueness.* New York: Harcourt Brace.

Taylor, Charles. 1985. *Human Agency and Language.* Vol. 1 of *Philosophical Papers,* 2 vols. Cambridge: Cambridge University Press.

—. 1991. *The Ethics of Authenticity.* Cambridge, Mass.: Harvard University Press.

Thompson, John B. 1984. *Studies in the Theory of Ideology.* Cambridge: Polity Press.

Thorne, Barrie, and Nancy Henley, eds. 1975. *Language and Sex: Difference and Dominance.* Cambridge, Mass.: Newbury House.

—, Cheris Kramerae, and Nancy Henley, eds. 1983. *Language, Gender and Society.* Cambridge, Mass.: Newbury House.

Torrey, H. A. P., ed. and trans. 1892. *The Philosophy of Descartes.* New York: Henry Holt.

de Tracy, Destutt. 1801–05. *Projet d'éléments d'idéologie.* Paris.

Trench, Richard Chenevix. 1892 [1851]. *On the Study of Words.* 22nd edition. New York: Macmillan and Co.

Vattimo, Gianni. 1988. *The End of Modernity: Nihilism and Hermeneutics in Postmodern Culture.* Translated with an introduction by Jon R. Snyder. Baltimore: The Johns Hopkins University Press.

Volosinov, V. N. 1973. *Marxism and the Philosophy of Language.* Translated by Ladislav Matejka and I. R. Titunik. New York: Seminar Press.

—. [1927] 1987. *Freudianism: A Critical Outline.* Leningrad: n.p. Translated by I. R. Titunik, and edited by N. H. Bruss. Bloomington: Indiana University Press.

Waters, Lindsay, and Wlad Godzich, eds. 1989. *Reading de Man Reading.* Theory and History of Literature, vol. 59. Minneapolis: University of Minnesota Press.

Weigand, Edda. 2002. "The Language Myth and Linguistics Humanized," Roy Harris, ed., *The Language Myth in Western Culture.* Richmond, Surrey, England: Curzon Press. 55–83.

Whitford, Margaret. 1991. *Luce Irigaray: Philosophy in the Feminine.* London: Routledge.

Whorf, Benjamin Lee. 1988. *Language, Thought, and Reality: Selected Writings of Benjamin Lee Whorf.* Edited by John Carroll. Cambridge, Mass.: MIT Press.

Williams, Bernard. 1985. *Ethics and the Limits of Philosophy.* Cambridge, Mass.: Harvard University Press.

Williams, Raymond. 1958. *Culture and Society.* London: Chatto & Windus.

—. 1976. *Keywords: A Vocabulary of Culture and Society.* New York: Oxford University Press.

—. 1977. *Marxism and Literature.* Oxford: Oxford University Press.

—. 1989. *The Politics of Modernism: Against the New Conformists.* Edited by Tony Pinkney. London: Verso.

Wilson, Frank R. 1999. *The Hand: How Its Use Shapes the Brain, Language, and Human Culture.* New York: Pantheon Books.

Wittgenstein, Ludwig. 1961. *Tractatus Logico-Philosophicus.* Translated by D. F. Pears and B. F. McGuinness. London: Routledge & Kegan Paul.

—. 1997. *Philosophical Investigations.* Translated by G. E. M. Anscombe. Oxford: Blackwell; London: Routledge & Kegan Paul.

Wollheim, Richard. 1987. *Painting as an Art.* Princeton, N.J.: Princeton University Press.

Wright, Robert. 1994. *The Moral Animal: Why We Are the Way We Are: The New Science of Evolutionary Psychology.* New York: Pantheon Books.

—. 1999 (December 13). "The Accidental Creationist: Why Stephen Jay Gould Is Bad for Evolution." *The New Yorker.* 56–65.

Young, J. Z. 1978. *Programs of the Brain.* Oxford: Oxford University Press.

Žižek, Slavoj. 1989. *The Sublime Object of Ideology.* London: Verso.

—. 1991. *For They Know Not What They Do: Enjoyment as a Political Factor.* London: Verso.

—. 1993. *Tarrying with the Negative: Kant, Hegel, and the Critique of Ideology.* Durham, N.C.: Duke University Press.

—. 1994. "The Spectre of Ideology." Slavoj Žižek, ed., *Mapping Ideology.* London: Verso. 1–33.

—. 2001. *Did Somebody Say Totalitarianism? Five Interventions in the (Mis)use of a Notion.* London: Verso.

Index